D0857978

KELLEY: The Story of an FBI Director

KELLEY
The Story of an FBI Director

By Clarence M. Kelley
and James Kirkpatrick Davis

Andrews, McMeel & Parker
A Universal Press Syndicate Affiliate
Kansas City • New York

Frontispiece illustration by artist Freda L. Reiter.

Library of Congress Cataloging-in-Publication Data

Kelley, Clarence M.
    Kelley: the story of an FBI director.

    Includes index.
    1. Kelley, Clarence M. 2. Police—United States—
Biography. 3. United States. Federal Bureau of Investigation—
Officials and employees—Biography. 4. Government
executives—United States—Biography. 5. United States—
Politics and government—1945-   . I. Davis, James
Kirkpatrick. II. Title.
HV7911.K37A3 1987   363.2'092'4 [B]   87-11482
ISBN 0-8362-7935-2

Contents

Foreword

by Elliot L. Richardson

THIS IS THE STORY OF A MAN'S CHARACTER—its shaping and testing under the pressure and heat of enormously demanding assignments.

The qualities that emerge with unmistakable clarity from these pages are those of fairness, firmness, discipline, and openness. We see them first in the episodes of early childhood that Clarence Kelley remembers as shaping influences. His most cherished recollections of his father, an engineer for the Kansas City Power and Light Company, are of discipline fairly administered and fair-mindedness tempered with love. It is easy to believe that these examples do indeed, as he tells us, account for his becoming a person dedicated to justice and law enforcement.

It was to be expected that fairness, firmness, discipline, and openness would be associated with honesty, and this too is stamped on every page of the book. As a lawyer and investigator, Clarence Kelley learned to look facts in the eye. His descriptions of people and scenes, whether of Richard Nixon at the end of his rope or J. Edgar Hoover's outer office, inner office, and inner-inner office, are notable for the accuracy with which the details have been observed and described. His portrait of J. Edgar Hoover is unsparing, but again it is the fairness and honesty that stand out.

Clarence Kelley is equally unsparing with himself. We believe his unadorned account of his own accomplishments because he tells us with equal matter-of-factness about his mistakes. Having seen during his twenty-one years in the Federal Bureau of Investigation the costs exacted by J. Edgar Hoover's increasing rigidity and remoteness, Clarence Kelley made it a point to be innovative and open. At his first general press conference as chief of police of Kansas City, he announced that his department would never hide behind "no comment" and assured the press that they could call him at any time. At his confirmation hearing as director of the FBI, he made it clear that he would welcome congressional oversight. During his fifty-five months as director, he spent more time before congressional committees than Mr. Hoover did in forty-eight years.

When I became attorney general in May, 1973, the search for a new director of the FBI was already under way. For the Department of Justice the selection was of course a critical one. In addition to being keenly interested in it, I took it for granted that I could block any appointment that did not have my concurrence. Judging by the manner in which the White House approached me on the subject, the president's men shared the same assumption. Although my colleagues and I had discussed various possible candidates, we had none of our own when General Alexander Haig called me to propose Clarence Kelley.

My first meeting with Chief Kelley (prophetically, he had been given the nickname "Chief" while still in school) was no mere courtesy call. We had a long talk, and I came away from it convinced that he did indeed possess both the qualities and the qualifications required by a dauntingly demanding task. Inquiries to friends who knew him and whose judgment I trusted confirmed by favorable impression. This book makes plain the underlying basis of this impression in language that speaks convincingly—and revealingly—of the man.

In June of 1973 when Chief Kelley took charge of the FBI, the relentless unfolding of the sad and sordid abuses collectively labeled "Watergate" dominated national attention. The presidency itself was shadowed by a mushrooming cloud of scandal. Even the FBI was implicated in violations of constitutional rights. Long-suppressed criticisms of the Bureau were breaking into the open. Morale was disintegrating.

At this time of unprecedented stress, Clarence Kelley brought to the Bureau a powerful combination of assets. Among them were unshakable integrity, long experience in the Bureau itself, the knowledge thus gained of its strengths and limitations as well as its potential, and a capacity already demonstrated in Kansas City to seize and exploit opportunities for administrative and investigative innovations. He and William D. Ruckelshaus, who had been acting FBI director and then became my deputy attorney general, formed a solid and constructive partnership based on mutual trust and a common commitment to the rights of the citizen. They had my total confidence and support.

Rather than content himself with giving us a conventional autobiography chronicling his life from year to year, Chief Kelley has organized his experience into chapters focusing on the events and challenges that most engaged his energy and concern. The result is not only to illuminate events of genuinely historic significance but to point up the lessons to be drawn from them. From my own standpoint, this is particularly true of the role of the FBI in the immediate aftermath of the "Saturday Night Massacre." The book is thus not only of absorbing interest but enduring value.

It is a testimonial to Clarence Kelley's character that he was able so quickly to restore both the internal morale and the external image of the FBI. Fairness, firmness, discipline, and openness were never more vitally needed nor more effectively brought to bear. As a citizen as well as a former colleague, I am grateful to Clarence Kelley for giving us this solid and thoughtful record of his service to the nation.

Memo from the Chief

EXCEPT AS STATED in the Acknowledgments, this entire book has been constructed from the dusty files, yellowed memo copies, frayed diaries, and all-too-human memory of Clarence Marion Kelley. Where references are made to published materials, the source has generally been given. The only exceptions to this are the dozens of books, newspaper and magazine feature stories, and news items that have been used to support recollections. Dialogue has been added to enhance readability. If the word-by-word replay is not precisely what was said, the tenor of the conversations, the ideas expressed, and import of the words have all been checked for what might be called accuracy-integrity approval.

—CLARENCE M. KELLEY

April 1987
Kansas City, Missouri

1

Fairmount, Missouri: 1911

"I remember my mother's vigil of love and my dad's fairness at all times."

WILLIAM HOWARD TAFT was president of the United States. The first automobiles had just started to appear on the dusty streets of Kansas City. World War I had not yet begun—nor, in Fairmount, Missouri, was it even imaginable. It was a time of family, homemade ice cream, and apple trees in the backyard.

It was 1911, and on October 24 of that year I was born, the only child of my loving parents, Minnie Brown Kelley, originally from Whiting, Indiana, and Clarence Bond Kelley of Iola, Kansas.

I was raised in Fairmount, a quiet hamlet nestled between Kansas City and Independence. It was a peaceful place, so peaceful in fact that I cannot remember ever hearing of a crime being committed in our town during my entire boyhood.

My father was an electrical engineer for the Kansas City Power and Light Company. He had only a third-grade education, but had put himself through night school for seventeen years, ultimately earning his college degree.

My youthful life was quite uneventful. It was marked by an absence of wealth but an abundance of love that filled our modest five-room stucco bungalow on Ash Avenue.

When I was about four years old, I remember that my mother, father and I boarded one of those dazzling new electric-powered streetcars that raced—at speeds up to ten miles an hour—from Independence to Kansas City.

This particular day we were off to Kansas City, the big city. Mother and I went to the back of the car where I sat down next to her as my father paid the fares. When he came back to our section, Dad asked me to get up and sit on the other side of the car, across the aisle. I balked, and said no. I was determined to stay next to my mother. A short discussion ensued.

Suddenly Dad lifted me out of my seat and sat down in it himself. Still holding me, he put me over his knee and gave me an impressive spanking, short in duration, but powerful in effect.

The spanking on the streetcar ended quickly—and so did my balkiness. I sat where I was told and Dad took his place next to Mother. But that incident made an impression on me that has accompanied me throughout the years: authority must be reckoned with, and while resistance to authority can at times be tolerated, even listened to, in the end authority must prevail, hopefully by persuasion but sometimes by force.

I was happy that my father did not hold a grudge against me for my stubborn behavior, and I did not tempt him to repeat his punishment thereafter. Though my mother was all mama (and of course indulged me in all ways), my father maintained a level of discipline which I came to respect without ever feeling burdened by its presence.

One spring day, when I was about twelve years old, my dad bought a new red lawn mower, a very fine machine, but a very heavy one. Also, a very expensive one for our family.

Cutting the grass was my job at that time, but putting the lawn mower away was always *our* job, Dad's and mine. I remember the struggle it was for me, trying to get that big machine down those storm-basement stairs into the cellar where we stored it. I guess Dad wanted me to feel like I was an important part of putting the mower into its proper place until next time—because I always felt that if he didn't have me there to help him, he'd surely not have been able to manage it alone.

Well, one day after doing the mowing, I decided to show Dad

that I could do the job all by myself. What a nice surprise it would be for him to come home from work and not have to worry about wrestling with that red monster.

I remember the first step was easy. I just let it roll down a bit while I braced myself at the top. Step two wasn't much more difficult: I was still able to dig my heels in at the top. But that next one! Suddenly the mower was on step three, I was on step one, and I felt like I was going right over the top of the machine to the concrete cavern below. Lucky for me I caught hold of the bannister at the last second.

Lucky for me, but not for the mower. It broke loose from my grasp, and started its final journey down those cement stairs to the floor below. It clattered and crashed down to the bottom where it shattered into dozens of pieces. The beautiful red cast iron wheels and shaft were broken, the machine was ruined, and I was in trouble for sure.

Though fearful of the punishment that awaited me when Dad got home, I knew I had to report the accident to him. I then spent the rest of the afternoon wondering just *how* I was going to tell him.

That evening Dad listened to my story, remaining silent throughout. He then said something I'll never forget.

"Son, I'm sorry this happened. I think you used bad judgment, but you were just trying to help. I think I used bad judgment, too. I should have realized that the mower was just too heavy for a little guy like you to manage. I was at fault. We'll just go back to using the old mower, and your dad will try to do better in the future."

I cried with relief—also in happiness—because Dad was so obviously a good guy and a fair man. This incident has often come to my mind over the years. Even now when I recall what happened, I have tears in my eyes. In fact, I think that perhaps I became a person dedicated to justice and law because of my father's love and adherence to fairness.

Dad's innate fair-mindedness is probably best demonstrated in an episode about some stolen apples.

One day a friend and I—we were both about thirteen at the time—were accused by a neighbor of stealing apples from his apple tree. The man came to my father to report the theft. Dad heard the man out, and told him he would talk to me about it. Dad then reported the story to me. I told my father truthfully that I hadn't stolen the apples, and I didn't think my friend had either.

"Son, I believe you're telling the truth. I guess our neighbor must be mistaken about this one." Dad reported my version to our neighbor who, while still convinced of my guilt, chose not to pursue the matter any further.

On the other hand, when my alleged accomplice's father was told about his son stealing apples, he took a different course of action. He confronted his son, who also pleaded innocent. The father refused to accept the denial, and gave the boy a good spanking.

Some days later the owner of the apple tree came over to our house to apologize to my dad, telling him that neither I nor my friend had done anything wrong. Two other youngsters were the true apple-snatchers, he had discovered.

The owner also went to my friend's father and told him the same story. But my friend's dad never told his son that he knew the true story about the stolen apples, never admitted that he learned the boy was innocent. Later my friend heard of his father's refusal to admit the mistake he'd made. Years after the episode, the matter arose in conversation between the two of us. My friend still harbored resentment against his father, not because of the spanking, but because his father had never told him the truth and admitted his own mistake.

Such incidents have a great bearing on the development of children. Certainly my experience was most memorable and favorable. I had a pretty good dad, I came to believe. He was also a deeply religious man, who for many years was chairman of the board of the Fairmount Christian Church.

My mother was a wonderful woman, a large part of whose life was dedicated to her husband and son. At age eleven I contracted typhoid fever. My mother stayed with me night and day until the sickness was past. For five weeks she never left my side. Unquestionably, she saved my life through her great love and caring. I remember being terribly frightened because of the fever and weakness. I also remember her being always with me. I have never forgotten her love or her round-the-clock attentions to my needs at that time.

A woman of her time, my mother never learned to drive a car, nor did she handle the family pocketbook. Her world was her home and her family, and that was all the world she seemed to need. She was a wonderful cook—I particularly remember the desserts—and enjoyed the expressions of appreciation heaped upon her by Dad and me. She was not prominent in our church, but always attended services (with a not-always-willing son in tow), and assisted in planning church dinners and cooking.

My mother—a good person—was sometimes quite pointed in her comments about anybody she felt was "no good." She was comfortable in her world, and throughout times of worry, trouble, and pain was always a source of love and inspiration to me.

I regard my boyhood as normal—middle class, middle America, and a little dull. As a teenager I played third base and then outfield for a local sandlot baseball team called the Fairmount Merchants. I fielded well enough, but I'm afraid I never learned to hit a curve ball.

I graduated from Washington Elementary School, then went to Northeast High School in Kansas City, where I maintained a B average. To tell the truth, though, I was less concerned about my grades than carrying home the books of a pretty girl named Ruby Pickett—the woman I was to marry in 1937, during my second year of law school.

As a youth I had very few encounters with minority groups. We had a grocer whose name was Abacar, a native of Syria. Few of our neighbors socialized with him. I could not understand this and it seemed unfair.

I also remember there was some interest in the Ku Klux Klan in our small town; I didn't know what those people stood for, but apparently they felt some need to "put blacks in their place," an especially curious mission in our town in the 1920s because there were no Negroes where we lived. I wondered then why there had to be such hatred for people who were different from us but who didn't harm us in the least, indeed people whose presence we were scarcely aware of.

It wasn't until I went to the University of Kansas that I had a real conversation with a black person. He and I were in the same psychology class and, on several occasions, we exchanged comments, very short but pleasant enough. I was curious as to how he felt about our talks and often puzzled over why we were almost forced to keep at such a distance from each other. Unfortunately, my college career did little to broaden my understanding of minority groups.

After entering the FBI in 1940, another agent and I were waiting for an elevator when my friend began bragging about his hoard of pistol cartridges. He said he felt "nigger rich" in them, and he wanted to go down to the firing range and use them. Unfortunately, he said this just as the elevator door opened; the black operator had heard his remark. My friend told the man that he was sorry—and he hoped the man realized that he was just using a stupid cliché.

The elevator operator said nothing, but later reported the incident. It eventually came to the attention of our agent-in-charge. He called us in and reprimanded us for the careless language, saying how it had hurt the man's feelings. This was my first such experience, and it had a lasting effect on me. I was taught to respect the dignity of man and I believe racial slurs are always unacceptable, even when unintentional.

I graduated from the University of Kansas in 1936 with a bachelor of arts degree, and obtained an LL.B. degree from the Law School of the University of Kansas City in 1940.

One day, during my final weeks in law school, the FBI special agent-in-charge of the Kansas City office spoke to our class, extolling the Federal Bureau of Investigation, and describing the tremendous services a lawyer could provide the nation through a career in the Bureau.

Though I had never given serious thought to a career in law enforcement, I reviewed my situation: The year was 1940; the nation had not yet recovered from the Great Depression; I had a wife to support; lawyers were not in great demand anywhere. I decided to join the FBI.

My dad had taught me justice and my mother had taught me dedication to duty and to those we love. Thus, from the beginning, I had an enormous advantage over those who had never received strong moral guidance. While pursuing my law enforcement career diligently I developed an acute compassion for those less fortunate. It was probably true that on occasion I was more concerned about the plight of a destitute and desperate wrong-doer than the plight of a victim. Thus, in some ways, I was probably a soft-touch, a charge that came back at me many years later when I headed the FBI as director.

During all of my law enforcement career the dregs of society passed before me. I saw drug addicts, murderers, thieves, procurers, con men, and other violators of the law. It was often apparent to me that the great majority of criminals were indeed the hopeless victims of an unhealthy and abusive youthful environment. In many cases, they were actually unable to tell right from wrong.

The penal system I observed early in my career rarely helped to rehabilitate anybody. In fact, even greater degradation often befell the wrong-doer, and rarely did one of these individuals rise successfully from the criminal environment. Almost always they were engulfed by the weight of their own problems, and continued to pursue a life of crime.

From my current point of view, after a career of four decades in law enforcement, I see genuine hope for our society. I believe that with the proper blending of our very considerable law enforcement and rehabilitation resources we will ultimately make substantial headway in lowering crime and its incredibly destructive effects on our society.

As we today view crime less as a sin to be punished and more as a disease to be cured, rehabilitation of the criminal to a respectable place in society will become the rule, not the exception.

Many of us were fortunate to have had healthy childhoods, leading to productive, happy, law-abiding lives. Just as I was influenced by my wonderful mom and dad so are other Americans directed by their parents, or significant people in their lives, toward an understanding of the values of civilization—freedom, justice, respect for all people.

In the final analysis, the best weapon against crime is not a weapon at all. It is the family unit itself—the guidance and creation of values and self-esteem by a loving mother and father.

2

Inside the FBI: 1940-1961

My Years Under Hoover

HE WAS FBI DIRECTOR under sixteen attorneys general and eight presidents.

He first took office under Calvin Coolidge in the Roaring Twenties; served during the Herbert Hoover presidency, marked by the Wall Street crash and the gangsterism of the early 1930s; flourished during the three-plus administrations of Franklin Roosevelt, embracing the depths of the Great Depression and our triumphant victories over the Axis in World War II; continued in office during the Harry S. Truman years, through the emergence of the Cold War and the trials of the Korean conflict; directed the FBI as the U.S. global power role grew during both terms of Dwight D. Eisenhower; led the Bureau into the storm-thrashed 1960s, serving John F. Kennedy and Lyndon B. Johnson during the Vietnam War with all of its tumult; and died in office at the age of seventy-seven near the end of the first administration of Richard Nixon.

In all, forty-eight years of service to his country spanning the decades from the 1920s to the 1970s—an unbroken record of service unmatched by any other government official in the history of our republic.

At his funeral in May 1972 he was eulogized by the Chief Justice of the United States Supreme Court, Warren Burger:

> John Edgar Hoover, who was known to his intimates as Edgar and to two generations of Americans as J. Edgar

Hoover, was a man who epitomized the American dream of patriotism, dedication to duty, and successful attainment.

From modest beginnings he rose to the pinnacle of his profession and established a worldwide reputation that was without equal among those to whom societies entrust the difficult tasks relating to enforcement of the laws.

Most members of the U.S. House of Representatives and the Senate paid similar tributes to Hoover. Senator Harry F. Byrd of Virginia said he was one of "the really great Americans of our time."

He had, during his career, received honorary degrees from George Washington University, New York University, Westminster College, Georgetown University, the University of the South, the University of Notre Dame, Rutgers, not to mention more than a dozen others.

At his death, condolences came to Washington from every corner of the globe. Indeed, when J. Edgar Hoover died, a major figure of twentieth-century America law—and lore—passed into history.

J. Edgar Hoover was born January 1, 1895, in Washington, D.C. He grew up in the Washington area, and received his law degree from hometown George Washington University in 1916.

From that year forward he spent his entire working life in government. The next year he entered the Department of Justice and served from 1919 to 1921 as a special assistant to the attorney general. From 1921 until 1924 Hoover served as assistant director of the Bureau of Investigation, which was then a small department in Justice. The young, hard-working J. Edgar was soon noticed by Attorney General Harlan Fiske Stone, who later offered him the job as director of the Bureau of Investigation, then an organization of about eight-hundred employees.

According to a news account of his appointment, when offered the directorship Hoover said, "The Bureau ought to be divorced from politics, appointments made solely on merit. Promotions ought to be made on proved ability. The Bureau ought to be responsible only to the attorney general." Stone, who later was to become an associate justice of the United States Supreme Court, told Hoover, "That's exactly the way it's going to be."

Speaking of the challenge accepted by Hoover at the time he became head of the Bureau, the *Chicago Tribune* noted:

> The Bureau was in disarray when Hoover took over. He was equipped with a law degree and was tough-minded. The job he faced was formidable, for the Bureau had degenerated into a scandal-ridden haven for political hacks. Hoover's thorough housecleaning turned things around. In a short space of time, the Bureau was on its way to becoming a respected, world-famous organization admired for its detachment and integrity.
>
> Instead of creating a Bureau which people might fear, Hoover developed an investigative and law enforcement section of the Justice Department which earned the respect of all Americans.

Under Hoover, the Bureau of Investigation grew quickly.

Year by year, Congress added to the investigative scope of the organization. In 1933 Congress changed the name of the Bureau to the Division of Investigation. At about this time the agency began its prolonged battle against organized crime.

In 1935 the name of the Bureau was officially changed to the Federal Bureau of Investigation. Concurrent with the name change, the Bureau was entrusted with the responsibility of investigating crimes that related to the internal security of the United States—sabotage, treason, conspiracy, and the like.

During these remarkable growth years it is important to recognize that J. Edgar Hoover was, without a doubt, the prime driving force behind the Bureau. By his will, his vision, his single-minded dedication to forging the FBI into the law enforcement instrument he knew the growing nation would need, J. Edgar Hoover almost alone built the FBI. But it was even more than will, vision, and dedication. Two other critical faculties Hoover had in abundance made it all come to pass: his skill with politics (and politicians), plus his uncanny sense of public relations, made it possible for him to achieve all of his goals for the FBI.

Hoover never married. He did not have a family. His outside social activities were few. The Bureau became his family and his purpose in life. Its people were his family. If his rule became patriarchal—and it did—we should not be surprised.

The FBI, which by 1935 had developed a vastly enlarged General Intelligence division, gradually became involved in the tracking down of subversives—also in gathering intelligence information. Throughout his career, Hoover used data gathered by General Intelligence in the Bureau's war against alien threats and, following the Second World War, the Communist Party influence in this country (real or imagined). But antisubversive warfare and counterintelligence activities came later; first there was the war against the Public Enemies of the 1930s.

And this all began with Bruno Richard Hauptmann.

A dramatic turning point in the Bureau's history and development came with the kidnap and murder of the infant son of Charles Lindbergh. The subsequent manhunt, capture, trial, and execution of Hauptmann only flamed the public passion for greater control and protection against such enemies.

Thus, given impetus by a shocked nation, Congress passed the Kidnapping Act of 1934-36. Known as the Lindbergh Law, the measure made kidnapping a federal crime, hence a responsibility of the FBI. Additional federal legislation during the mid-1930s gave the Bureau jurisdictional authority in bank robberies and the authority to carry firearms.

The FBI became front page news; the G-man, a national hero.

As a result of dramatic gun battles between FBI agents—G-men—and such characters as John Dillinger, Ma Barker, and Machine Gun Kelly, the Bureau catapulted into national prominence. The concept of "public enemy" was developed, with the FBI widely known as the nation's number-one crime buster. Attired in business suits, white shirts, and ties, the FBI agents became America's good guys in the battle against crime.

Ovid Demaris, in his book *The Director,* has discussed at some length the massive FBI publicity campaign which developed largely during the 1930s and which aided in "transforming Hoover's G-men into household words. It was a triumph of virtue over evil. The G-men movies replaced the gangster movies."

In time—just as soon as a man named Melvin Purvis could be moved aside—J. Edgar Hoover became the living symbol of the nation's crusade against crime and evil. In fact, one public opinion poll after another reflected the country's infatuation with Hoover. During the heart of the Depression, three magic names kept appearing at the top of all "most loved/respected/admired" lists: Franklin Delano Roosevelt, J. Edgar Hoover, and Shirley Temple, not necessarily in that order.

FBI crime statistics became the nation's yardstick in the battle against crime. The FBI was extolled in movies, on the radio, in books, magazines, and on toys and clothing for youngsters. Much of the publicity was generated by the Bureau's Crime Records division. All of it was engineered by the Director.

World War II produced yet another period of phenomenal growth in the responsibility of the FBI. The Bureau was extraordinarily successful in finding and jailing potential enemy aliens. In fact, not one case of foreign-directed sabotage took place in the United States during all of World War II because the FBI assisted in preparing security measures for war production plants in the U.S. A number of spies were captured; in some cases the Bureau persuaded the German agents to work for us. Eight German spies actually came ashore in this country. All were captured by the FBI. The Bureau's record in protecting the internal security of the United States during World War II was practically flawless.

New challenges were soon to follow.

At the end of the war, with the collapse of Germany and Japan, the Communist threat and the Cold War developed. This new menace to the United States presented the FBI with a new set of responsibilities.

In a perceptive article written for the *Washington Post,* William Greider described these new changes:

> With the Cold War, it was Communists. FBI men figured out the Soviet plot through which America lost its monopoly on atomic weapons, an event that traumatized the nation for

a generation. FBI agents so thoroughly infiltrated the Communist Party of America that it was said, only partly in jest, that the federal government's dues were keeping the organization alive.

The same basic FBI tactics were also used to infiltrate and undermine the Ku Klux Klan in the 1960s. And, later in the same decade, the targets for "neutralization" expanded to include leftist groups, antiwar demonstrators, and student militants on college campuses.

But J. Edgar Hoover warned against going too far with this.

In fact, Hoover predicted dire consequences if Nixon's White House aides actually implemented their more bizarre ideas for domestic intelligence schemes. On a number of occasions Hoover simply refused to coordinate and/or execute the illegal strategies advocated by that administration's more radical elements. After Watergate, author Sanford Ungar wrote that "President Nixon later claimed Hoover's veto was the reason he (Nixon) found it necessary to establish the Special Investigations Unit—better known as the 'plumbers'—in the White House."

Interestingly, historian Arthur M. Schlesinger, Jr., notes, in *The Imperial Presidency*, that President Nixon received a complaint from one of his aides about Hoover's concern that the civil liberties of people being investigated might become jeopardized. Schlesinger points out: "The civil liberties people had not known that J. Edgar Hoover cared, and it may well be that he did not care all that much about civil liberties; but he did care supremely about the professional reputation of the FBI."

In my opinion, this alleged Hoover disdain for civil liberties has been oversold. I prefer to believe that Hoover saw a vast difference between Communist spies and student antiwar demonstrators. They were not the same, and I believe he treated them very differently.

Speaking of civil liberties, another aspect of the J. Edgar Hoover legend that even today I am frequently asked about is the fact or fable of the "Hoover files."

One thing is certainly true: Hoover kept personal files. What *kind* and what *for* are two different issues that I can't answer.

Were they salacious and lurid, used to blackmail politicians into compliance with his will?

I don't know about that. I doubt it.

Were the files personal indictments of public figures—from movie stars to millionaire businessmen? Again, I have a hard time believing that.

The subject of the files never would go away.

I discussed the matter at considerable length throughout my term as director of the FBI, so I have no qualms about talking about it now. I was questioned about the files several times during my Senate confirmation hearings in June 1973. The subject also came up at hearings of the House Subcommittee on Civil and Constitutional Rights.

In my personal correspondence as FBI director, I wrote to several congressmen about the files. Each time we attempted to provide a definitive answer on the subject, we would find more disagreement. People tend to believe what they want to believe about almost everything. More so with J. Edgar Hoover, I have discovered.

I had about ten thousand things on my mind when I became director. As a result, I couldn't apply myself solely to the problem of coming up with answers that would put the question to rest. In *The Director*, Ovid Demaris asserts that Ugo Carusi, an executive assistant to six attorneys general, said he never saw the files. But William C. Sullivan, the Bureau's number-three man until forced into retirement in 1971, said that there were extensive personal files. Emanuel Celler, the late Democratic representative of New York, agreed with Bill Sullivan. On the other hand, former Attorney General William P. Rogers said he never saw them.

The subject was initially raised by Senator Birch Bayh at my confirmation hearings on June 19, 1973:

> *Senator Bayh:* Chief, could you tell us what you know about the compilation of congressional dossiers? Are there any, and if so, where are they?

> *Mr. Kelley:* Senator, I don't know a thing about them. I have never seen one and I know nothing.
>
> *Senator Bayh:* Would it be too much to put that on your list . . . and find out if there are any down there . . . how we get them destroyed? We understood from your acting predecessor that there were some, but for some reason or another there wasn't any authority to destroy the darned things!
>
> *Mr. Kelley:* I will look into it as soon as I have the position, yes.

Shortly after the hearings, I told a Washington reporter that while I hadn't been through all the FBI files personally, I pledged that if anybody can find one on a member of Congress, "I'll eat it."

The subject of Hoover's private files arose at the hearings of the Subcommittee on Civil Rights and Constitutional Rights, September 26, 1973. The questions are from Committee Counsel Alan A. Parker:

> *Mr. Parker:* You also referred to earlier this morning, and characterized some materials which had been, as I understand it, destroyed, that were personal to Mr. Hoover. Could you describe for me what you mean by personal?
>
> *Mr. Kelley:* Letters to friends, his financial investments, the investment matters concerning his will and that type of thing, and his legal counsel. I have no definite listing.

Later, however, we did learn that some files had been destroyed.

I promptly told Attorney General Edward Levi that Mr. Hoover had evidently kept 164 files of his own locked in an adjoining office. I later discussed the matter of these particular files on the "Today Show" with Douglas Kiker:

> *Mr. Kiker:* . . . Miss Helen Gandy was for forty years, I gather, the private secretary of Mr. Hoover. She took thirty volumes of his private files and burned them. Did she exceed her authority? Who gave her permission to do this?
>
> *Mr. Kelley:* These were personal files of the former director.

Our investigation revealed that he gave the order for the destruction of those personal files before his death.

What then should we say in summary about the files? Will we ever know the truth?

First, as you can see, the subject generated considerable attention from the media and Congress. It was felt that once Hoover had died, the real truth would come out. The alleged secret files were in my opinion a matter vastly overrated. Hoover never said that he had such files, but then he never denied it. In my view, by saying nothing about them over the years, Hoover allowed the legend of the files to grow to incalculable dimensions, and they increasingly took on an air of mystery.

Second, we will probably never know what was in the files that Helen Gandy destroyed. She has said they were purely personal files. But that doesn't clarify much, does it? I said earlier, now let me repeat: I do not believe that Hoover maintained confidential or salacious files on elected officials in an effort to intimidate them or maintain his position in power. That was a myth. Period.

No discussion of the life and career of J. Edgar Hoover would be in any way complete without describing two men who certainly helped to shape the career of Hoover and the FBI: Bill Sullivan and Clyde Tolson.

William C. Sullivan was with the Bureau for more than thirty years. Sullivan, a hard worker, spent twenty-eight of these years in Washington, and by age fifty-nine had worked his way through the ranks to become assistant to the director for all investigative activities. When Hoover demanded Sullivan's retirement in 1971 because of policy differences, the position was widely believed to be the number-three position in the Bureau. For many years, Bill Sullivan was thought to be the successor to J. Edgar Hoover.

I first heard of Sullivan after he had been with the FBI for about ten years. He was, I soon learned, regarded as a "fast mover" and as the top authority within the Bureau on communism.

Somewhat professorial in manner, Sullivan was a rather short, slight man with a fabled disinterest in how he looked. His attire, to put it mildly, was disheveled. In personality, he was eccentric, at times loud, at times explosive, and at other times sullen and moody.

In a tidy, neat Hooverian world, Sullivan maintained a chaotic office and profile. Accordingly, he was tagged Crazy Billy by some. Frequently he was described as one so immersed in his own political philosophy and in researching the fields of espionage and Communism that he was generally divorced from other aspects of the Bureau, of Washington, and of the world.

But there was a second side to Sullivan.

Notwithstanding his eccentricities, he was a brilliant student of the inner workings of the Bureau. A sensitive, intelligent man, he constantly reflected on the problem of maintaining an investigative police force in a democratic society. In his book, *The Bureau: My Thirty Years in Hoover's FBI*, Sullivan describes his opposition to many of Hoover's policies. He made several strenuous efforts to modernize the Bureau. He wanted to improve relations with other policing agencies, sought new methods of reporting statistics, and tried to improve personnel policies. But Hoover nearly always resisted his efforts. Nevertheless, Sullivan was working, I believe, for what he felt was in the best interests of the Bureau, the country—and J. Edgar Hoover.

Sullivan clashed repeatedly with Hoover over such matters as the Ku Klux Klan investigations, the Nixon wiretaps, domestic intelligence activities, and the FBI coverage of the 1968 Democratic Convention. Both men exchanged angry letters privately and publicly over Bureau policy.

Finally, Hoover demanded his resignation in 1971.

I spoke with Bill Sullivan several times before his resignation. On one occasion, we discussed the controversy he seemed to provoke. He was most disturbed about this. He was concerned about rumors circulating throughout the Bureau that he was not supportive of the FBI and, more specifically, that he was saying things that were very harmful to Hoover. He had spent a lifetime trying to build a better FBI; how could anybody think he was not loyal to it? And he believed that he proved his loyalty to Hoover every day—by trying to improve the FBI.

William C. Sullivan, however, in making his perceptive analyses of the internal conditions of the Bureau, highlighted what he believed to be the negative effect Hoover had on the direction of Bureau policy. Sullivan's analysis included, of course, the argument that Hoover's autocratic rule of the Bureau discouraged independent and creative thinking within the organization. As a result, the FBI was not keeping pace with the times. Moreover, Bill Sullivan believed that the Director's harsh personnel policies discouraged individual agent initiative, hence effectiveness.

Sullivan made a multitude of additional recommendations, most of which were in conflict with Hoover's will (and therefore doomed to failure). Bill Sullivan deserves special mention because he was one of the few individuals who had the courage to criticize J. Edgar Hoover both publicly and privately.

Personally, I believe that had Sullivan's point of view prevailed more often, the FBI would have been a more effective organization—as well as a more rewarding place to spend a career.

Although Sullivan may not always have been right, I believe that he was attempting to temper Hoover's autocratic rule and, by doing so, create a better FBI.

If Bill Sullivan was Hoover's loyal opposition, Clyde Tolson was his alter ego.

Tolson, the associate director of the FBI until 1972, was probably J. Edgar Hoover's only close friend. He joined the FBI in 1928 and in 1947 became associate director: in effect, the number-two man in the FBI. He and the Director, both bachelors, were virtually inseparable for years. They lunched together almost every day, vacationed together, spent most of their leisure time together, and, of course, worked together.

He served as Hoover's chief of staff and it is believed that Hoover consulted him on virtually everything. When Tolson became sick, he would usually move into Hoover's house, and when Hoover died, Tolson moved into his home permanently. At his death, Hoover left his estate to Tolson.

Rumors of a homosexual relationship between the two circulated for years, but nothing was ever substantiated. There are no concrete facts pointing to such a relationship. I always believed it was probably more of a mentor-protegé relationship. They were just two old friends, completely at ease with each other at all times, nothing more. I still feel the same way today.

My own personal relationship with J. Edgar Hoover, which was never close, goes back many years.

I was appointed as an FBI special agent on October 7, 1940, and I received my academy training at the FBI National Academy, in Quantico, Virginia. Study at the Academy was conducted in a businesslike atmosphere and the freedom of exchange and informality of the college classroom was absent. Agents were trained in a profession which demanded their full attention and undivided loyalty in an arena of intrigue sometimes charged with danger.

Sprinkled throughout our classroom lectures were references to Mr. Hoover, or as he was most often called, the Director. He was held in awe. New agents were expected to give him the most deferential respect, and any breach of acceptable conduct could mean the end of an FBI career.

During training, I first met Hoover at a short reception in the Mayflower Hotel in Washington, D.C. We, as well as several other classes of new agents, were brought in to meet one another and, more importantly, J. Edgar Hoover, on an informal basis.

First, however, we had to learn the Bureau rules of deportment.

Before actually meeting him we were told to straighten our ties, comb our hair, to smile, look alive, and be alert. We were to stand the instant he entered the room, and rise again when he departed. Any visit from J. Edgar Hoover was always preceded by FBI officials and associates who determined that all was in proper readiness for the Director's visit.

When it came time to actually meet him, we were to stand in

line. The line then passed in front of Hoover, who shook hands with us (one pump per man) as we came face to face with him. I will always remember that moment. It flashed through my mind that he was shorter than I had imagined, not more than five-eight or -nine. He had that tough, bulldog face with that jaw he liked to thrust forward. And eyes that could stare down a crocodile. In dress, he was immaculate. He handled himself extremely well, courteous and friendly, but kept a certain distance. From head to toe, he looked and performed exactly the way this brand new agent thought an FBI Director should look and act.

Having been introduced to all of us, he withdrew to one side of the room where he was soon surrounded by new agents who wanted to talk with him.

One member of our class was particularly vocal in expressing his great affection for the Bureau, and his admiration for Mr. Hoover. He went on (and on) about how for so many years he wanted more than anything else to become an FBI agent.

He was from the deep South. Apparently Hoover was quite taken with his southern accent. Later Hoover mentioned to one of the training division people that the young man seemed to be outstanding. He had thoroughly enjoyed talking to him and listening to him.

On occasion, however, the Director could be initially displeased with a new agent. After another reception he mentioned to his aides that one man had a "slovenly appearance." A second agent, he felt, seemed somewhat "uncouth." He also observed that one particular FBI Academy graduate had "an unusually small head . . . a pinheaded fellow." Whenever Hoover made comments like these, there was always a flurry of activity by his aides-de-camp to correct these perceived defects; otherwise, the man would be permanently marked.

In the case of the man with the unkempt appearance, efforts would have been made to have him dress with more care. Successful or not, if J. Edgar Hoover ever again said that the man presented a slovenly appearance, the agent would, in all likelihood, have been asked to leave the Bureau. The man described as "uncouth" would have presented more of a problem for the aides. First they would have had to determine exactly what the Director meant; in what way was he uncouth—was it his dress, his language, or his appearance? Having determined what Mr. Hoover was talking about (or *guessing* what Hoover meant), they would then have taken steps to improve the man's manner—or manners.

However, in the case of the man with a very small head, the aides were faced with a problem that defied solvability. First of all, exactly who was he talking about? Then, what could they do about it?

Several of the agents at that reception might have had small hat sizes—but which one was "pinheaded"? It was impossible to determine which agent was the object of Hoover's remark, and it was imperative, if the fellow was to survive in the FBI, that the situation be corrected.

I have no idea how this was resolved, but I have heard the same story told over and over again whenever ex-agents get together. Most of us field men agreed that pinheadedness in headquarters wasn't something that ever got anybody fired, so we universally hoped that he had found a permanent place in Washington.

At the graduation reception I attended, conversation between the new agents and Hoover had just begun to get rolling when Clyde Tolson approached the Director and whispered something in his ear.

Hoover abruptly cut off further socializing, bid us farewell, and hurried out to his waiting limousine, parked curbside in front of the hotel.

I was a twenty-nine-year-old lawyer at the time, fresh from Kansas City, excited about being a member of the elite Federal Bureau of Investigation, and totally captivated by the Director's whirlwind appearance among us—and departure from us.

More than whirlwind, it was regal. Wherever he went, pomp preceded him—and accompanied him.

Already a legend, Hoover fueled every Bureau activity, from the way we were taught in the Academy to the way an agent conducted himself in the field. The way we looked was according to Hoover. And I do mean *looked*. You looked serious, alert, and attentive. You walked briskly, never running unless you had to. And if you had to, you ran damn fast. The way the Director wanted you to run.

Mr. Hoover was the most important man I had ever met, and only in retrospect am I certain that this had some bearing on my assessment of him.

Only later did I come to feel differently about these receptions. It was then that I began to wonder how he viewed himself on these occasions. Whatever he felt, I think they added very little to the stature of such an important man. He didn't need our awe to pad his ego. Such events, so carefully staged by all those Bureau aides to further the Hoover image, were a short-term gain. Hoover, an extremely intelligent man, was fully aware that he was the center of attention. He wanted to project the best possible profile for himself and the Bureau . . . and one can only guess that he believed theatrics like this helped both the FBI and J. Edgar Hoover in this respect.

I believe that Hoover himself deliberately chose to appear only briefly at these receptions to instill in the new agents the belief that his enormously responsible position allowed him only so much time for such ceremonies. Hence Tolson's whisperings, the numerous aides hovering about, and the closing-curtain performance of his hasty departures. All very programmed, and very artificial. Somebody should have told him. Somebody else.

On another occasion, Mr. Hoover visited one of our classrooms at the FBI National Academy.

We were told in advance that the Director was on his way and he would speak to us for a few minutes.

Again, his visit was preceded by aides who determined that everything was in order for the Director. I remember it well: the blinds in our classroom were straightened and adjusted to a uniform height. Chairs were aligned; the blackboards were wiped clean. One man, an associate director no less, was a key member of the advance squad. His job was to scurry down the hallway in front of the Hoover entourage picking up cigarette butts because he knew the sight of these butts—even on that old concrete floor—was especially distasteful to Hoover.

When Hoover arrived, a hush fell over the room, broken only by the simultaneous rising of us all. And, in unison, we sat down when he said, "Good afternoon, gentlemen. Please be seated."

We then heard a torrent of words, spoken in that staccato, snap-crackle-and-pop voice that he always affected for his lecturing. I was so impressed by the drama of the occasion that, for a moment, I forgot to take notes. Observing the feverish pen and pencil activity of my classmates, however, I began writing immediately. Hoover spoke for about ten minutes focusing on the range of an FBI agent's responsibilities. Vast. Through it all he was the consummate actor, maintaining the mantle of aloofness and authority one would expect from the nation's number one policeman. Another theatrical performance—so impressive to the impressionable.

Following graduation, my pay was $3,200 a year. Not a princely sum, but in those days—and especially in the depression-wracked hills of West Virginia—very adequate. Huntington, my first assignment, lasted but three months.

In 1942, I was transferred to the FBI training center in Quantico, Virginia, as a firearms instructor. I was assigned to this post because my handgun score was consistently in the high nineties out of a possible one hundred. Not a God-given gift, my proficiency in firearms developed only after one of my superiors read me the riot act about my initially poor performance. My instructor said that my inferior marksmanship would be of more danger to a fellow agent than to any fugitive we might be pursuing. This was definitely not the kind of report a young agent wanted Mr. Hoover to hear. My superior's scolding bore fruit. Within a short time I became an expert marksman.

It was during my tour of duty as an instructor at Quantico that I saw Hoover again.

His behavior during this visit proved a unique insight into the Hoover personality and legend. The occasion was significant enough, a visit by the Duke of Windsor, who was in the United States in 1942 for a personal tour and a general ambassadorial mission. Because the duke had expressed an interest in learning about the FBI, the government decided to take him to Quantico to listen to some of the discussions at the FBI Academy and also to view firearms instruction. A carefully planned schedule of events was arranged.

An amusing sidelight occurred while preparing for the visit and during the visit itself.

During preparations, it was decided that our one baldheaded firearms instructor would stay in the back of our facility and not be exposed to the visiting entourage because of his lack of hair. Two thoughts struck me at the time. First, the agent made no complaint about the action. It seemed that he went along with being sequestered in order to maintain the image of youthful vitality that was a hallmark of the Bureau. Second, there was a bona fide concern that Mr. Hoover might come under some criticism because an obviously middle-aged man with little or no hair would be in the public limelight when the Duke of Windsor visited. Hoover's image—and speculation on what was good for his image—influenced the thinking of everyone.

When the day arrived, Hoover accompanied the duke and his entourage through the academy grounds. Everything went smoothly until the group came to the area where the shotgun demonstration was scheduled to be held. The duke asked to fire a weapon. Of course, he was immediately granted permission to do so. An agent suggested that he don a padded shooting jacket (which we wore to prevent bruised shoulders). He refused the jacket, but went ahead and shot at the target. He did a more than workmanlike job of handling the gun, hitting the target with a tight dispersion. Good score!

Hoover's next move stunned all of us.

One of the duke's aides turned to the Director and asked him to describe the velocity of the bullet and the grain weight of the powder in the gun's cartridge. Hoover, not knowing the answer, looked at the man as if he were speaking a foreign language. Then he simply walked away—and began talking to another group. The question was finally answered by an FBI instructor fully versed in such things.

Such behavior was typical of Hoover. Though there wasn't a reason in the world why he should have known that technical information, he did not want to reveal an ignorance of anything. To do so would have been a loss of dignity. The Director wanted everybody—especially FBI men—to believe he was all-knowing. It seemed impossible for him to relax and join the ranks of human beings.

Another interesting sidelight to the Hoover personality was his near obsession with the almighty importance of the Bureau . . . notwithstanding anything.

In early 1944 I sent a letter to the Director advising him that I had decided to leave the Bureau to enter the U.S. Navy. I told him that I had enjoyed my service in the FBI, and that I was leaving with nothing but admiration and respect for the organization and its people. However, I had some misgivings about the importance of the service I was then rendering to my country. With the nation at war, I believed my time and efforts would be of more value to the U.S. Navy, wherever they might want to use me, than to the FBI in Des Moines, Iowa. I wrote to FBI headquarters, explaining my feelings, and giving a three-week notice. My letter of resignation apparently reached the Bureau the next morning because that same day—not three weeks later—I was terminated from the Federal Bureau of Investigation.

At the time it was very disturbing. But I can't say I was surprised. The Director couldn't understand anything ever being more important than his FBI.

Then, in 1946, having served almost all of my time in the Navy aboard ship, I returned home thinking how much I would have liked to rejoin the FBI. But my speedy dismissal in 1944 made me doubt my chances. Even though my abrupt termination from the Bureau had occurred a full two years earlier, I knew Hoover wouldn't have forgotten any "disloyalty" to him.

Shortly thereafter, with nothing to lose, I filed my application for reemployment with the Bureau, requesting assignment in the Kansas City office. Within a couple of weeks I received a letter informing me that my application had been approved—and I would be reinstated to the Kansas City office. I was delighted, of course. It was nice to know I'd be going back, and under what I felt to be "my terms."

As a returning veteran, I was entitled to my job again. But getting the Kansas City assignment as requested was icing on the cake. To this day, I don't know why Mr. Hoover allowed me to have it my way.

I worked for the Bureau in Kansas City as a general criminal investigator and supervisor until 1951. Later that year I was transferred to the Washington, D.C., FBI Headquarters as a supervisor. This new move was, I felt, a good promotion for me. I later learned that this specific supervisory assignment had been given to me as a direct result of the recommendation by a key Hoover lieutenant who was making a general inspection of the Kansas City office.

Inspections were important to an agent's career. And you had to know how to play the game.

Field office inspections were standard FBI operating procedure and were conducted in each field office every twelve to eighteen months. Individual inspectors interviewed all field-office supervisors, and all special agents-in-charge were informed individually when the inspectors wanted to see us for a review. As always, we were expected to be prompt for inspection interviews. As always, it was mandatory to have a notebook and take careful notes.

For the Kansas City field office inspection, I appeared as scheduled and walked into the inspector's office on time.

The inspector naturally said he appreciated my promptness and was particularly glad that I had brought my note-taking paraphernalia. He told me he had recently interviewed another one of our supervisors, but this person had been tardy and did not bring his notebook with him. Absolutely nothing further was said about the reason for his visit. We chatted for a few minutes, and I was excused. Clearly, the man simply wanted to see if I would arrive on time with pencil and notebook in hand. Within a few months I was transferred to Washington, D.C., as a supervisor.

I worked as a supervisor in the Investigations Division in Washington, D.C., for less than a year.

About six months into the assignment, a rumor surfaced: a significant reduction in my division's supervisory personnel was supposedly in the works. Apparently, J. Edgar Hoover felt that there were too many supervisors in the Washington Investigations Division and, further, he wanted many of these more experienced personnel transferred to field offices. And of course when Hoover wanted something, he got it.

Once again thinking that I had nothing to lose, I asked the assistant director in charge of our division if I might return to the Kansas City FBI office.

"My family did not come to Washington with me, and I have been unable to sell our home in Kansas City. If my suggestion would save the government—and the FBI in particular—the expense of transferring our furniture to Washington, I would be more than happy to return to Kansas City."

The transfer was approved almost immediately.

Apparently, I had stumbled onto a clever way to request a move and in the process it avoided the fuss that some agents had made when their transfers came through. Indeed, as far as I know, my transfer was the only one that was happily granted and willingly received. I was not aware then of the shrewd thinking I had applied to this situation. In any case, I was able to move back to Kansas City to be with my family.

My career and those of other agents evolved within narrow Bureau guidelines established and monitored by Hoover. After thirty years as FBI Director, he was (from any distance) the ultimate monolithic figure, dictating every change or move in all our respective careers.

Generally, if an agent worked hard, maintained "acceptable" statistics, and followed Hoover's rules, his career would move forward something like this: he would be given an assignment for specific on-the-job training as a supervisor's aide in a field office. If successful in this assignment, he would next be sent to FBI headquarters in Washington, D.C., as a supervisor. Or he could be designated as a supervisor in a field office. In the latter case, the supervisor might also be sent to Washington if a vacancy arose. The order to go to Washington for training was normally seen as a very notable event in an agent's career (not always a positive note, however, as we will see later). There was no doubt that all major decisions of this type came from the Director.

However, organizational frictions did exist.

There was a distinct difference in the perceptions of service to the Bureau between agents in the field and those at headquarters.

Having worked in both areas extensively, I can say that the staff of the FBI at Washington headquarters felt that accomplishments by people in the field were a direct result of the guidelines provided them by headquarters in Washington. On the other hand, the individuals at the field offices felt they were the ones who did the hard work and conducted and completed most successful investigations. There was, quite naturally, some jealousy on both sides and, with some duplication of efforts both in the field and at headquarters, certain differences of opinion existed.

In some cases, orders affecting an agent's career appeared to be made quite subjectively. An agent could benefit enormously, or his career could be destroyed—all with no apparent reason. Other than Mr. Hoover wanted it that way.

In the truest sense of the words, Hoover's wish was everybody's command.

An agent sent to Washington as a supervisor would remain there for an extended period of time. The exact length of time was determined by his performance or by his "sponsors" at the higher levels of FBI management who could give his career a boost. In some cases, an agent supervisor could be sent to the field at his own request. On the other hand, he could be sent to a field office because his performance at headquarters was unsatisfactory.

Generally, following a two-year term in Washington or in the field as a supervisor, an individual was usually considered ready to become an assistant special agent-in-charge of a field office. After a satisfactory three-year term in this position, he could then be considered for promotion to the position of inspector and, after that, conceivably could become a special agent-in-charge of a field office.

Whatever happened, however, one thing was certain: every FBI agent's career unfolded under the sometimes inexplicable direction and management of Hoover himself—J. Edgar Hoover and his finely tuned machinery in Washington.

More often than infrequently, abuses did occur.

In some cases highly qualified individuals were passed over. Other times it appeared that men were promoted without any proven performance record. I once encountered a field manager—a special agent-in-charge—whose experience in the field was abysmally shallow. He was totally unprepared for such an important management responsibility. Also, I saw some agents promoted to positions of high responsibility in Washington because of their acquaintanceship with men at the top. (Astonishing to me was the Bureau practice of promoting men from the field to Washington to get rid of them—the thinking being they could do less harm in the bureaucracy of headquarters than in the field. This widely recognized reality always cast a shadow on any transfer to headquarters.)

Fortunately for me, I was able to remain in Hoover's good graces throughout most of my twenty-one years with the FBI. I was happy to return to Kansas City in 1951, and the move back indicated to me that I was held in a benevolent light by Hoover. I knew all along that my "let's save moving expenses" argument wouldn't have held much water if J. Edgar Hoover hadn't chosen to smile.

In 1953 Mr. Hoover transferred me to the post of assistant special agent-in-charge of the Houston office.

I was transferred to Houston to replace a man who, in my opinion, was a diligent agent who had done a good job in the

Houston field office. But he fell victim to the myopic and harsh personnel treatment of which the Bureau under Hoover was certainly capable.

Word got back to Washington that this agent had been involved in something questionable while investigating a crime on the high seas. During the routine course of doing his job, he made a visit to the ship and, while there, bought a pair of boots from a member of the ship's crew. Undoubtedly, the agent purchased the footwear for less than he would have paid in the States. For this minor violation, he was summarily demoted, without a hearing. Notwithstanding, the agent knew the rules of the game. He took his demotion in stride, made no vocal protests, didn't rock the boat, and soon was assimilated into the investigative staff in the Kansas City office. I'm sure that this was a Hoover-inspired decision and, in my opinion, clearly an unfair one.

After I became an assistant special agent-in-charge of the Houston field office in 1953, I was called into Washington every year for my annual conference with J. Edgar Hoover.

For me, this was always a time to be on edge. One had to be at the top of one's game when it came time for a private session with the Director.

In fact, any meeting with Hoover was an event that became permanently etched in an agent's mind. To a large measure, these meetings with the boss determined an agent's ultimate success or failure with the Bureau. The chemistry didn't have to be good between you and Hoover, but it better not be bad. No matter how many times you met with and dealt with J. Edgar Hoover, you always seemed to come out where everybody else came out: an unusual man, complex in so many ways, messianic in his dedication to Bureau excellence—and yet somehow so profoundly simple.

An agent always had so many factors to keep in mind as he called on the Director.

First, every agent always knew that this meeting between him and Hoover might be their last, the last before you got a significant promotion—or before you were told that you better start looking around. And rarely would the agent know what he did or said to win a great victory with Mr. Hoover, or suffer such a devastating defeat. The stress this caused grew over the years I spent under Hoover, perhaps because he was growing more irascible, or perhaps because the superstructure of the Bureau had become so unmanageable for all.

Second, if an agent was to be on time for any event in his life, this was it. Stories of Hoover's almost uncontainable wrath over tardiness were legend throughout the Bureau.

In one case, a special agent-in-charge, a highly respected career man, did not report on time for his appointment with the Director—through no fault of his own. In fact, his tardiness was traced to an error made by the Director's own clerical staff. Nevertheless, when the special agent-in-charge did not report at the precise time indicated on Hoover's calendar, the roof fell in. He was refused another meeting with Hoover, reduced in rank, ordered returned to his field office, and censured. The agent in question was a skilled and respected veteran and, as a result, knew the ropes. He correctly felt that it would be detrimental to his future with the FBI to proclaim his innocence.

He, therefore, accepted his demotion without protest. None of Hoover's office staff ever came forward to admit the error. No doubt they too feared for their own jobs. Errors of this type were simply not permitted. And for every error, somebody was at fault. For every fault, blame was to be assigned. Well-meaning and well-intentioned individuals within the Bureau who might otherwise admit a mistake were restrained by Hoover's rigid rules of conduct and retribution.

Fortunately, in this particular case, the agent was a good soldier and later recovered his former rank. This move, I always suspected, was engineered by the people who themselves had been responsible for the error. They appreciated his course of action in not creating a scene—thereby getting them into hot water too.

A third basic rule in having a meeting with J. Edgar Hoover, in addition to being on time and looking properly deferential, was to bring a pencil and a notepad. There are several cases where meetings with the Director were actually aborted because the agent involved did not bring these two essentials to his meeting.

Waiting in J. Edgar Hoover's outer office at the power center of the Bureau headquarters was an experience an agent rarely forgot.

I can recall from my own visits there that the personnel in the outer office are as accommodating as possible. They certainly make every effort to put you at ease, but, unhappily, none of their efforts were of any real comfort in view of the impending encounter with the Director. In fact, the nicer they were, the greater the stress.

But no tension could equal "getting it on the first buzz."

Let me explain.

The telephone system in the headquarters' reception area consisted of a number of office lines, buttons, switches, and so forth, in a large telephone console. The console was designed to accept incoming calls as well as internal calls. It was an absolute mandate that when Hoover's buzzer sounded, the receptionist must get it on the first buzz. Everybody in the FBI, the world around, knew how critical it was to get that first buzz. If he had to buzz twice, not only was the receptionist in hot water, but the Director would be most unhappy. And the den of a most unhappy J. Edgar Hoover was the last place a fresh-from-the-field agent wanted to enter.

Well, one time I was sitting there on my pins and needles, wondering what the fates held for me that day, when a call came in from the outside. No sooner had the receptionist taken the call when Hoover hit the buzzer. I thought, get rid of that call, answer that buzz!

To the caller, the receptionist said, "I'm sorry, sir, but I can't understand you."

Forget him, get that buzz, I thought.

"I'm sorry, sir, but you'll have to talk slower."

Slower? Forget him, get that buzz.

"I'm sorry, sir, but I can't make out what you're saying. Our connection must be bad."

"Forget him, get that buzz," I blurted out loud.

And with that, she pulled the cord on the outside caller, and got the buzz, glowering at me.

"He'll see you now, Mr. Kelley." She paused, then broke into a smile, and added "Good luck—and relax" with more warmth, humor, and understanding than I deserved.

Normally, after fidgeting for a few minutes, an agent would be called in to see the Director.

The trip to see him from the outer area included a journey along an oak-paneled corridor about fifty-feet long after which the agent would go through a solid oak door. This door led into a large conference room adjacent to Hoover's private office.

The conference room featured a splendid fireplace over which hung an oil painting of Harlan Fiske Stone. Lining the walls were chairs and sofas upholstered in black leather with bright brass buttons on the cushions. To me they always looked like new, shiny pennies.

Occupying the center of the room was a glass-top conference table, which ordinarily could seat as many as twenty people. Beneath the table was an enormous oriental rug that covered most of the floor. One would then pass through the outer office and come directly to Hoover's smaller private office. In this inner sanctum Hoover worked . . . hard and long. The furnishings here consisted of Hoover's large, attractive, and very traditional desk, which had very little on it except an in-box, out-box, and telephone. Visits to the Hoover inner sanctum tended to follow a similar pattern: first the amenities—then pencil and notepad.

As the agent entered Hoover's small, rather spartan office, the Director would stand up and extend his hand.

"Welcome back to Washington, Mr. Kelley."

He would greet the agent formally, say he was glad to see him, and then invite him to sit down. Always he would proceed to discuss "matters of substance" almost immediately.

At this point the agent pulled out pad and pencil and started writing. He would have to scribble anything, at a feverish pace, even if it was nonsense.

The Director, a master of human psychology, knew instinctively—indeed, saw to it—that virtually everyone who came to see him was, in some manner, intimidated. His desk was cleverly arranged so that it and his chair seemed to be on a platform, higher than the very low-slung guest chairs. Thus, anyone invited to his inner sanctum had to look up to him during the conference. Also, the office blinds were left open in such a way that the sunlight came over Mr. Hoover's shoulder like a spotlight right into the visitor's eyes. Hoover, speaking in his staccato, lecturing style, dominated the conversation. It was very difficult for anyone to get points across to him. He really didn't want to know what you had to say. His mind was made up. He was convinced he was right. Why would he want to hear from anybody else? He didn't even want to allow questions. He might not know the answer.

Often a guest would sit there wondering to himself: "Am I looking intelligent? Am I responding all right? Am I writing fast enough?"

As I said, I personally didn't care for these meetings. I never met an agent who did. And I wouldn't have believed him if one said he did.

Quite often Hoover would discuss something on his mind that had nothing to do with the reason for the visit, and often had no significance at all for the visitor. Going off on tangents that might last as long as forty-five minutes without interruption, Hoover would talk about some congressman or senator who was stepping on his toes or simply irritating him. Nothing, nobody was sacred. Government spending, the attorney general, big business, proposed legislation he personally disliked—anything—it was all discussed in that rapid-fire delivery. One thing about those tirades that always stumped me: I never knew whether to look like I was taking notes when he talked that way. I didn't want him to think I was writing down his every word, but I also knew that one was supposed to take those notes.

As for responses, a "Yes, Mr. Hoover," or "I agree, Mr. Hoover," was about all that was necessary. Just enough to show you were awake—and listening.

I usually went away from such meetings awed by the Director's command of the language. In addition, each meeting with Hoover invariably contained the veiled threat that if a field office did not have good statistical accomplishments, "it might be necessary, as in the Ford Motor Company, to close the office for lack of production." I must have heard that speech a dozen times in twenty-one years. Occasionally, the Director used colorful locker-room language with me. These meetings, however, followed a free-form routine that nearly always was, in a word, bewildering.

There was, however, a way to alter the general pattern of these meetings with the Director—if one had the nerve to do so. A peculiarity of the Hoover personality emerged over the years. We found that he liked to receive presents.

On one occasion an agent, whose field office statistics were not good, arrived at a meeting with the Director. The agent came dutifully equipped with a pad, pencil—and a gift wrapped in an octagonal package. The meeting began in normal fashion. The agent listened and Hoover talked. However, the package placed on the Director's desk was a challenge Hoover could no longer resist. The lecture stopped abruptly.

"What is in the package?" Hoover asked.

The agent explained that it was a present for the Director.

A present! Suddenly the nature of the meeting changed. Hoover opened the package. In it was an inexpensive wristwatch, one having all number fives in place of the normal numbers on the face. It was a "cocktail hour" watch. Hoover was delighted. The day was won. Not only did the Director forget about the Ford Motor Company lecture on the agent's poor field office statistics, but the meeting concluded pleasantly.

Another agent, known to this day as "Coconut Cake," faced an unpleasant meeting with Hoover over his limping stats. Fearing the worst but hoping for the best, the agent was willing to try almost anything to have an amicable meeting with the boss. He heard through the grapevine that Hoover enjoyed, of all things, coconut cake.

With this in mind, the resourceful agent bought one before he left on his trip. He carried the cake on his lap during the plane ride to Washington for his session with the Director. Extraordinary as it might seem, the agent presented the cake to Hoover just as the boss was swinging into his statistics lecture. Bingo! The Director was thrilled. It goes without saying that no one had ever dared (or even thought) to bring a coconut cake to J. Edgar Hoover's inner sanctum office before. The prospects of an unpleasant discussion about field office statistics vanished as Hoover buzzed Helen Gandy, instructing her to bring two cake plates, two forks, and two cups of coffee—at once.

The lengths to which some agents went to earn the Director's good graces were amazing.

During the many years that I was involved with J. Edgar Hoover I tried earnestly to do as good a job as I could. But never was I able to engage in these machinations. Nevertheless, I (like most of my fellow agents) was always apprehensive about my personal dealings with him.

While I enjoyed my work in the Houston field office from 1953 to 1955, I always knew that Hoover was the only person truly in charge of all FBI offices. That fact influenced our behavior and the nature of the regular reports sent to Washington.

One memorable incident in Houston illustrates, I believe, the "creative reporting" techniques we would use to elude criticism from Washington. In this case, I led a group of agents from the field office to apprehend a dangerous fugitive known to be working as a hired hand on a large ranch outside of town.

This episode was a near disaster.

We converged on the ranch just after dawn that morning, sped into the yard, and spotted the fugitive on a tractor. He was driving directly toward a large barn when we pulled up alongside him in our car. I jumped from the car, ran over to the tractor, pulled the fugitive off while the tractor was still running, and physically subdued him.

In the meantime, the tractor, still in gear, chugged and sputtered along, slamming into—and through—the barn. Incredibly, it stopped just short of hitting an Appaloosa horse valued at about five thousand dollars. Had the tractor not stalled right then, it most certainly would have killed the valuable animal and probably leveled the barn—at a cost of several thousand dollars more.

I obviously did not always go by the book.

This type of criminal apprehension was not exactly standard FBI procedure. But I was the agent in charge of the operation. So I knew that I had to write the report. And I knew that Hoover would probably read it. Thus, to put the event in the most favorable light, I wrote that "in making the apprehension, I assisted the subject in getting off the tractor." I later learned that Hoover did indeed read the report, and I've always wondered how he felt about having such a courteous and polite agent in Houston. Whatever doubts he may have had about my story, however, were apparently placated by the fact that the arrest was made—so he overlooked my "gallantry."

In another case, two FBI agents had, after a long search, captured a highly sought-after military deserter. It was necessary to transport the fugitive about sixty miles. He was handcuffed with his hands in front of him and placed in the back seat of a government sedan. The prisoner was alone in the back, and the two FBI agents rode in the front seat. While in transit, the prisoner, in a desperate move, opened the back door of the car, jumped out of the moving car, rolled to the shoulder of the road, and, amazingly, bounded to his feet and vaulted over a bridge railing into a stream below. All this while wearing his handcuffs!

The agents' astonishment was matched only by their chagrin.

They searched in vain for the man for the next several hours—only reluctantly enlisting the aid of local law-enforcement personnel. At last, following the all-day search, they recaptured the fugitive just before nightfall.

Unfortunately for the two agents, the whole episode received a full round of publicity, all focusing of course on the angle "LOCAL POLICE COME TO AID OF FBI"—not one of Mr. Hoover's favorite themes.

Needless to say, with all of the newspaper attention it got, this story had to be sent to Washington pretty much as it happened.

Granted, the agents had made several mistakes.

First, they should have handcuffed the prisoner with his hands behind him. Second, they forgot to lock the sedan's back doors. Third, the prisoner should never, under any circumstances—handcuffs in front or in back, locked doors or not—have been left alone in the back seat.

Prisoner back in custody, case closed. Now the report had to be sent in. All of the newspaper coverage minimized the possibilities available for coloring the episode. So the epistle dutifully indicated that the agents had conducted an immediate search for the escaped subject, had quickly enlisted the efforts of local enforcement officers and succeeded, at last, in recapturing the fugitive. The report did not focus on the errors that the agents made.

When the report was read by Hoover, he immediately rejected it as a fabrication. He refused to believe that the escapee could swim wearing handcuffs! The fact that the stream wasn't deep enough to swim in made no difference. The fact that no reference had been made to swimming made no difference. The fact that the Director missed the whole point of the story made no difference. The two agents were censured because he did not believe a portion of their story that the agents hadn't thought to hedge on. Hoover never questioned how the man could have jumped from the car in the first place. At any rate, the demerits were enough to cost the men their periodic salary increase for a couple of years—a painful conclusion to another bizarre FBI story.

It is not surprising that very little bad news was passed along to J. Edgar Hoover.

Most reports sent to Washington were written, rewritten, edited, scrubbed, and cleaned and pressed a dozen times before they were put in the mail. Reportorial accuracy was seldom a consideration. Almost everyone in the organization was usually afraid to tell Hoover the truth for fear of upsetting him—and for fear of the inevitable punishment. As a result, Hoover often had to rely on information that had been sugarcoated for him. This tended in many cases to isolate him from the greatest potential resource for creating a better FBI: his own people. I felt that the penalties imposed in the handcuffed swimmer incident were extremely heavy. However, if the truth had been revealed or a protest presented, an even harsher punishment would have resulted.

His posture as Director was so domineering and his power over his people so intimidating that communication from those of us in the Bureau was not always a bona fide source of information for the boss.

There were instances, of course, when episodes were not reported to headquarters at all.

One such situation happened to me when I was a young agent. I and another agent, also a rookie, were attempting to capture two burglary suspects. An informant had told us that the fugitives could be found in a local tavern. The two of us drove there and immediately spotted their car by the tavern's front door. We then circled the block, and parked our car just where the book says you should: at least a hundred feet behind the car you're to follow. My fellow agent got out to go make a phone call. I remained in the passenger's seat, my eye on that front door. Sure enough, as my companion was making his call, the suspects came out of the tavern, got into their car, and began to drive away.

I immediately moved over to the driver's seat and reached for the ignition. I was ready to apprehend them myself. And I would have done so except for one thing: no keys. My companion had taken them with him. The fugitives turned the next corner and sped out of sight.

A simple but frustrating mishap, but one we thought was kind of funny. We knew Mr. Hoover wouldn't laugh, however, and we weren't especially anxious to report our story back to our field boss.

In this situation the local agent-in-charge was equally reluctant about submitting this report to Washington.

"I'm not going to make any report to Washington now. But you guys better find those two, and find them fast."

It took us six more weeks but we finally caught up with them, and made the arrest, thus bailing out the boss—and ourselves. Had Hoover ever found out what really happened, all three of us would have been censured. Two of us might have been fired.

The report to Washington was all laudatory, however. It talked in glowing terms about the two brave young agents who apprehended the dangerous outlaws . . . without mentioning the two clowns who let the men escape six weeks earlier.

My next direct dealing with Hoover was in 1955. That year I was promoted from assistant special agent-in-charge to inspector. A good promotion for me and an indication that my performance as an agent had met or exceeded the generally accepted standards of Bureau competency and performance in the field.

I went home the evening of my promotion and announced my new responsibilities. I explained that my new position would entail a good bit of travel, with extended absences from home. My family listened very carefully, and it was clear they were pleased with my promotion.

However, my son Kent, who was eight years old at the time, had a concern.

"Daddy, how much of the time won't you be home? I think we will miss you too much."

I was touched. This was the first time I had experienced such deep feelings from my son. "Kent, I don't think I'll be away that often . . . or for any long periods of time. But if we all feel that I'm away more than we like, I'll talk to Mr. Hoover, and I'm sure he'll do something about it."

My wife, Ruby, looked at me as if to say, "Okay, now how will you ever get yourself out of *this* one?"

Nevertheless, with my promise made, I was determined to stick with it.

"If ever any one of the three of you feels that Daddy is away too much, you just let me know, and we'll do something."

Off to Washington we went. For nine months I was as good a

field inspector as I could be—or as good as the system would let me be.

In my assignment I had to travel to FBI field offices in many major American cities. Inspections generally followed certain established FBI routines. As a result the inspector neither improved the caliber of work performed at the field-office level, nor was he expected to improve things. His responsibility was to merely report to Washington what he found out there.

On many occasions I saw the opportunity to initiate changes that would have produced better investigations by the Bureau. However, my experience with headquarters' officialdom cautioned me against any departure from FBI norms. Essentially, I did what others had done before, and rocked no boats. But that wasn't the real problem with this new post. Time away from home, that was my main concern. Me and three others.

After an extended tour of inspections to the West Coast kept me away from my family for almost a month, I knew I was going home to face the music.

As I came in the door, Ruby said, "Okay, Mr. Promises, get ready to hear from all three of us."

I allowed that I was ready to hear what they had to say.

We called the children, and sat down in the living room.

They all wanted to talk at once.

"Suppose you let me say it for you," I suggested.

"Dad," I said, "you've been away too often . . . and too long. Your new promotion might be great for you, but it's terrible for our family. What are you going to do about it, Dad?"

Kent jumped in. "You said you would talk to Mr. Hoover."

Ruby gave me the same look she'd given me the night I first announced my promotion—and made my promise.

"I'll take care of it," I said.

Ruby gave me that look again.

The following day I called the Director's office and asked for an appointment with Mr. Hoover. There was no need to specify why I wanted an appointment with him, so I gave no reason.

I was called the next morning and advised that I had an appointment with the Director at 2:30 P.M. that day.

Word raced through headquarters that I had requested a meeting with Hoover. Because it was quite unusual for anyone at my level to request time with the Director, everybody wanted to know what was up. "Are you quitting?" most of them asked.

"No," I said. "I'm just going to ask that I be relieved of my position as inspector. I want to spend more time with my family than this job will allow."

"Oh, you *are* quitting," they said.

"You just don't *do* this, Kelley," they said.

"Kelley, you don't tell Mr. Hoover that your family is more important than your job."

"It'll be all right," I said with more assurance than I was beginning to feel. "He'll understand."

"How *can* he? Did you ever see *his* wife and children? When was the last time *he* took a month-long business trip?"

Needless to say, before my friends got through with me, I was wound up as tight as an alarm clock. By the time 2:30 came around, I wasn't looking forward to making my speech.

But at the appointed hour I managed to get myself to Mr. Hoover's office. I survived the short wait in the reception area without any "first buzz" problems, and was soon summoned to his office.

From the start, unlike any other time I'd ever spent with him, Mr. Hoover was quiet and reserved. He simply looked at me and said:

"Well, Mr. Kelley, what is it you wished to see me about?"

I explained my son's request many months ago. I told him of the promise to my family, and my prolonged absences from home were of paramount concern to me.

I related my meeting with my family, and told Hoover that my wife, daughter, and son all wanted me to change positions so that I could spend more time with them.

"It is my desire, sir, that I be released from my current duties as an inspector, and be assigned to another office. I think I can be of greater service to the Bureau in another position, and I am fully prepared to go anywhere you might wish to send me— under most any conditions you might want to impose."

Hoover stared at me, as if in disbelief. He said nothing.

Finally, I played the best card I had.

"I would like you to grant me this request so that I can continue my career with the Bureau." I did not mean that statement as a threat, but as a commitment, and Mr. Hoover took it in the spirit that I offered it.

Silence. The Director continued to look at me, saying nothing.

Then he closed my manila-bound personnel file quite slowly and deliberately. He stared at the ceiling, deep in thought. I thought, he *doesn't* understand. My friends were right. But I was determined not to say another word.

Hoover finally looked directly into my eyes and said, "Thank you for coming to see me, Mr. Kelley. I appreciate your telling me what is on your mind. I will have an answer for you in a few days."

He gave no indication what that answer might be. I didn't know whether he was pleased or displeased. I could detect absolutely no emotion on his face or in his voice.

We shook hands and I left.

Curiously, even though I couldn't know the outcome, my tension was gone.

As I left the building, several of my friends asked me how the meeting turned out. With all good intentions, they spoke admiringly of my integrity and fortitude. Their eyes and smiles gave them away, however. They thought the prospects of me lasting out the week were zero. This was not altogether comforting.

That evening, I replayed my visit with Mr. Hoover to my family. Ruby's eyes and smile gave her away, too. She thought my chances of lasting out the week were *less* than zero.

The following day, in the afternoon mail, I received a letter from Mr. Hoover's office on his own private stationery. My fumbling hands almost could not get it open.

I'll never forget the words: "Your request is approved . . . move to Birmingham, Alabama, as special agent-in-charge." The head of the office! A clear and significant promotion!

The next day I handwrote a thank-you note to Hoover. Initially, I felt that my good fortune represented Hoover's understanding of my family's genuine needs. I believed the boss had been impressed by the story of my son's wishes to see more of his father. There was, of course, no way I could know all of the reasons for my favorable treatment.

I was soon to learn the full story. The previous special agent-in-charge of the Birmingham field office had been gored by various Birmingham law-enforcement and civic officials, chiefly the commissioner of public safety—a man who called himself "Bull" Connor.

In light of the fact that the Birmingham office had more than its share of problems, it struck me that Mr. Hoover had given me that assignment as a "special treatment" response to my request. Because I had been blessed with special treatment, I would therefore devote extra effort on behalf of the FBI. I, it seemed, was just the man for the troubled situation in Birmingham.

Whatever Hoover's motives, however, I will always think of it as a gesture of kindness on the Director's part. He handed me an assignment I deemed attractive and, at the same time, solidified my family's ties, allowing us a new closeness. Even if problems awaited me in Birmingham, I felt I had much to be thankful for. Given all the options in advance, I still would have chosen Birmingham, and handwritten my thanks to the Director for the opportunity.

I remained special agent-in-charge in Birmingham for more than two years. At least once a year I reported to the Director on the status of the Birmingham field office. In my first month in Birmingham an incident occurred that again demonstrated Hoover's management style, his iron-fisted control over the rules and regulations of the Bureau.

The assistant agent-in-charge of the office had scheduled some time off to return to his hometown in order to sell his parents' house. He asked me if he could go ahead with his plans. I told him there was no reason why he should not, so he left on a three-week leave.

In the meantime, I searched for a place to live in Birmingham, soon finding a comfortable home in a good neighborhood. I immediately called my wife and told her that the furniture should be shipped to Birmingham and that she and the children should follow soon thereafter. A few days later my wife informed me that the furniture was being sent and would arrive in a few days.

The day before its arrival I sent a telex to Bureau headquarters in Washington informing them that I would be at my new home, and that a telephone had been installed where I could be reached. Further, I said that I was taking time off as part of my annual paid vacation to supervise the arrival of my furniture and my family in Birmingham.

The telex was dispatched to the Director's office where the news caused a furor.

Immediately an assistant at Hoover's office was on the phone.

"Mr. Kelley, you know the FBI rules do *not* allow *both* the special agent-in-charge *and* assistant special agent-in-charge to be out of the office at *the same time.*" He paused only long enough to make sure I knew I was in trouble.

"Moreover, Mr. Kelley, this rule has been in force for *quite* some time, and you *should* have been aware of it."

I protested, saying I was very much aware of that rule. "However, I am not going to be away. I will be in Birmingham, but, at another telephone. I can be reached at any moment. My own people know this, and my purpose in informing Washington was simply to let you know where you could reach me . . . here in town."

The assistant didn't want to see it my way.

"No," he said. "You are in violation of a Bureau regulation." Another pause for effect. All I could think of at that moment was that this was beginning to sound like Gilbert and Sullivan.

"Mr. Hoover expects *all* his regulations to be followed to the letter. You will definitely hear more about this from the Director himself."

"You've got to be kidding me." I knew he wasn't.

"We'll see," he said, and hung up.

As predicted, a scorching letter of censure for my failure to observe the letter of the law arrived the next day. Through his management staff, Hoover again demonstrated that the penalty for even the most minor and questionable infraction could be a reprimand from the top.

In looking back at this episode, I wonder how much of the story actually reached J. Edgar Hoover's desk. It is my feeling now that this was one of those times when people who worked for Hoover at headquarters, looking for a way to bop some agent in the field, overreacted. In the field, you never knew whether some staff functionary was doing what he thought Hoover wanted him to do . . . or what *he* wanted to do. In turn, Hoover felt pressure to enforce his rules and regulations—to the letter—so he went along with this gamesmanship.

Such domination of the headquarters staff by the Director was all the motivation most of them needed to come down as hard and as often as they could on the agents in the field. And field men were always playing it safe for fear of appearing to step out of line. In retrospect, I think it's a wonder that field and head-quarters people got along as well as we did.

With time, however, the gulf between us widened.

I and my colleagues in the field gradually developed a grow-ing detachment from the headquarters. We began to feel that the Washington Bureau had little concern for the field except to make sure we followed every rule in the book and kept our statis-tics up . . . just like that automobile company.

After I had been in Birmingham for about two years, I received a call from "Bull" Connor. The same Connor who had caused my predecessor so many headaches, the same Connor who later became notorious throughout the world during the sit-ins and freedom rides to Montgomery and other cities in the South.

"Can I come and see you?" the soft, mellow voice of Connor asked.

"Yes, of course, Mr. Connor. But can you give me some idea what it's about? Maybe I really can't help you."

"I don't want to talk about this over the phone," he said. "I want to meet you and discuss it in person."

He sounded reasonable enough. "When would you like to see me?"

"How about right now?"

"I'm busy right this minute. Can we make a date for later in the week?"

"This is really important," he said.

"How about the end of the day?" I suggested.

"Okay, but I'm coming over right away. I'll just sit outside your office until you can talk." Not waiting for a response to that, he hung up.

He was in the outer office within the hour. The receptionist called to announce his arrival. I told her to tell him to have a seat, that I'd see him in a minute. She called back in exactly a minute.

"He's pacing back and forth out here like a caged animal. He makes me nervous."

"Have him come in."

Entering my office, he made himself clear at once.

"I want to go to Washington. I want to talk to somebody in charge of civil rights enforcement. Who would that be? Can you help me get an appointment with him?"

I told him I didn't know exactly who he should see. And I thought he could make his own appointments with whoever that person would be.

Connor went into a lengthy monologue. He wanted to talk to the person in charge of civil rights. He had a need to talk to this person. He wanted to explain the difficulties that he, as public safety commissioner, was having in Birmingham.

"The men in your Justice Department really don't understand the problems we're having with Negroes here in the South. If I could just get to the head man, I know I could make him see the problems we have here."

He looked at me and asked, "Would you please help me?"

"I really don't know who you should talk to," I protested.

"I can understand that," he said. "Can you find out?"

"I wouldn't know where to start," I said.

"Somebody in Washington will know. I need your help, Mr. Kelley."

He was being reasonable, calm, persistent—and very persuasive.

Against my better judgment, I said I would try to find out who he should talk to, but I couldn't commit to making an appointment for him.

"You just do what you can, Mr. Kelley. I'm sure you can arrange something for me." And he was gone.

Despite my gut-level feelings, I prepared a telex to the Bureau which outlined Connor's complete request.

The response was fast and scorching. Within a couple of hours, I heard that I had apparently been "snookered" and I should inform Mr. Connor that he should get his own information, and make his own appointments.

Furthermore, I was ordered to Washington to report to Mr. Hoover, and give a full explanation.

This is ridiculous, I thought. To be called on the carpet for this . . . what an overreaction. But I wasn't surprised at all.

A few days later, I was summoned to Washington.

At FBI Headquarters I was given an appointment for late that afternoon. I had two or three hours before my appointment, so I went to see friends and associates at headquarters. Word had gotten out that I was in hot water, although it was not generally known why, and that I was to be disciplined.

I sensed that some of my friends were unwilling to be seen talking with me. When a man was in trouble with the Director's office, and until that trouble was resolved, contact with him was minimal. Many felt that too friendly a conversation with anybody who displeased Hoover might be interpreted as evidence of lack of allegiance to the Director.

I reported to Hoover's office and was ushered in for what turned out to be a meeting of only five minutes. He was abrupt and critical. He said, "FBI agents aren't appointment secretaries. You don't make dates for outsiders with anybody in government." He paused as if to say, I thought you knew better than this, Mr. Kelley.

Aloud, he added: "Please confine yourself to relevant matters within the FBI. You know how to turn aside such requests." He shook his head.

"A man of your experience, Mr. Kelley . . ." He shook his head again.

All I could think of was that word somebody had used when all this began. Snookered. I knew I'd been "snookered" all right. But not so much by fast-talking "Bull" Connor as by a handful of tattletales in Washington. I was boiling mad, but I knew I had no one to blame but myself.

The Director concluded by saying that I should return to Birmingham, and let this be a lesson to me. The Bureau and *its* interests should be considered paramount in the conduct of my office.

Then he suggested that I go see Clyde Tolson, "my associate director," he said, in the event I did not know who Clyde Tolson was.

This was a new one on me. I never heard of anybody being sent to Tolson. What was *he* going to say? However, I did as I was told.

I entered Tolson's office, and described the interview and counsel given to me by the Director.

Tolson was nonplussed. I had the feeling this was a new one to him also. Not knowing exactly what was expected of him, he said, "Mr. Kelley, this is a good lesson for you."

"I'm sure it is, sir," I replied, thinking I didn't need any lessons from Washington. And I was sick and tired of hearing about it.

"I would suggest that you get the next flight to Birmingham," he said. "You have important work to do there."

"Yes, sir, I know that my work there is very important," I said in a way that suggested learning my lessons in Washington wasn't very important at all.

Outside the office, I saw a couple of fellow agents in the hallway who wanted to know what happened. I told them that I had been sharply criticized by Hoover, and then recounted the let-this-be-a-lesson-to-you message from Tolson.

They just shook their heads. They'd been through it, too.

"I am still the agent-in-charge of the Birmingham office," I said, as they tried to imagine me as I learned my FBI "lesson" from Clyde Tolson.

Smarting under the Hoover–Tolson, one–two reprimand, I left the building wondering how many more of these sessions I was going to be able to take. I felt I had been initially excoriated by those under Hoover not for what they felt was wrong, or for an infraction of any important FBI rule, but for what they thought Hoover might be thinking. They took this quick and aggressive action to show the Director that they were on top of things.

And despite Hoover's pointed criticism during our meeting, I had the distinct feeling that the boss was somehow emotionally detached from the whole affair.

I recall thinking, maybe we're *both* geting too old for this.

In the air on the way back to Birmingham, I again reflected on the insanity of the day: The aides out-Directoring the Director in order to prove their worth and their loyalty. To be less than sharply critical of me, they perhaps believed, would have represented a breach of allegiance to the Director, and have earned his wrath.

And because they reacted like automatons, they were of no real service to him. One assistant director, I knew, actually kept a card file that contained expressions or opinions made by Hoover either privately or publicly. The file was used by the assistant to arrive at policy decisions that would please the Director. Occasionally Hoover would express surprise when a new policy was written into the book. He is known to have asked, "Why do we have that rule?" He was always told, "We put that in there because of what you said, Mr. Hoover." Oh.

In the fall of 1960 I was transferred to the Memphis field office as special agent-in-charge.

This assignment was to be my last with the FBI under Hoover. I did have one conference with him while I was responsible for the Memphis operation. It was an annual review of performance. Like others, this last "conference" consisted of an analysis of the statistics of my office, and a thorough review of any special problems that he thought I might find in Memphis. I don't recall him asking what problems I thought I might have, however.

On the subject of statistics, there was the perennial threat that if we didn't increase our numbers, he would have to close the office—"just like the Ford Motor Company."

I heard the usual monologue about the importance of apprehending those fugitives and recovering those automobiles. And I listened to an accounting of the problems he was having with the attorney general, Congress (both houses, both parties), and every other personal grievance that was on the Director's mind at that time.

As usual, I heard nothing about office expenses. In all my years with the Bureau, I was never asked about office expenses. Had I been asked, I couldn't have answered. As special agent-in-charge, I was not responsible for budgets, costs, or expenses. I was responsible, inescapably responsible, for the statistics of my office. But not the financials.

Agents, particulary special agents-in-charge, normally stayed with the Bureau until age fifty-five and perhaps well into their sixties. In 1960 I had been with the Bureau for twenty years and I was getting pressure from my family to go back to Kansas City, where many of our friends and relatives still lived.

I decided to make a career change.

Through contacts, I heard that the police department in Kansas City was looking for a new chief of police. As that was home for both Ruby and me, and we had been talking a little about how nice it would be to go home again, I decided to apply for the position.

I wrote Mr. Hoover advising him that I was interviewing for the position. In return, I received a very cordial letter saying that he appreciated the notice, and he hoped that I would be successful. I had the feeling that he meant that for both of our benefits. He knew I wasn't the same Clarence Kelley who stood so much in awe of him back in 1940.

When the Kansas City position was offered, I accepted at once.

I immediately telephoned Washington and told one of Hoover's aides that I would be leaving the Bureau.

There was silence at the other end of the line.

I said, "Mr. Hoover knows all about this. I've kept him informed about my actions."

That was all he wanted to hear.

"Oh, that's good. I'm sure he'll be very happy for you. What is your timetable for leaving?"

"My timetable is very flexible. The people in Kansas City understand that I have obligations here, that it will take some time for you to interview or consider other agents for Memphis. They will be very obliging, I know."

"Good. You have no timetable with them, then?"

I repeated that I did not. The people in Kansas City would understand that after twenty-plus years, my first obligation was to the Bureau.

"They would like it to be a couple of weeks," I said. "But maybe Mr. Hoover would want me to stay for a month. It's up to him. I do not wish my leaving to create any hardships for either the Bureau or the Director."

"Maybe three weeks would be a good compromise," he said.

"Three weeks sounds very fair to me," I said.

This call was made at approximately three o'clock in the afternoon. Shortly after five, as I was preparing to go home, I got a return call from the same aide.

"Mr. Kelley, upon reconsidering everything, we have decided to clear the way for Kansas City."

"What do you mean—clear the way?" I asked.

"We have decided that you can consider this your last day."

Déjà vu! After twenty-one years with the FBI, I was terminated on the very day I announced my resignation. Just like 1944.

Why, on two occasions, was I terminated with less than a day's notice? I was angry. As I was in 1944. Why were such abrupt responses necessary? What lesson was to be learned from this? I think they probably were designed to create a feeling throughout the Bureau that it is incomprehensible that anyone would want to leave such an organization, and unforgivable if they do.

My new position of chief of police in Kansas City started late in the summer of 1961. I had no opportunity to see Hoover again until almost exactly one year later.

I had been asked to attend a meeting of police officials in Washington and I felt that it would be an opportunity to visit with Mr. Hoover while I was there.

At least two weeks before my arrival date, I wrote to the Bureau saying that I would like to see Mr. Hoover and introduce him to one of the officials of the Board of Police Commissioners of Kansas City, W.H. "Bert" Bates. A reply confirmed the meeting at the time and on the day I had requested.

My companion and I arrived in Washington, checked into our hotel, then went to the FBI building and to Hoover's outer office. Mr. Hoover would be unable to meet with us at the time scheduled, we were informed. We should keep in touch with the office throughout the afternoon, for when time became available, we would be advised.

We left and visited with other acquaintances of mine on the Director's administrative staff. We checked back with the outer office at regular intervals.

Late in the day I checked with Mr. Hoover's appointments secretary for the fourth time.

"I'm sorry Mr. Kelley, the Director will not be able to meet with you at all today."

I later learned that the cancellation of our appointment was necessary because of preparations for the following day's graduation ceremonies at the FBI's National Academy. President John F. Kennedy was scheduled to speak and, as a result, Hoover was so tied up with the details of the appearance that he could not handle additional commitments.

I must admit that I was irritated and embarrassed by the cancellation, especially since I had requested—and confirmed—the appointment two weeks previously. The Director, I knew, had many qualified persons within the Bureau who were capable of helping him handle the details of a presidential visit. In fact he had experts at handling such arrangements. In addition most, if not all, of the security details of the president's visit would routinely be handled by the Secret Service. How curious a way to treat an employee of more than twenty years, I thought.

All was not lost, however.

As we were leaving the Bureau I saw a close friend of mine who had been a reporter in Seattle. He was now attached to the press office of Attorney General Robert F. Kennedy. The friend asked me if I'd like to visit with the attorney general. My companion and I were then taken to Kennedy's suite and, after being announced, promptly ushered into the attorney general's inner office.

RFK was then the second most powerful man in Washington. Seated behind his desk in shirt sleeves, Robert Kennedy was deeply tanned and much more muscular than he appeared in photographs or on TV.

His desk was strewn with papers—not at all austere like Hoover's or President Nixon's. It was obvious that he was at the hub of Justice Department action. Amazingly, there was a real football on his desk, next to his telephone. I commented on it and Kennedy laughed out loud.

"When things get tough in here my friends and I throw the ball back and forth to relieve the tension."

We had a pleasant, rather lengthy conversation. He spoke informally and recalled a visit he had made to Kansas City. He said he was very familiar with—and very pleased with—the direction of law enforcement in Kansas City. He complimented me for that. I never forgot that RFK personally wrote a letter to officials in Kansas City recommending that I be selected as chief of police.

As we departed from this unscheduled visit, my friend made an interesting observation.

"Here we came to see Hoover, with a date already arranged,

and were turned aside. But, without asking for it, we got to see Robert Kennedy within a few minutes after the request."

The contrast between the two men and their styles was not lost on my friend—or myself.

The last time that I saw J. Edgar Hoover was when I was called to Washington to participate in a conference with President Richard Nixon. Several chiefs of police had been invited to discuss local law-enforcement problems with the president and the FBI Director.

In a private morning meeting at Bureau headquarters, before the White House conference, Hoover was most cordial and spoke of the continuing concern he had about violent crimes in the United States. He was in command of the situation and, as in past interviews with him, I responded only when spoken to and was, as always, attentive. I no longer took notes, however.

Later that day we went to the White House and were seated in the cabinet room. The president came in and, of course, we all stood up.

Nixon sat directly across from me, Hoover sat on the president's right, and John Mitchell on his left. There was an exchange of pleasantries, a few lighthearted remarks, and then Nixon and Hoover spoke of their desire to assist local law enforcement as much as possible and to be as helpful as they could to stifle the riots and deal with other problems plaguing cities throughout the country. In addition, they affirmed their confidence in local police forces throughout the country. As a result of the meeting, the chiefs could return to their cities and report that the federal government was aware of their difficulties and, further, would be as helpful as possible.

One sidelight seemed to me significant.

Rumors were about that Hoover, because of advancing age, was physically declining. As we were seated around the table in the cabinet room, coffee was served. I was most attentive to the way in which Hoover picked up his coffee cup and returned it to the saucer. I scrutinized his movements for a sign of a quivering or tremor in his hand. Hoover's movements were steady, however. I saw no evidence of physical deterioration.

After we adjourned, several of the local law-enforcement people gathered outside the White House. Comments were made that Hoover appeared to be in good health, and that was the consensus. It was, however, the last time I saw J. Edgar Hoover.

On Tuesday, May 3, 1972, I was in Washington, D.C., to address a large group of law-enforcement personnel.

I had just begun my speech when I was handed a note. It said that Hoover had died the night before, May 2.

We later learned that he died during the night, alone in his Washington home overlooking Rock Creek Park. His housekeeper, Annie Field, discovered his body beside his bed about nine o'clock the next morning. She summoned his personal physician, Dr. Robert V. Choisser. The Justice Department announced that he died of natural causes.

Dr. James L. Duke, District of Columbia coroner, described the cause of death as "hypertensive cardiovascular disease," which is associated with high blood pressure. Dr. Duke said the immediate cause might have been a heart attack, although no autopsy was planned.

The Director had worked a full day as usual on Monday. He left his fifth-floor office at Ninth and Constitution at 5:00 P.M. with his closest friend, Clyde Tolson. They dined together at Tolson's home. Although his own health was failing, Clyde Tolson briefly became acting director after Hoover's death.

Notification of the death was immediately given to the members of the Bureau.

As might have been expected, someone at the FBI felt that a subterfuge was necessary to avoid premature publicity. Accordingly, a station wagon, rather than an ambulance, was sent to transport Hoover's body to a mortuary. This tactic enabled the FBI to make the announcement of the Director's death, rather than have it "unofficially" reported by any other source.

Funeral arrangements, it was decided, should include a carefully selected group of chiefs of police from around the nation. As one of the chiefs perceived to be closest to Hoover, I was invited to attend the ceremony.

While making preparations to go to Washington, I received word that the invitation had been withdrawn . . . because of "insufficient room." Dismayed but not entirely surprised, I first thought of the circumstances surrounding my two resignations, but then I learned that other chiefs had received similar withdrawals. Later we learned that funeral preparations were revised because of procedural difficulties. Even in death, it seemed, Mr. Hoover and his rules generated discord. Had he been in charge of the funeral arrangements, however, I know that things would have been definite, down to the last detail.

Hoover thus became a legend in American history.

What, in retrospect, does one say about his man? Scholars, historians, and many others have chronicled the life of J. Edgar Hoover in an attempt to understand the kind of man he was. Psychologists and other researchers may one day shed more light on his unusual personality. But I believe much is revealed by looking at his actions in office, his leadership style, and the organization he created.

His story was the FBI story. Its growth mirrored his own. When both were young, they reflected a great vigor, a drive for knowledge, and a great ambition. Hoover had a law degree but not a college degree, a distinction not possible today.

He lived all of his life in Washington. And aside from the Bureau, dining with friends, collecting antiques, and going to the racetrack, he had no other activities. His compulsion to control was extreme. He, for example, fiercely opposed drinking coffee in the office. There were times when people who were caught drinking coffee in the office were penalized. Drinking coffee is not a great concern to most people. It was to Hoover.

Only occasionally would he take vacations, and when someone would comment on it, he might snap, "I wasn't on vacation." He tried to maintain the fiction that this was not rest but work.

The matter of dress was important to him. He was well tailored, wearing only white shirts, subdued ties, and dark suits. Penalties befell those who violated his FBI dress code—until the day the Director wore loafers to work. This meant, of course, that it was acceptable for anyone else to wear them.

He was gifted in many ways.

Hoover had an acute sense of drama, sound ideas on how to help law enforcement—such as training local law-enforcement people—and made advances in the identification field. But he wasn't what I would call an innovator. He rode a crest of publicity in the 1930s and then over the years benefitted enormously from the legend that grew up about him.

Some have theorized that his domination of conversation in his office was an attempt not only to control others but also to ensure that he was not caught off-guard. My own experience confirms that theory.

Doubtless, Hoover constantly protected his position as Director. I know of many individuals in the Bureau who had great promise. But they posed a threat to the boss, it seemed. They were usually transferred to a field office or actually encouraged to leave the FBI of their own volition.

Finally, a question frequently asked: Did Hoover stay in office too long?

Yes.

No one man can for decades dominate an organization like the FBI without help and have it last as a successful operation. The Bureau could not have changed under his leadership unless there had been a change in his philosophy, which was unthinkable. He needed ideas and counsel from younger men. Equally unthinkable.

In later years Hoover began to slide. Massive and glaring difficulties surfaced in the Director's performance during the late sixties and early seventies. Ferocious collisions occurred with the more radical elements of American society—antiwar protesters, Black Panthers, civil rights demonstrators, the New Left, and Students for a Democratic Society, for example. In some cases, there were excesses in the FBI's treatment of the radicals.

By 1970 Hoover had, regrettably, broken off most communication with other intelligence agencies in government.

And it became common knowledge that FBI crime statistics were not always reliable. In consequence, public confidence in the Bureau waned. As difficulties mounted Hoover's internal discipline of his agents became more rigorous . . . and more unreasonable.

In sum, J. Edgar Hoover undoubtedly stayed in office too long. He personally suffered for it, as did the FBI.

A great comfort for the aged is the memory of the past, undamaged by the realities of the present. But no longer was the Bureau beyond criticism and no longer could Mr. Hoover cast aside his critics. When detractors attacked the Bureau itself, the criticism gendered a strident response from Hoover. The Bureau and its boss were one.

Hoover eventually withdrew from almost all social life. His only contact with the outside world was the thinning line of visitors to his inner sanctum. Mercifully, his death was sudden, sparing him of even more criticism, and from efforts to remove him from office—which surely lay ahead.

The death of the Director brought many changes in Bureau procedures, policies, and personnel. In my opinion, all were necessary—and long overdue.

Nothing that happened after the Director's death can alter or detract in any way from the glory of his past. His life was one of triumph for both the man and the country he loved and served so well for so long. He championed a noble cause: dedication to order.

As a young man, before a time even the oldest of us can remember, he built an agency of government that was to gain worldwide fame and respect. If his later years were beset by turmoil and trouble, it was because his own personal style—as well as his management style—was so egocentric. But that is not all bad. Indeed, in the final analysis, his own belief-in-self, his exalted self-esteem, are what made the Federal Bureau of Investigation the agency it was to become. Problems arose only because the agency grew beyond the grasp of one man; and the times changed faster than the man could.

As I reflect on my own life, review my own goals and see how short I so often fell, I find it more and more difficult to be critical of others. I hope that nothing I have said here will be weighed without balancing it with the other side of J. Edgar Hoover. Committed to law and order, admiring and respectful of physical courage, Mr. Hoover left a legacy of dedication to his country.

Would that every man might have such an epitaph.

3

The Kansas City COP

"I liked the sound of that!"

IN THE FBI, Memphis was known as good duty.

A fine place to live, this beautiful old Southern city on the Mississippi featured a relaxed profile that made it especially appealing to FBI veterans. In the spring of 1961, newly transferred there as special agent-in-charge of the Bureau field office, I should have been looking forward to the assignment.

Unfortunately, I didn't feel that way.

I thought the FBI had changed. I know I had changed. Approaching fifty, I was ready to return to Kansas City and reestablish roots in my old hometown. Since joining the FBI in 1940, I had served in Huntington, Seattle, Kansas City, San Francisco, Des Moines, Houston, Pittsburgh, Altoona, Johnstown, Birmingham, three different hitches in Washington—and now Memphis. For more than twenty years I had filled about every role an FBI agent could fill: from firearms instructor to investigator, to supervisor in headquarters, to inspector and, finally, to the highest level of field-office command, special agent-in-charge.

My experience, I knew, could be of real value elsewhere. I felt I would gain greater rewards in another kind of law-enforcement responsibility. I knew where my wife, Ruby, and I would be most happy. The only question in my mind was: How do I make all of this add up to something that would be right for me in Kansas City?

Then, out of the blue, it happened.

Several months after my arrival in Memphis, a call came through from an old friend, Mark Felt, special agent-in-charge of the Kansas City field office.

Mark knew that I was anxious to return home.

"How would you feel about coming back to Kansas City?" Mark opened the conversation that day.

"Good idea, Mark. What do you have in mind? An even-up trade, with you moving to Memphis? Or how about a three-way deal . . . I go to K.C., you go to Washington, and we send Clyde Tolson to Memphis?"

"Seriously, my friend. Kansas City is looking for a new chief of police and you'd be perfect for the assignment. The town needs you, and so does the job."

I told Mark I'd enjoy talking to the commissioners. The idea sounded pretty good to me. In addition, during my travels with the Bureau I was able to observe, firsthand and closeup, the operation of police departments in many metropolitan areas. These observations could be valuable during a second career in law enforcement. The more Mark and I talked about it, the better it sounded.

"Don't be too sure," he cautioned. "There are some unusual problems here. It's kind of a mess right now."

I thanked Mark for the call and told him I'd discuss the matter with my wife.

As I had hoped, Ruby's feelings were the same as my own. I immediately began to pursue the position.

I wrote to J. Edgar Hoover and told him of my interest in this opening. I suspect my letter was no surprise to him, and within a week this reply came back to me.

July 19, 1961

Personal

Mr. Clarence M. Kelley
Federal Bureau of Investigation
Memphis, Tennessee

Dear Mr. Kelley:

I have your letter of July 12, 1961, and want to

assure you there is no objection to your applying for the position of Chief of Police in Kansas City, Missouri.

If you were appointed to that office, you could cease active duty in the Bureau on October 24, 1961, or any date between now and then. Whatever that date might be, you could be carried on annual leave until October 24, 1961, and would receive pay for any unused annual leave.

Your thoughtfulness in writing and the kind comments you have expressed are indeed appreciated.

Sincerely,
J. Edgar Hoover

A friendly, understanding note, totally lacking any of the rancor that I would later perceive when I formally submitted my resignation. Is it any wonder, I think every time I reread this letter, why so many came to believe Hoover was victimized as much as anybody by the bureaucratic pettiness of his own organization. By 1961, after all these years of total power, who could know what the real J. Edgar Hoover was like?

Landing the position of Kansas City Chief of Police, I soon learned, was no piece of cake. The police board had conducted almost thirty interviews with many well-qualified prospects. A special search commission appointed by the governor of Missouri had talked to approximately the same number. Additionally, perhaps a dozen other interviews were conducted privately by individual board members.

On August 16, 1961, I went to Kansas City for my first, and only, interview. I appeared before the five-member board—and about fifteen other persons who had been appointed by the governor to choose the new chief of police. It wasn't so much an interview as a free-for-all, with questions being fired at me from all angles.

Frankly, I didn't dazzle the panel with my great in-depth knowledge and understanding of metropolitan police work. Fortunately for me and my aspirations, they knew in advance that my background was all FBI, and their admitted interest was in the integrity of the man they were to choose for this assignment. In this respect, the FBI's reputation for integrity was very much in my favor.

One gentleman asked me a question that went on for about three or four minutes, winding a labyrinthine path through his own feelings about hiring and firing people before asking what my thoughts were on the subject. Or that's what sense I made from the question. In essence, he asked if I believed a supervisor or a department head should be careful about firing people. I could tell the spellbound crowd was awaiting an answer that would be as circuitous as the question. But I also knew the question could be answered with a single word.

"Yes."

Everybody seemed to think that was the funniest thing they'd ever heard. Maybe, after months of searching in vain for a chief of police, the committee was beginning to get a little punchy itself.

All laughing aside, what startled me most about this entire line of thought was the possibility a chief could dismiss an officer—or any other member of the force—without substantial basis. The tone of the question, and all that was behind it, left an indelible impression on me. I certainly would never have allowed an employee to be fired capriciously.

At any rate, I enjoyed the interview-conference with my twenty interrogators, and returned to Memphis to resume my responsibility as agent-in-charge of the FBI field office there. I had work to do in Memphis, and all thoughts of Kansas City had to be put aside.

In a few days a call came to my home.

"Mr. Kelley, we'd like to talk to you again here in Kansas City. We're very close to making a decision, and we feel another conversation would be in order. Can you make it this way in the near future?"

"Would the day after tomorrow be all right?" I suggested.

Two days later I was offered the job.

Suddenly, and for the first time, the impact of what I had just done hit me. I was about to enter into a completely new and different life. True, I was to continue in law enforcement, but on a level I'd only observed from the outside. The crimes now to be confronted by me would range all the way from parking violations to homicide. What happened to that confidence, that bravado I voiced on the phone the day Mark Felt and I talked?

With my head still spinning from the excitement of this dramatic career move, I again returned to Memphis and my family. My wife Ruby told me she had received a phone call from a reporter in Kansas City who asked her several questions about how she felt.

"What do you think about coming back to Kansas City after all these years?"

"How do you feel about your husband leaving the FBI?"

"Do you look forward to being the wife of a chief of police?"

"Are you happy about leaving the FBI life behind you?"

Plenty of room there for controversial—or negative—publicity, but Ruby must have handled herself well because the story that appeared in the *Kansas City Star* was entirely favorable to us.

Fortunately Ruby and I had previously discussed the possibility of just such a call. We knew we were about to lose the insulation from the public eye that the FBI always provided for the wives and families of its agents. We were moving into a fishbowl, and we were going to be on our own in a way that we'd never been during the years under Hoover.

Even our children, eighteen-year-old Mary, and thirteen-year-old Kent, were about to be thrust on stage as the children of the chief of police. But we were in it together, and the ties of love bound us closer than ever before. This was one aspect of the move to Kansas City that I didn't anticipate, but one benefit that I have always treasured. As rewarding as an FBI agent's life can be, the very nature of the assignment seldom allows the closeness of home ties that I found possible as chief of police in Kansas City.

There was another thing about my chief of police position that I had never thought about until the moment of truth arrived—the uniform! Now that was something that took a lot of getting used to but, I have to admit, the self-consciousness passed. As I became accustomed to my new position, I soon grew very comfortable in my handsome uniform.

When it came to making adjustments, however, the one that took the longest for me had to do with the size of the weapon. As an FBI special agent, I had always carried a .38 calibre snubnosed revolver. Lightweight and easy to conceal, it was in sharp—and visible—contrast to the conspicuous four-inch-barrel magnum frame six-shooter constantly at my side during my chief-of-police days. Then, too, in the FBI I attended target practice six times a year, thus keeping my marksmanship skills quite sharp. As the C.O.P. in Kansas City, my practice was limited to once a year. But as a former firearms instructor, my skills, learned so painstakingly, remained sharp. Marksmanship—like riding a bicycle—once learned, is never forgotten.

Our move to Kansas City was a bittersweet experience for my wife and me.

Going home, for us, was like a dream come true. Fond memories of earlier days, however, were intertwined with the good times of twenty-one years of life the FBI had provided us. I knew I was saying goodbye to work friends that I'd probably never see again. One always pretends that the goodbyes will be followed by visits in the near future. Christmas cards are exchanged for several years, then the break comes—and old friends are old memories, always valued, but never to be seen again.

Except for a brief tour of duty in the Kansas City office at the end of World War II, we had been gone for nearly a generation. We knew we were not the same young couple who had set out on that FBI journey in 1940. Nor was our hometown the same.

Before the war, the entire Kansas City two-state area was made up of a few counties with a population of less than a half-million. It was a big, lovable cowtown. By 1960, it was a fast-growing metroplex of more than a million people, the center of the burgeoning midwestern agri-business industry. No longer a cowtown, to Ruby and me it was still as lovable as ever.

Since 1940 we had lived in a dozen or so cities, coast to coast and nearly border to border. We had raised (almost) two children. My career advancement through the ranks in the FBI, while not mercurial, was solid and steady. During that career I had seen human nature at its most sublime (agents risking their lives in the line of duty) to its basest (people who kidnapped children for money). We had known so many wonderful people, and I had been associated with the finest and most sophisticated investigative agency in the free world. Only Scotland Yard is its equal.

Ready or not, here I came. Prepared for this new career, or woefully short in the experience I was going to need in a hurry, I was the Chief of Police, the Kansas City "COP"—and I liked the sound of that. I didn't know it at the time, but I was in for twelve of the most stimulating, most rewarding, and fulfilling years of my life.

Shortly after I was sworn in, one of the commissioners asked me a question that really jolted me.

"Mr. Kelley, is this job going to be used by you as a stepping stone to something bigger and better?"

He hit me just like that. I was confused by what was behind the interrogation. Had I given the impression that I was not a dedicated lawman? Racing through my mind, I considered my position in life, my personal goals, even my abilities.

It dawned on me then, perhaps for the first time, that I was already enjoying my new post, that in many ways I had been preparing for this role for twenty years. I sincerely believed that there was much I could do to make life safer, more secure for the people of Kansas City.

My response to the question was a resounding one.

"No. This is not a stepping stone to anything. Whatever the future might hold for me, this is what I have chosen for myself now. This responsibility will be given my time, my attention, and my fullest dedication."

The vehemence of this declaration made my interrogator step back. He may have felt I was going to hit him. I could understand his reaction; I surprised even myself. I knew then I was committed to making the Kansas City Police Department the finest organization of its kind in America. So I found my goal, and if it was a bit lofty, at least I could always say that as I began my new assignment I was reaching for the stars.

It was certainly true from the beginning that the people I found in the KCPD were worthy of my total commitment. They gave me theirs.

I recall my earliest concerns about this very thing. I was about to go to work with men and women who, I feared, would view me less as a returning son than as a meddlesome interloper. In my imagination I could hear them asking each other, "Who does this hot-shot G-man think he is?" It's strange what your thoughts can do to you. I soon found that I was among people who only wanted me to succeed. Though their pride in themselves had been shaken by a series of police corruption charges (many of which were unsupported and later dropped), they never lost their fundamental self-esteem. From the beginning they welcomed me, gave me their respect and cooperation—and asked only that I would give them a chance to do their best for me and the department.

Twenty-one years of FBI experience had taught me that the two essentials of any successful law enforcement operation were solid public support and high quality personnel. From the beginning, I knew that I had both.

Moreover, I knew that the road to success in law enforcement must be preceded by thorough planning and disciplined, professional performance. There is no other way. I had also learned, from the example of J. Edgar Hoover, how autocratic leadership can stifle initiative and individual effectiveness. Where discipline ends and autocracy begins was an issue I had yet to encounter. All I knew at the time was that I intended to combine the skills learned during my FBI years with my best personal— and interpersonal—efforts to build a police department that I, the department itself, and the people of Kansas City could be proud of. Though I knew my FBI background had not trained me for every part of this new assignment, I was certain it would be of great benefit to me, and it was my intention to use it for all it was worth.

I took the oath of office as chief of police on August 28, 1961, before a gathering of about 150 officials, family members, and friends in the city council chamber of City Hall in downtown Kansas City.

On the same day I faced my first crisis. A twenty-six-year old Kansas City policeman was shot and killed in the line of duty.

Thus, within my first few days in office, I was investigating a police homicide and making arrangements for a funeral with full police honors. Once again the dangers of police work were brought home to me and I was reminded again that in a moment life can be snuffed out like a candle flame.

In the ensuing years in Kansas City we were to have eleven more deaths in the line of duty. Each touched the department deeply, drawing the force into a tight group—like a death in any family.

After being in office only a few weeks, I discovered that relations between the police and minorities were at a low point. I was told in no uncertain terms that blacks and other ethnic groups "simply did not trust the police officers who patrolled their neighborhoods." The American Civil Liberties Union had committed itself to doing something about this situation . . . if the new chief of police didn't.

Then there was the matter of the mishandling of funds in the municipal court clerk's office. I had to oversee an investigation of a grand larceny charge made when a CPA audit revealed a shortage of more than two-thousand dollars.

All of the conditions were compounded by the fact that Kansas City—like so many other municipalities throughout the U.S.— had not allocated funds for the advances of modern technology such as data processing and computer recall of vital information.

Most of the problems, however, were attitudinal. People problems. So they did not lend themselves to easy, cut-and-dried solutions. As I have said, the most serious attitude situation had to do with department morale. It was down. People, good people, did not feel appreciated. Some people, not so good, didn't like the threats being made by the ACLU in behalf of minority groups.

One man, an officer whom I did not know, walked into my office early one evening and asked if he might have a moment of my time. He had something very important he wanted to say to me. Nothing very flattering, I surmised from his attitude.

"I'm anxious to hear it," I told him.

"I am turning in my badge, Chief. And you're the reason why."

"What have I done?" I asked.

"You're not supporting your people. Pressure groups are pushing you around. Those of us who are walking beats in ugly neighborhoods feel that you're not behind us."

"That's a serious charge," I said. "In what way haven't I supported you?"

"You're under the thumb of the NAACP and that civil liberties bunch, and we're getting the short end of the stick out there."

"I really don't know what you're talking about. What's different today from, say, last year?" I asked.

"You are, Chief Kelley. You should walk a beat in this town. You should know what we go through in some of these crummy neighborhoods. Sometimes a knock on the head or a kick in the stomach is the only way to keep peace out there. And now you're taking that away from us." Suddenly he was no longer belligerent, and I could only think that nothing in his nature was compatible with "police brutality."

"I can't allow you to kick people in the stomach to maintain law and order, you know that," I said.

"What are we supposed to do? That's all they seem to understand."

"I don't believe that. But even if it is true, it's the only language you've ever used with these people." I paused. It was the-chicken-or-the-egg all over again.

"You're in a vicious circle . . . and *you've* got to break it," I said.

The room was silent. The man finally said, "I don't know how, Chief. And that's why I'm here to turn in my badge." He placed his badge on my desk. Very deliberately. He was not angry, only tired and sad.

"I will keep it here until you change your mind. I hope you can do that overnight. Will you try?" I asked him.

"I have tried. I only want out," he said as he left.

I never saw him or heard from him again. He was one of many who walked away in those days because they could perform only by excessive force.

I said I had people problems—attitudinal. But what was this—a bad attitude? I don't think so. It was more of a *conditioned* attitude that wasn't right for the rapidly changing times. Fortunately, I inherited a department of people who were strong and good and not at all convinced that they had to kick stomachs. For them, the big problem was how to teach this new chief exactly how much he had to learn.

My greenhorn status hit me—for the first time—about the third or fourth morning on the job. I arrived early at police headquarters and got on the elevator in the basement of the building. My destination, of course, was the chief of police's office on the third floor.

The elevator stopped at the first floor to pick up five or six uniformed officers. I moved to the back of the elevator, and unknowingly stepped into a compartment reserved for prisoners who were being taken to the city jail on the top floor.

As we started our ascent, one of the officers turned to the elevator operator and said, "Is that guy back there some kind of nut?"

The other passengers, apparently aware of who I was, remained silent until I got off at the third floor. I have often wondered what conversation took place on that elevator after I departed. Whatever was said, it was apparent to me that I needed to do something to gussy up my image.

A couple of weeks later I got my chance.

I was invited to attend the police department's annual picnic. I welcomed the opportunity to meet more of the department members—I always enjoyed the company of police officers.

Arriving at the picnic, I was amused to see the mountains of barbecue—and the well-stocked bar.

I was immediately greeted by a young officer who shook my right hand as he put a rich amber whiskey and soda in my left hand. No sooner had I finished that drink than another young man handed me a second drink. It felt good to be so warmly received, and accepted so enthusiastically into the ranks of the men. I continued to drink to their friendliness and hospitality, noting with some suspicion that each drink seemed to appear more amber than the one before. I was relieved when we finally sat down to eat.

As we were eating, I noticed several officers in whispered conversation. Later I learned that they were exchanging thoughts about the new boss's "hollow leg."

In fact, I did not—and do not now—have a great capacity for drinking, but I had anticipated the possible direction of their efforts to welcome me into the group. Before leaving home, I had eaten a sufficient amount of chili with bread and butter to avoid finding myself face down in a platter of ribs. My precaution worked beyond my every hope. Though members of the department were to challenge me in many ways during the years ahead, no one in the Kansas City Police Department ever again challenged my capacity for whiskey and soda.

I worked long hours during those exciting early months and, frankly, I expected others to do the same.

I was at my desk most mornings by 8:30, and I stayed until the day's work was completed. I met with the full command of staff twice a week, a meeting that could run nearly a full day. The staff at that time consisted of five division commanders, all lieutenant colonels. Attendance at the meetings varied, but normally we had about ten people there.

The meetings were long and fatiguing and hard work for all. I wanted it known that I intended to be a stern, no-nonsense chief, but, I hoped, always fair and reasonable. I made it clear to all that I would stand behind my people, except in those cases where an officer had been dishonest, was guilty of police brutality, or had mistreated his family.

"This is the way we have always done it" was not a good reason for perpetuating anything. From the first day in office I took the position that no Kansas City Police Department procedure was sacred, and that the way everything had been done was now open to question and study. My immediate goal was to develop a talented, open-minded group of senior and middle-level police administrators so that together we could transform the department into a fully professional and effective organization.

From the beginning I felt the need to break with the past. Fresh new ideas were more than welcomed; they were called for.

In particular, the younger officers were encouraged to undertake additional training and enroll in academic courses that might bring new thinking into the department. Examples of the training I emphasized included instruction in crowd control, advanced first aid, defensive tactics, review of city ordinances, weapons handling, law, community relations, and psychological training and evaluation.

Academic courses at two local colleges were made available to all police department personnel. Areas of college-level study included police law, public administration, state and local government, police administration, and criminal psychology. It was stressed to all officers that advanced training and education would improve their chances for career advancement and, of course, salary increases. I wanted to develop, at all levels, the most advanced participatory police management possible. Moreover, I wanted to stay in touch with day-to-day law enforcement while planning and building toward a future of law enforcement enhanced by science and technology.

To avoid the danger of being like the general who mounted his horse and rode furiously in all directions, I disciplined myself— and my staff—to establish and adhere to strict first-things-first priorities. We took care not to attempt too much too soon, thus lessening our effectiveness. New ideas in police management and administration were introduced at a programmed rate of speed.

One of my initial tactical moves was to apply a proven FBI technique to the police department's detective bureau: personal involvement of one specific detective on every case. Because this procedure reduced specialization within the bureau, two benefits accrued to the men. One, our detectives began working on a wider variety of case types. Not only did this make the work more interesting, but each man had an opportunity to develop a broader array of skills. Two, they now handled investigations from beginning to end. Instead of the almost assembly-line way cases had been handled, now each case was given to a man who knew that he was responsible for its solution.

We also decentralized the detectives. Traditionally, the detective bureau operated out of the downtown police headquarters. We changed it so that more and more of our men worked out of district substations. Big multi-district cases were soon the only ones handled downtown.

As was true also with the FBI, these changes were designed to encourage initiative among detectives, and ensure their best professional performance. It worked almost at once. The new system enabled the men to become more deeply involved in cases—and to respond more quickly. Morale in the bureau jumped dramatically, and effectiveness followed. The public got much better service.

During the fall of 1961, we introduced a system for tracking cases within the department. And what revolutionary new idea launched our new system? Each case was assigned a number!

Until the introduction of our new Central Complaint System, every case had been given a title, or a name. For example, the theft of a Cadillac owned by R. J. Johnson from the driveway of his home on Ward Parkway might have been filed under: "Cadillac Theft" or "Johnson Car Theft" or "R. J. Johnson Car Theft" or "Ward Parkway Theft" or "Automobile Theft: Johnson"—or almost anything else the recording clerk wanted to call it. And it could be found in the files under the C's, the J's, the R's, the W's, or the A's. As often as not, it was never found at all. Before our magic new "system" was put into effect, cases were often lost, some forever.

With the new complaint system, tracking procedures became far more effective and efficient. Assume, for example, that an automobile has been stolen. The victim calls the police. The dispatcher immediately assigns the incident a complaint number, which will stay with the case until it is resolved. All reports go to the file under that number, and the file is finally handed over to the prosecuting attorney.

In addition to allowing us greater tracking efficiency, the system ensured the overall accuracy of crime statistics in Kansas City.

Another innovation, unique to Kansas City, was the establishment of the Law Enforcement Intelligence Unit—better known as the "hoodlum squad." A completely separate unit within the police department, created to monitor the activities and whereabouts of known underworld figures in Kansas City, it consisted of just eight of our best men, selected for their outstanding skills, and their unquestioned integrity.

Working long, grueling hours, always under the most stressful conditions, the LEIU squad functioned hand-in-glove with the FBI, federal, and state narcotics agents, and other police departments throughout the United States to give highest possible visibility to the comings and goings of Mafia members and other professional gangsters. Because, as a rule, hoodlums don't very much appreciate being spied upon or having their activities scrutinized, LEIU duty was always a risky, nerve-wracking tour for these men. Though the work was primarily surveillance, we gathered information by a number of covert techniques. Mafia contacts were very much aware of who our men were, and, all too often, where they were.

I recall that on one occasion several Mafia figures became aware of the precise location of one of our LEIU stake-out units stationed in a downtown hotel. Our people learned that the underworld was coming after them. The confrontation would have been unpleasant. Just in the nick of time, the LEIU staff climbed out of the fifth story window and went down the fire escape, carrying all of their surveillance equipment with them. Within three floors of the ground, the rickety old fire escape became impassable. The men put their equipment down, leaped from the fire escape to a telephone pole, shinnied to the ground, and got away. They returned after dark to pick up their recording and tracking equipment.

Undaunted by this hair-raising escapade, the squad returned to work the very next morning as if nothing had happened. It is certainly an understatement to note that the LEIU squads provided solid intelligence information which, on both local and national scales, often led to the arrest and conviction of underworld figures. How do you adequately compensate people for doing work like this?

In my report to the board of police commissioners for the year 1961, after I had been chief of police less than six months, I noted that the number of offenses solved by arrests and convictions in Kansas City had increased by 23 percent. I didn't know whether that was good news or bad. Was crime on the increase? Or were we getting better at taking care of it? Also, though the city experienced an overall gain in traffic accidents (bad news), the report showed a 36 percent decrease in fatalities (good news). The report also said that we planned substantial and prudent increases in foot patrols, as well as the expansion of our German Shepherd K-9 Police Corps.

I felt that while we had a long way to go, solid achievements were being made. Especially encouraging, though unmeasurable, was the general feeling among department officials that morale at every level of the force was on the rise. Our officers and staff were meeting the challenges, and I was proud of them.

In January 1962 I established the important position of public information officer. This person provided the media with complete background on all police department happenings, personalities, and activities.

We had excellent media people in Kansas City, who, I felt, deserved to be treated with every consideration. At my first general press conference as chief of police I told the assembled reporters that they were entitled to all of the news about police department activities that they believed to be newsworthy.

"And you will get this information," I said.

"We will hold nothing from you except those stories where publication would adversely affect the solution of a crime. I personally will not hide behind 'no comment'—and I invite you to call me at any time about anything," I added.

During my years as Kansas City's police chief I felt that news coverage by local reporters, though not always favorable, was almost always complete and fair. With one serious exception (which we will get to a little later), I felt that the media members stuck to the facts, and kept opinion out of news reporting. I've always enjoyed working with reporters, and I believe that they knew that I was being straight with them.

My next move was again based on my FBI experience. We began to lay the groundwork for enlarging and improving our information-gathering procedures through the use of paid informants. This enlarged network would in time provide us with essential and often-times missing information on Kansas City crime.

Then we took a look at our police patrol-car system. Of the existing forty-four patrol areas in Kansas City, twenty-seven were designated higher crime areas. In these areas we assigned two officers to each patrol car. Thus, we gave critical backup protection to the people working these more dangerous areas.

In July 1962 we initiated an exciting concept called "traffic-copter." This venture represented a joint effort between the Kansas City Police Department and a local radio station. A two-person helicopter, provided by the radio station, monitored and coordinated morning rush-hour traffic. The chopper carried a pilot and one of our officers to apprise motorists of traffic conditions as they were developing. On the ground and in the air, we were using our manpower far more effectively.

As we continued our work to improve the department, we succeeded in attracting not only more officers but also a higher quality of police recruits. I felt that our officers deserved the highest salaries and the best working conditions we could provide. Actually providing these things was not always easy. Annually, we did obtain funds for better working conditions, better overall fringe benefits, and more education and training opportunities. Unfortunately, we were unable to fund some of the new and technically advanced programs we had planned.

Early in my term, new codes of conduct and ethics were formulated and discipline was considerably tightened. Not only were the rules loosely defined when I arrived in Kansas City, but the observance of them was as now-and-then, maybe-so-maybe-not as anything I'd ever experienced. To come from Hoover's buttoned-down FBI to Casual City was a culture shock for me. In an effort to further professionalize the department, rules for more disciplined behavior were inaugurated—regulated overtime, proper dress, defined vacations, uniform health benefits, penalties for unexplained absenteeism and chronic lateness. All such areas were treated in a new employee manual that spelled out what we expected of our people, and what they could expect from us. Employees who broke the rules were reprimanded. Second-offenders were required to take in-service training. If all else failed, repeated violators were subject to dismissal.

My 1962 report to the board of police commissioners stated that the crime rate in Kansas City had increased by 2 percent. I thought we were still on our treadmill until I saw the national average. The great American unrest of the mid- and late-sixties was being foretold on police blotters all over the country.

The same year, traffic fatalities also increased, by a deplorable 40 percent, to a tragic fifty-six deaths. On the bright side, the decentralization of our detective bureau had resulted in far more efficient investigations of crimes by the department. And we expanded our K-9 Corps, which supplemented the effectiveness of our regular police patrol activities.

During these early years I had three things going for me. First—despite my long absence—as a native Kansas Citian, I knew the city and how it worked. This helped in many ways, especially in the very beginning. Second, my lengthy FBI background gave me credibility and stature. Third, and of equal importance, I personally knew many members of influential city groups—not the least of whom was the mayor, H. Roe Bartle— and most members of the news media. Thus, to my everlasting gratitude, I was entrusted to run the Kansas City Police Department pretty much as I and my top officers felt it should be run, receiving very little interference from outside. We had the freedom we needed to improve and administer the police department, which continued to be insulated (as many police departments were not) from partisan politics.

In March 1963 our office layout was redesigned to bring together the offices of the chief of police, the press group, the legal department, and our personnel department. The changes reflected our new working philosophy and method of administering the police department.

This was a time of growing racial unrest in Kansas City.

In May the governor of Missouri appointed an advisory committee on human relations specifically created to work with the police board and the Kansas City Police Department on matters related to racial policy. Later the same year, both before and after the Kennedy assassination, Kansas City experienced a flurry of racial violence, a series of confrontations that were minor in consequence, but ominous to those of us in law enforcement. We immediately initiated an intensive training course on crowd control. In addition, we developed special police units within the department to deal with unusual emergency situations.

At year's end, I expressed my concern about the fact that we were faced with a record number of unsolved murders (eight) in the metropolitan area. Two had taken place across the state line, in Kansas City, Kansas.

It seemed to me that as the metroplex continued to grow, there would be more jurisdictional problems and duplication of efforts by the various police forces. If we were ever going to succeed at solving common police problems we had to get the local forces working together.

The greater Kansas City metropolitan area is divided by the Missouri River into four major parts. They include Kansas City, Missouri; Kansas City, Kansas; North Kansas City, Missouri; and northern Johnson County, Kansas. What's more, the state line between Missouri and Kansas divides many of the area's suburban communities into separate, autonomous municipalities. Indeed, the city even has a State Line Road—policed on one side by Missouri authorities, and on the other side by several suburban Kansas police forces.

After studying the multijurisdictional problem for some time, I proposed on December 5, 1963, that area law-enforcement authorities consider the development of a quick-actioned, skilled forty-person squad authorized to cross city, county, and state boundaries to investigate major crimes. Such a squad would act at the request of any law-enforcement agency within the multi-county metropolitan area. The squad, made up of highly trained individuals, could go to the scene of a major crime and begin to investigate all aspects of it simultaneously. Wherever it went, the unit would be under the supervision of the chief administrator of that municipality's police agency. The idea was well received, and I announced that the Kansas City Police Department would contribute twenty men to the squad.

On January 2, 1964, after an extensive study and review process, we selected twenty of our finest officers as our contribution to the new Metro Squad. The team, under the command of Lieutenant Elza N. Hatfield, was ultimately composed of ninety-three officers, representing more than thirty law enforcement agencies throughout the greater metropolitan area. The entire squad received advanced specialized training in the new methodologies necessary for this coordinated, highly mobile police work. The final training was handled by three veteran FBI agents, specialists in this type of work. The two-state Kansas City area was the first major metroplex in the United States to make this idea work. Again, here was a concept I picked up from the FBI, whose Major Case Squad was organized this way for many years.

The fully trained Metro Squad was utilized for the first time on February 14, 1964, when the body of William F. Kirchner, a robbery and homicide victim, was discovered in Kansas City, Kansas. Ted Peacock, chief of that city's police department, and also a member of the Metro Squad board of directors, activated the squad and within two hours the entire unit had assembled ready for assignment. Approximately twelve hours later the Metro Squad broke the case. This immediate success was followed by the solving of another homicide and forty-seven burglaries throughout the Kansas City area. This was just the beginning of a successful new venture in local law enforcement.

We used the Metro Squad repeatedly with outstanding results. Years later, after becoming director of the FBI, I spoke often about the pioneering spirit that made the Metro Squad possible. The Metro Squad was conceived and founded as a means to span city and state lines, and to mobilize the best personnel and equipment available to solve major crimes, wherever they occurred, in the Kansas City metropolitan area. That it proved effective—and became a model for other metropolitan areas—was a tribute to the selflessness of a great number of people who put aside jurisdictional jealousies for the common good. The leadership of our local Police Chiefs and Sheriffs Association was especially to be commended for its spirit of cooperation, which made the Metro Squad such an effective tool for all.

Later in 1964, in our attempt to use every available resource to fight crime, we devised "Operation Barrier."

This novel program enlisted private citizens—drivers of hundreds of radio-equipped vehicles like taxicabs, utility vehicles, delivery vans—to give us "hundreds of additional eyes to observe the criminals," as a newspaper article later said. We asked for and received the help of those hard-working people. They watched for and reported suspicious or criminal activities. In some cases, crimes were reported to police only minutes after they took place. More than once a crime was reported as it was actually happening.

As was apparently becoming my style, I continued to push for more and better training, and for new ways of doing things. It was a never-ending process. Courses on crowd control, leadership, human relations, first aid, report-writing, investigation, handling mentally disturbed people, firearms training, and many other subjects, were taught by division commanders and our personnel department. Many of our officers took advantage of the local college programs. Officers were allowed to coordinate their shifts around college schedules. The police department underwrote tuition and books if the courses were related to law enforcement.

The new training and the new programs paid off for us, although not as dramatically as I had hoped. In 1964, despite our many efforts, crime rates inched up in several categories. I again took little consolation from the fact that our increases were below those of the rest of the nation.

By 1965 I had moved or transferred into most top administrative posts those officials who generally shared my philosophy of police administration and law enforcement. We questioned our administrative procedures and our assumptions time and again. I made strenuous efforts to remain open to new ideas, staying innovative in our own thinking. Though we had made some progress in improving the overall performance of the Kansas City Police Department, always the questions remained: Is there a better way? Where is the department heading? Can we use our limited resources more effectively? How can we do a better job? What about computerization?

Because I wasn't satisfied with our progress, I asked the Public Administration Service to analyze the department and provide us with new ideas that might improve our performance.

The Chicago-based Public Administration Service, a division of the International Association of City Managers, at that time conducted special in-depth case studies. We felt they could help us.

From an administrative point of view, the PAS study was both comprehensive and beneficial. For example, many departmental activities were regrouped to improve efficiency. In-service training was expanded to include all departmental staff members. (In-service training is conducted in two ways. Veterans teaching special police skills—either on the job, or in the classroom.) A board of inquiry and recommendation, a self-policing board, was set up to investigate possible departmental misconduct or police brutality. We also began to utilize the Universal Time System (twenty-four-hour clock). A high percentage of our police officers came from the military, where they became used to, and learned to prefer, the Universal Time System. Because the police department runs twenty-four hours a day, such a system helped eliminate mistakes.

The revisions and changes were fine as far as they went, and I am certain the Public Administration Service was at its best helping fine-tune a strong organization. But strength was exactly what we were trying to build. The PAS recommendations, almost all of which we implemented, still did not give us the extraordinary, innovative results that I felt were necessary to make us a top-flight organization.

I began to wonder if anyone was capable of giving us the kind of hard data and recommendations necessary to build a first-level police department. There had to be a better way to do things. We were improving, for sure. We had worked hard, trying a variety of innovative (for us) and, in some cases, totally original programs. More was needed. But what?

After much soul-searching, I directed in 1965 that we submit results of the Public Administration Service study to the President's Crime Commission for analysis and review. I say "soul-searching" for two reasons. One, I wasn't sure about the propriety of giving the PAS report to the President's Commission for review—and criticism. The PAS people had done a thorough and conscientious job for us; we had already implemented some of their suggestions and we were still considering others. Two, the President's Crime Commission had earned a reputation for hip-shooting in some instances. Very long on staffers who knew the crime problems of the East Coast megalopolis, "the PCC style" did not always set too well with some of the more laid-back, midwestern folks who had worked with them. Regardless, I asked the President's Crime Commission what it thought.

In time, the PCC's report came back to us. It was a bombshell. We pored over it with mixed feelings.

The reviews, which examined both the PAS study and our situation in Kansas City, were not all favorable. Which, in itself, was all right. We were looking for help, not pats on the back. But the report was rife with controversial recommendations unsupported by any verifiable data.

Once again I was frustrated. No one seemed able to help us.

Then it began to dawn on me. No one person or organization, public or private, was capable of knowing exactly what our problems were—so no one source could give us the ideas or techniques that would translate into a decline in our crime statistics. Our needs were ours alone. There was no cause-and-effect study that we could superimpose over our problems to solve them.

I realized at last what I should have known all along: Our effectiveness, our strengths, our skills—they would all be what we ourselves made them. From the chief of police to the newest recruit on the force, we had to do our jobs together, or improvement would never come.

Going slowly, and altering suggestions to fit our specific needs, we did utilize a number of the suggestions made by the President's Crime Commission, especially those concerning public relations and procedures. We revised our policies on riot control and dealing with crowds by adopting the use of nonlethal weapons. We developed performance ratings for individual officers. We broadened the scope of community service officers to include women. And though we made other changes as well, none of the new policies made any significant impact on crime prevention and/or detection.

In the fall of 1965, at the International Association of Chiefs of Police Convention, we learned of the dramatic potential of advanced computerized equipment and data systems for improving police work. Later that fall, we began planning for the purchase of our first equipment.

Particularly exciting to us was the idea of interlocking police agencies coast-to-coast via a computer network. This could reduce the entire data information and retrieval process from days to minutes. Although great strides were made, even today the systems throughout the country are not interfaced completely. Assuredly, they will all be joined in the not-too-distant future.

But the 1965 IACP meeting had its dark side, too.

At the same convention it was predicted that the tragedy of Watts was just the beginning of racial strife in the nation. The tensions that caused the looting, burning, and killing that summer were not exclusive to Los Angeles. "Any city with an inner city is in line for the kind of violence that befell Watts," we were told.

The mood of the nation was such that race riots and violence could sweep the country at any time—with the least provocation, we heard. Inner-city life, in conflict with the "establishment," could no longer tolerate the unfairness of the status quo. Revolution, not evolution, was the theme of the day. These predictions, which were to come only too true for so many cities, led to discussions about the conditions that were believed conducive to causing racial unrest.

Traditional law enforcement attitudes must give way to the fact that the growing cry for "equality now" was uncompromising. Every chief of police heard the same theme: a dramatic change in police philosophy regarding the treatment of minorities was required. Urgently required.

We heard that racially explosive conditions in urban areas could not, and would not, be contained by merely expanding police patrols. New approaches were already being considered (and tried) in many cities: better understanding of minority viewpoints, community meetings that encourage tolerance and communication, educational opportunities for minorities, and continuing education for police officers. All were suggested as ways to head off the inevitable.

We were told that the hour was very late, and we had better expect—and prepare for—the worst.

I recall returning to Kansas City full of anticipation and

excitement about the help that computerization could mean for us; and full of anxiety and apprehension about violence in the streets of our city. Would it hit us, too? If so, how? And when?

In early 1966 a series of articles appeared in the local press that said that the Kansas City Police Department was racially biased, that we tended to see blacks as simply "a class of criminals" and that police recruits were trained to think that way. Of all the charges contained in those columns, I found this last the most grave. The first two were opinions, prejudiced themselves—and whose prejudice do you subscribe to? But to accuse us of training recruits to think and act in a racially biased way was far worse than nonsense. Given the temper of the times, it was dangerously irresponsible. Also, with the growing number of recruits who were themselves black, how in the world could we get away with training new people to mistreat blacks?

Though I thought—and said—that the articles were distortions, I knew they could not simply be ignored. The charge that an entire police force would characterize any single racial group as a "class" was outrageous. Our denials, however, were words in the wind. Deeds were in order.

With the reality of Watts and the warning I'd heard at the IACP convention just a few months earlier, I feared that just such newspaper talk might itself trigger violence.

Thus, in my speech to the 101st class to graduate from the KCPD Police Academy, I headed into it. I stressed the need for law-enforcement officers to maintain a proper and balanced attitude regarding civil rights and minorities. I repeated this need in staff meetings on several occasions. In addition, I instructed our personnel department to double its efforts to recruit blacks for our department. Suddenly we needed blacks to do more than patrol our streets or operate our computers; we needed their enthusiastic, vocal support based on the reality of the KCPD as they knew it to be in these perilous mid-sixties. Recalling the American Civil Liberties Union threat of September 1961, I felt we were being nailed—four years later—with a charge that if once true, was now obsolete.

The year 1966 was to be one of transition. Discarding more of the old, trying the new.

Much of the year was spent enlarging and revising many recommendations of the Public Administration Service and the President's Crime Commission. Early in the spring we formed the Bureau of Tactical Operations, designed to solve unusual or special police problems: for instance, those requiring a concentration of law-enforcement personnel at a single site—like riots, protests or disturbances, or a sniper barricaded in a house with a gun.

We also began, with great success, a program of citizen education and involvement in crime prevention. "Crime Alert" asked citizens to call police to report suspicious-looking individuals or activities.

Then, in a further effort to streamline our intelligence and administrative operations, the Staff Administration Division, Training Division, and Inspection Division were consolidated under the Staff and Inspection Bureau. This bureau assumed full responsibility for all criminal intelligence operations. In September, our newly revised Command Staff Training Program, which outlined new training responsibilities for all officers above the rank of sergeant, was implemented. Next, the Police Reserve Section was reorganized to provide a pool of manpower that would be available to all units in critical situations. In the following month, our electronic data processing and computer operations were reorganized to meet our growing requirements.

Notwithstanding these activities, traffic fatalities climbed to the new height of 108 that year. Because traffic accidents can be linked to ineffectual policing of traffic codes—such as speeding, failure to give right-of-way, running stop signs—a city's number-of-accidents and deaths-per-accident statistics can often be revealing. In Kansas City, we were not proud of our 1966 numbers, and I was determined to find their cause.

The news was not all bad, however. Our new Crime Alert program, which ultimately enrolled some 125,000 citizens, paid huge dividends. Crime dropped well below that of the national average.

In the spring of 1967 our patrolmen were for the first time issued mace and heavy-duty helmets as part of their regular gear. And that summer we formed the Police Rifle Squad. Composed of police marksmen and sharpshooters, the squad could be rapidly deployed in critical situations.

I was fond of the police officers I came to know during these years as chief of police. Each had his own brand of humor, and storehouse of tales about law enforcement. Work which is so deadly serious is eased with humor.

On one occasion an officer told me that he had routinely stopped a speeder the day before on a busy street. He went up to the driver and asked for his license. The driver simply gave him a blank stare. The officer repeated his request. The driver then pulled out a paper and pencil and wrote down that he was a deaf mute and handed the pad to the officer. The officer wrote out what the man had done wrong and then penciled in: "Slow down! You can go!" The deaf mute drove away. That evening, off-duty and out of uniform, the officer went to a neighborhood bar and there saw the same person telling his friends how he had fooled a policeman by pretending to be a deaf mute. Fortunately for the "deaf mute," the officer could laugh this one off.

In the fall we began what turned out to be the most exciting project of the year. Project '67 was in fact, a joint venture between the Kansas City Police Department and the Hughes Tool Company of California. We wanted to test the effectiveness of using helicopters as a crime deterrent, particularly when used in close coordination with fast-moving police patrol operations. The Kansas City around-the-clock police chopper patrol system was the first of its kind in any major American city.

At the same time, my commitment to improving our technology began to pay dividends. First, the KCPD became the focal point in the metropolitan area telex system. Then we became the region's liaison in the newly developed National Crime Information Center System, which extended throughout not only all fifty United States but also into parts of Canada and Mexico as well. This program, eventually known as the Automated Law Enforcement Response Team (ALERT), enabled a policeman to report a license number or a name and receive information back in less than twenty seconds.

As the year came to a close, I felt we were at last making strides toward our goal: building a first-rate police bureau for the citizens of the Kansas City metroplex. We had momentum on our side. We needed it. The assassination of a great black leader, less than a hundred days away, would test our every resource.

With the new year, 1968, came a change in the emphasis of our intelligence activities. Civil disturbances and organized crime would each receive greater attention. We implemented plans for extended individual training in riot control for all of our officers—skills that would be put to use almost immediately.

On April 4, tragedy struck. In Memphis, Tennessee, a white sniper shot and killed the single most influential figure in the history of black America: Martin Luther King, Jr.

Predictably, violence erupted at once.

All the forewarnings came to pass. My memory went back to the words I'd heard just six months earlier: "any city with an inner city" would suffer the violence of Watts.

More than 100 cities across the United States were consumed by paroxysms of black rage. In Kansas City, we prepared for the worst. There was no reason why we would be spared. While we had no Bedford-Stuyvesant, we did have our own inner city.

For five tense days violence spread across the United States: in Washington, D.C., Boston, New York, Chicago, Toledo, Philadelphia, Pittsburgh, San Francisco. The skies were gray with plumes of smoke; the sidewalks glittered with broken glass—shattered windows and smashed whiskey bottles. Some twenty-thousand people were to be arrested coast-to-coast. And thirty-nine would lose their lives in riots and confrontations.

And for five tense days we waited for it to happen here.

Then, on April 9, the plague spread to Kansas City.

It all began innocently enough. At 8:40 that morning a group of junior high-school students planned a walk-out to coincide with Dr. King's funeral in Atlanta. A confrontation with police ensued. The situation intensified, with local pockets of trouble escalating the turmoil until it reached a tortured crescendo the next night. Almost from the beginning the Missouri Highway Patrol, the Sheriff's Department, the fire and police departments of various adjacent municipalities, and the Missouri National Guard—called in by Governor Warren E. Hearnes—were involved.

At noon on April 10, a dramatic confrontation had occurred between police and black rioters near police headquarters in downtown Kansas City. The blacks were dispersed with tear gas. Incoming dispatcher calls reached headquarters in record numbers as the violence spread to many parts of the inner city. That evening matters nearly got out of control as savage firefights erupted between what was predominantly a white force of lawmen and black rioters. Blacks had armed themselves with various weapons, including handguns, firebombs, and high-powered rifles. Our main concern was to contain the violence in order to avoid a full-fledged race war that might consume the entire city.

A traumatic and exhausting experience for everybody, it was hellish for me. I recall that we went without sleep for two days.

The next day, April 11, violence broke out again. That evening everything exploded at once. A fast-moving caravan of cars swept through inner-city streets, passengers throwing firebombs in all directions. Terrified residents had fled and the area was deserted. By 7:45 furious firefights were raging in many parts of the city. Casualties mounted on both sides. One officer compared the scene to wartime conditions—flames and smoke filling the night air, emergency messages, constant dialogue on two-way radios, sirens screaming throughout the city, all accompanied by alternating sporadic and sustained weapons' volley. At 10:30 several fires were burning out of control.

Then, suddenly, it ended.

By 11:00 P.M. all stations reported that the violence was at last coming under control. At the time I didn't know whether the rioting fell of its own weight, or if the few months of training and preparation had been enough for Kansas City.

The costs in terms of human life and property damage were incalculable, but at least the violence had ended. For those who lived through the ordeal, more ghastly episodes were witnessed than will ever be told. But of those on record, a particularly sad episode resulted in the tragic misfortune of a man being in the wrong place at the wrong time. One of the victims that night was an innocent man who had been sweeping his screened-in porch adjacent to his apartment. The light was dim and the man was standing in the shadows holding a broom. A passing officer saw the man, and in the extreme tension of the riot atmosphere, mistook it for a rifle or shotgun. Thinking that he was about to be fired on, the policeman shot and killed the man.

The officer, horrorstruck by the magnitude of his error, had no alternative but to turn himself in, throwing himself on the mercy of police administration. Given all the circumstances, what could I do? The officer and I later met with the dead man's wife at police headquarters. She said that though she bore no resentment or anger, she did expect an apology from us. We expressed to her our most heartfelt regret over the tragic mistake. She understood that it was an error made under the most severe conditions. Her forgiving attitude and acceptance of what was clearly an act motivated by self-defense was a humbling experience.

After so much violence and bloodshed, I knew that it would be some time before wounds were healed and life in Kansas City was back to normal. And even though things were getting back to normal, I knew that it would be some time before the tension eased. Nevertheless, for the overall handling of the riots, our department and personnel received a great deal of praise, from civic groups, other government agencies, and hundreds of citizens.

The Mayor's Commission on Disorders, composed of blacks and whites, conducted an exhaustive investigation into the riots. Though there were some sharp differences of opinion, the commission decided that the leadership of the department was "capable and competent." While this was not exactly a rave review, I felt the commission had exonerated us from responsibility. In spite of this, however, it certainly was not lost on me that six of our citizens—all black—had died in the riots. With that, I intensified our plans for the addition of still more black officers to the force.

By the end of 1968, two extraordinary programs were in place and operating efficiently. The first was our helicopter patrol system, already discussed. The second program was our new computer system.

After a lengthy trial period, the Kansas City Police Department data system had shown itself, beyond anyone's expectations, to be an invaluable police tool. The installation of the system was a long and involved process, but I knew that eventually it would greatly improve the performance and efficiency of our department.

Planning for the computer system began as far back as 1965. But in September of 1967 the Board of Police Commissioners approved the purchase of the IBM 360/40 computer and related equipment. The cost was slightly over one million dollars. The equipment, delivered in May 1968, was operational two months later.

The conversion was not, however, without human problems, primarily because we were the world's pioneers in the use of computerized systems for law enforcement. The installation of our computer was a long, complex, and exceedingly difficult process. Our programmers were selected from the department, a challenge few were prepared for.

I recall one individual for whom the installation of the computer simply became too much to bear. This poor guy arrived at work one day at his normal time, went into the computer room, and sat down in a chair facing the equipment. As he sat there his rage and frustration mounted. Finally, unable to control himself further, he jumped up, ran over to a fire axe hanging on the wall, took it down, and began a furious attack on the machine. Department co-workers, hearing the terrific noise, subdued him before there was extensive damage. Two months of rest and rehabilitation (and a transfer to another department) solved the problem.

From its inception, it was designed to help the police officer on the street, in the squad car, or in the helicopter. Now an officer on patrol could call our dispatcher's office for information on wanted persons, stolen vehicles, or for identities of habitual criminals suspected of a crime, and receive background information almost instantly. Gaining such information in the past had been a time-consuming process of making telephone calls—and waiting for information to be looked up, sometimes manually.

To put it in practical terms, the computer systems worked this way. A police officer sees a license plate that he wants to check. He calls the number into the information center where six to eight dispatchers, operating CRTs, await. The operator then enters the number into the computer. A search of Kansas City Police Department files is made. All information on the plate number and any outstanding warrants flash up on the screen. If no local statistics come up, the computer spins the plate number off to Jefferson City, the Missouri state capital, to determine who owns the car and if there are statewide warrants outstanding. If there's still no information, the computer automatically searches FBI files in Washington, D.C., for other out-of-state or federal charges pending. The computer will print this information on the CRT video display unit—within the minute.

Later we installed CRTs in many Kansas City police cars. These radio-controlled computer display terminals enabled a police officer to punch in his request for information and quickly retrieve all local, state, and federal information on his own display terminal. This, again, was the first such system anywhere in the world.

Kansas City's computer system also detected repeated patterns of activity. For example, it calculated the percentage of probability where traffic accidents were likely to happen and where major types of crimes were likely to take place. This helped compensate for manpower shortages. The data-processing system also gave us the ability to catalog crime records more professionally. This facilitated a much greater number of arrests, even though our manpower base remained constant.

However, as always seems to be the case, good mingled with bad. Despite all our advances, our woeful, almost desperate, shortage of manpower made it impossible for us to win our war on crime.

By late summer in 1969, as I approached my eighth year as chief of police, I returned to what was becoming my perennial theme: Our advanced systems and technology must be utilized in conjunction with adequate and fully trained manpower. Our men and women were perilously overworked. In 1969 we had 958 officers (only sixty-five more than we had in 1961), yet the population of Kansas City had grown by some 115,000 during the same period. It was a fact of life that if we did not increase our manpower, crime in our city would increase. Certainly crime on our streets would continue to be high. By now I was convinced that our alarming traffic statistics were almost totally the result of under-policed streets.

Later in 1969, I encountered two of the most outrageous charges in my nearly thirty years of law enforcement. They came at me one on top of the other. The Kansas City Police Department was accused of selling firearms to a local right-wing organization known as the Minutemen; and, at the same time, we were charged with covering up an alleged insurance fraud involving our office and a local insurance company. These latter charges, startling beyond comprehension, were brought before the Jackson County Grand Jury. The grand-jury hearing lasted for about an hour-and-a-half.

The following day, December 5, I planned to hold a 3:00 P.M. press conference in my office at police headquarters to refute the charges publicly. At 2:50 P.M. four Black Panthers stepped off the elevator at the third floor of police headquarters and said they planned to attend the press conference in my office. Our men had expected problems of this sort. Consequently, the Panthers were met by eight of our officers who barred their way to my office. The policemen told the Panthers that the press conference was not open to the public. That's not what the Panthers wanted to hear, so they tried to force their way in. Pushing and shoving evolved into a full-fledged fistfight on the third floor of police headquarters. Reporters and office personnel could hardly believe their eyes as they witnessed the affair. After a noisy struggle and in the midst of unbelievable confusion, the Panthers were handcuffed and arrested. I couldn't imagine what was going on outside my office, and as I came out, the four Panthers were in the process of being led away.

Following the slight delay, the press conference was held. I flatly denied any and all charges: no insurance coverups; no sales of arms to Minutemen. With respect to the first allegation, the local insurance company supported me all the way, saying there wasn't the slightest indication that anything improper had taken place.

The idiotic flap involving the Minutemen also ended almost as quickly as it had begun. Unsupported by any evidence at all, the charges against us were withdrawn.

Such were the tensions of the time.

In summer 1970 I personally made my first arrest in many years. In June I was out for dinner, and while driving northbound on State Line Road, I heard a pickup order on my police radio for a fifteen-year-old wanted in connection with an attempted rape in nearby Mission Hills, Kansas. I saw a youth walking east on Sixty-ninth Street who fit the description exactly. I pulled my car to a stop and told the boy I wanted to talk to him. He was indeed the suspect. I radioed for assistance and had just finished searching the youth when other officers arrived. Ten years had elapsed since I had done anything like that. I was quite surprised when a newspaper article about the episode appeared in the *Kansas City Star* the next evening.

Later that summer I was named the outstanding law enforcement officer in the United States. The honor, called the "J. Edgar Hoover Gold Award," is presented annually by the Veterans of Foreign Wars.

What the award symbolized for me was the fact that we had at last achieved a law enforcement leadership status for Kansas City. Our police department was winning recognition for innovation and leadership—and effectiveness. Nine years of striving through trial-and-error had finally gained recognition for us all. I was proud of the award, but even more proud of what the honor meant for all of our law enforcement people, the men and women whose skill and dedication brought this award to our city. Though I received the lion's share of the praise, I knew where the credit should have gone.

A second blessing marked that summer. A supplemental budget appropriation was authorized by the city council for enlarging the police officer strength to 1,030 men and women, and for providing overdue salary increases for officers and many of our administrative personnel.

In addition, we received more than $430,000 in 1969 in the form of federal grants through the Demonstration Cities Act of 1966, the National Highway Act of 1966, and the Omnibus Crime Control and Safe Streets Act of 1968. These funds enabled us to acquire new traffic-enforcement equipment, radar, flares, and first-aid equipment, and to expand our computer data center and regional telecommunications system. The regional system involved the hookup of computers with different municipalities in the metro area for the exchange of information. This system allowed dispatchers to send and receive data within ten seconds.

We also prepared to interface our telecommunications system with a statewide information network, linking metro areas to a federal hookup with the FBI. Such a system could retrieve information in twenty seconds.

In 1970 we also expanded our fleet of helicopters to six. And of even greater significance, the public voted for increased funds for the Kansas City Police Department by way of a heavier earnings tax. Those funds enabled us to expand our strength to 1,300 people, an additional increase of 270 officers. By the end of that year, we had finally achieved an overall decrease in the rate of crime, the first sign of a downtrend in years.

During 1971 our performance continued to improve greatly. The years of long hours and painstaking trial and error were finally paying off. The Kansas City Police Department was beginning to gain national and even international recognition. Officials from other cities and other countries (England, Japan, and the Netherlands, for example), came to Kansas City to study our work. Assistant Chief of Police James R. Newman went to Belgium and West Germany to lecture Interpol officers on how our computer system worked. I received many invitations for speaking engagements to explain our new technologies and innovations.

Our growing reputation could not, however, be completely explained by computers, helicopters, or other technological advances. Our department had always stressed the training of quality officers. And those officers remained our most important asset and our greatest strength. Now they could use the latest technology to their best advantage. Our officers seemed proud to be identified with our growing fame.

In spite of our progress, our officers remained human, as I was often reminded. For example, one report noted that an officer had struck a private citizen in the mouth. I looked at the report, and at the accompanying complaint that the citizen had brought against the officer. I knew the officer and his record. The report, on the surface, didn't make sense. I asked the officer to come to my office and give me the details.

It seems the patrolman was in uniform, eating lunch in a local restaurant. The owner came to him and said that one of his female customers was being bothered by a man in the parking lot. Could the officer do something?

The policeman got up from his lunch, went to the parking lot, and observed the problem as described by the owner. The officer assured the woman that the man would stop bothering her. She was free to leave. With that, the woman got into her car and drove away.

The man who had been pestering her was enraged. This is a free country, he shouted. No cop was going to push him around. The officer merely stared at the man, who was making a fool of himself. This served only to anger him more. "If you cops think you are so tough," he shouted, "why don't you try to punch me in the nose?" The officer pondered the invitation a bit and accepted. A roundhouse swing at the man's nose missed, but landed flush on the mouth. I had to officially censure the officer for bad judgment, reminding him that he was technically guilty of "police brutality." I also considered censuring him for his poor aim, but did not.

In 1972 a series of Major Task Force studies—some of the most significant studies ever undertaken in the history of police administration—were financed by a grant from the Police Foundation. The Kansas City Police Department was selected as a test model. The in-depth analysis of such police procedures as personnel selection and promotion, preventive patrol effectiveness, gathering and analysis of data on criminal activity, and, interestingly enough, the testing and evaluation of mobile computer terminals, were all examined. The purpose was to increase officer patrol efficiency.

The portion of the Task Force on preventive patrols represented the most extensive study and analysis of preventive police patrols ever undertaken in an American city. The experiment itself, which covered a year-long period ending September 30, 1973, analyzed three preventive-patrolling methodologies. The first experiment completely eliminated routine preventive police patrols; officers responded only to calls for service. In the second experiment, routine patrolling procedures were maintained at normal levels. In the third experiment, preventive patrols were intensified by two or three times their normal levels. The results were extraordinary, representing a landmark decision on proper and efficient use of police manpower. The three basic types of patrolling did not differ from one another in altering the incidence of crime, the delivery of police services, or the citizens' perception of their safety.

By the end of 1972 it was clear that the department was having another banner year. Overall crime had decreased by 11 percent. This meant that the department, with all new systems in place and with fully adequate manpower, had reduced overall crime by 25 percent in three years. As we entered 1973 I was proud of what our people had accomplished.

Comfortably attached to Kansas City and the department, I looked back with great satisfaction. Much had happened in twelve years. Our budget had tripled, salaries had doubled, we had added 600 officers, and, reorganizing the force seven times in twelve years, we had built an entirely new department to meet the various changes in our society. We added the Metro Squad, helicopter patrols, a sophisticated computer network, and much more. Our people were, as I told them all many times, the best in the business. My greatest regret was that we lost twelve officers, killed in the line of duty, while I was chief of police.

I was confident that the department would continue to gain national recognition for its work on behalf of the citizens of Kansas City. But storm clouds were gathering over Washington. It was late spring of 1973 and Watergate was making headlines.

With J. Edgar Hoover dead for almost a year, Richard Nixon was considering who should be the next permanent director of the FBI.

On July 9, 1973, I was sworn in as Director of the Federal Bureau of Investigation in the presence of many friends and associates. In my acceptance speech I said the following: ". . . Then, to my associates in the Police Department, I say no chief has ever had greater support and no group of people has ever discharged its duties more capably. Thank you for all you have done—and all that your are."

This faithfully expressed my feelings then, and I still feel the same way.

4

Richard M. Nixon

In the Oval Office and Other Places

AT THE VERY APEX OF HIS CAREER, in the most triumphant days of 1971, Richard M. Nixon was described by journalist Allen Drury in his book *Courage and Hesitation,* as being a man who was "shy, lonely . . . much wounded."

Drury might have added: complex, star-crossed, tortured, contradictory, and enigmatic. Dozens of other adjectives could be added I am sure. My own experiences with the man were all of the above. I saw him at his best, and once, at the end of his presidency, I witnessed him at his most pathetic.

No study of contemporary American history could be written without focusing on the multifaceted personality and character of Richard Nixon. With varying degrees of prominence, he has been on the national political scene for forty years. And during this strangely enduring political career, his strident campaigns for public office (as well as his frenetic tenures in political offices), have taken him to the pinnacle of success—and to the nadir of defeat and desolation.

I first met Nixon in Birmingham, Alabama, during his 1960 quest for the presidency. I was then the special agent-in-charge of the FBI field office there. He was the forty-seven-year-old Republican candidate for the highest office of the land. Young and energetic, he was much more handsome than newspaper photographs of him suggested. He was deeply tanned and well-groomed and, in spite of the enormous pressures of the campaign, was quite relaxed. Most notably, he was personable and pleasant to those around him. Dressed in a dark, well-tailored suit, a well-pressed white shirt and subdued tie, he was the personification of a successful young politician, a winner.

The crowds in Birmingham were large and enthusiastic. His off-the-cuff remarks were, I thought, quite effective—logical, crisp, and hard-hitting without being derogatory. As vice president during the eight Eisenhower years, he was proud of his many accomplishments. And his confidence was real. He arrived in Birmingham amid enormous excitement, performed well, and left for another distant part of the country, as if it was all in a day's work. I was impressed.

I next saw Nixon ten years later, in 1970. He came to Kansas City to speak on behalf of Jack Danforth, Republican candidate for the U.S. Senate from Missouri. As chief of the Kansas City Police Department at the time, I had the responsibility of coordinating our efforts with those of the Secret Service to provide security for the president. We met with Secret Service personnel several times to arrange the presidential motorcade from the Kansas City airport to the downtown business district.

A presidential visit is a huge undertaking for all concerned. It consumed much of my time, as well as that of many of our officers and supervisory personnel.

When *Air Force One* flies into a city almost everything stops to make way for the president of the United States. Indeed, for sheer grandeur, power, and pomp and circumstance, nothing can match the scope of the American presidency. What other head of state can command, at an instant's notice, a transportation and communications network that extends throughout the United States and around the world? And, when you are the chief of police of a major American city, you become, automatically, an extension of that network.

Hugh Sidey, of *Time* magazine, offers in *A Very Personal Presidency,* his book on Lyndon Johnson, an interesting view of the power at the presidential fingertips. As I recall, it goes something like this: The president could simply leave the Oval Office (the door would be opened and closed for him), walk through the Rose Garden (an umbrella would be carried for him if it was raining, or if it was cold his coat would be produced for him), and board a waiting helicopter on the White House lawn. All travel, baggage, and lodging reservations (as well as countless other details) have been taken care of and are not of the slightest concern to the president. When the president comes within 100 feet of the helicopter, the pilot starts the engine and, as the president buckles his seat belt, the helicopter lifts off. Traffic behind the White House is stopped by White House command as the helicopter lifts off and heads for *Air Force One,* which is fully prepared and waiting at Andrews Air Force Base.

As the president's chopper lands, the *Air Force One* captain starts the starboard wing engines and, as the president enters the craft, the two portside jet engines are also started. Since all Andrews Air Force Base runway traffic is halted, the president's plane will taxi for less than four minutes before taking off. Since the skies have been cleared of all other aircraft, *Air Force One,* with the caption "United States of America" printed in bold blue letters on each side, is fully airborne in something less than thirty seconds. The skyways are cleared and swept clean of any aircraft so that there is no interference of any kind with presidential travel. *Air Force One* remains in continual radio contact with Washington and the world.

The day President Nixon landed in Kansas City the skies overhead had indeed been swept clean, and all airport traffic came to a halt while *Air Force One* touched down. Mr. Nixon had only to emerge from *Air Force One* to a waiting White House limousine, which had been flown to Kansas City in advance of his visit. Then, at motorcade speed, he went to his hotel, unimpeded by traffic or traffic lights—the limousine surrounded by four motorcycle patrolmen, and the entire route lined by untold numbers of foot patrolmen.

During the 1970 visit to Kansas City I had the opportunity to spend some time with the president under unusual circumstances.

Two Kansas City police officers had been badly wounded in a bomb blast on Twelfth Street in downtown Kansas City, a few days before Nixon's visit. They were sent to Menorah Medical Center in Kansas City for treatment. During the Nixon visit a few days later, my thoughts drifted to those officers wounded in the line of duty. Could I persuade the president to visit them while in Kansas City?

Everyone knows that the president has dozens of people vying for his attention every minute of the day. Moreover, he is surrounded by numerous aides who not only help him perform his duties, but also protect him from unwanted intrusions. Access to the president is not easily achieved.

On this occasion I was able to do no better than gain the unsympathetic ear of Press Secretary Ron Ziegler. He was not one of the Nixon entourage noted for his outgoing warmth. I approached him tentatively.

"Mr. Ziegler, I have an idea that the president might be interested in hearing. But in your capacity, I am sure you're the one to talk to about it," was my halting opener. Not quite good enough.

A sharp "What is it?" and a frown.

"It's about a visit to a local hospital I thought he might be able to make tomorrow," I told Ziegler. "I know that the effort will be worth . . ."

Frown. "No time, Chief. His schedule is full. You know that."

The conversation ended abruptly. I wasn't getting anywhere with Ziegler and I knew it, but he had given me an idea. I did know the president's schedule, and it was not quite full.

A little later, behind the rostrum, I chanced into Ziegler again. He frowned as I approached him.

"Ron, you gave me an idea a moment ago," I said.

Frown. If he gave me any ideas it certainly wasn't his intention to do so.

"You know the president has time in the morning before his flight," I continued. "He's not leaving until eleven o'clock—and in an hour-and-a-half, between about 8:00 and 10:00, he could score a major public relations coup with police and law enforcement people not only in this city, but all over the country. The idea of Richard Nixon making time in his busy day to visit two wounded young police officers in the hospital is something that could make him look awfully good to a lot of voters—and you know how that would fit his own law-and-order commitment. The PR would be great."

Frown . . . with a slight pause. Then a cool "I'll see what can be done, but don't expect too much. I don't exactly tell the president what to do with his open mornings."

"Thank you, Ron. The public relations will be great," I repeated, smiling like a politician.

We parted. Ziegler, still frowning, left with the presidential party for its suite in the old Muehlebach Hotel.

Why, I don't know, but through those last two frowns I thought I saw a glimmer of hope. My idea had merit and I felt Ziegler recognized it. Back at headquarters, yielding to my optimism, I told our people to start planning for a presidential visit to Menorah Medical Center the next day. "Alert some key people, and let's lay some groundwork for a visit in the morning. All unofficial now, of course," I said.

Much later that evening, around midnight, I received a call at home from the police dispatcher's office.

"Chief, we just heard from Ron Ziegler himself. Everything is 'go' on that Nixon visit to Menorah in the morning. Ziegler said he just got the president's approval a few minutes ago. How did you know about it today?"

"A gift you acquire when you get to be chief of police," I said. "Any specific news about when he'll be leaving?"

"They said eight o'clock in the morning, from the hotel. Ziegler wants us to call him back to confirm that you'll be there."

"I wouldn't miss it," I said. "Please tell him that I'll be in the hotel lobby at eight sharp."

I put all wheels in motion by calling several officials at the department and advising them of the visit. I went to bed that night confident that our standard contingency plan for an additional VIP visit would be in place by morning.

Arriving at police headquarters at 6:45 the next morning, I

first determined that all of our systems were operational for Nixon's motorcade. Then I took one of our squad cars to the Muehlebach. As we entered the hotel lobby, the presidential party was just getting out of the elevators—with Nixon in the lead. The president looked well rested and chipper. The waiting automotive entourage, nearly half-a-block long, consisted of several police squad cars, Secret Service sedans, four police motorcycles, and the black, bulletproof presidential limousine. All vehicles were freshly washed and polished, and, with engines running, were aligned in front of the hotel. The president approached me immediately and asked if I would like to ride with him in the limousine. Extremely flattered, I, of course, accepted.

Once the car doors of the limousine were shut, the motorcade quickly began to move. Red lights flashed, but sirens remained quiet, for security's sake. Every intersection on our route had been blocked off by our police officers, so we sped along with no interruptions.

I sat beside the president in the back seat. The driver and a Secret Service agent sat silently up front. Nixon and I talked casually.

"How large is the Kansas City police force?"

"Slightly over one-thousand officers, Mr. President."

"How do you like being back in Kansas City?"

Taken aback because I had no idea that he knew of my origins, I could only answer, "It's always nice to come home."

"I have good memories of Kansas City. I've always enjoyed myself here." He smiled, and added, "I think it's the steaks . . . and the wonderful music. Is Twelfth Street still the great jazz center it once was?"

And so the conversation went.

The president was personable, cordial, and completely relaxed. Much more so than I was, I have to admit. I was worried about the security . . . the timing on those traffic lights . . . what we'd encounter at the hospital . . . how the visit with the young officers would go . . . and almost anything else that might possibly go wrong.

Despite the fact that neither the press nor the hotel personnel had been given advance notice of this trip, I was anxious about what we would find along the way. I need not have worried. The motorcade route was virtually deserted. Our police personnel at all levels performed superbly. They had handled presidential visits before and I was proud of their professionalism now.

My chat with the president had been so pleasant that the ride seemed to pass in a few seconds. As we approached the medical center, I provided him with the injured men's names and the extent of their wounds. He remarked, "It's too bad that police officers are subjected to violence like that. By and large, I have found police personnel to be of very high caliber. They certainly need all the support you and I can give them."

As we pulled up in front of the medical center I noticed that the parking lot and driveway in front were almost empty. Good. The news blackout had worked. But if the word had been kept from the public, it was a different story inside the hospital.

Obviously, the entire hospital staff knew that the president of the United States was coming for a visit. The lobby was a sea of white. Doctors, nurses, supervisors, and many others milled about, waiting to greet him. The air crackled with excitement. At the forefront of the welcoming group was Dr. Jacob Kraft, physician for the Kansas City Police Department and in charge of treating the wounded officers.

Dr. Kraft immediately shook hands with the president and said calmly but with evident feeling, "Mr. President, we are very pleased to have you as a visitor, and it is a pleasure to meet you personally."

President Nixon shook hands with a number of other persons, waved to more, and, amid applause, walked to the elevator. He rode the elevator with Dr. Kraft and me to the third floor. There, lining the hallway, was another large group of medical personnel, visitors, and patients, some in wheelchairs. A great buzz of excitement, lots of chatter, more applause and waving accompanied us as we wound our way to the hospital room of Charles T. Robinson and Kenneth M. Fleming.

Upon entering, Dr. Kraft introduced the two policemen to the president.

Nixon greeted each man as if he'd known him all his life.

He shook hands with each and chatted with them for about twenty minutes. He told the young officers that law enforcement played a vital role in making our country a democracy that works. He was in no way patronizing them and the men sensed this immediately. The president asked about their injuries, their families, their work. He expressed his concern for the hazardous nature of their job—hazards the two wounded officers knew only too well. He emphasized that the federal government was a solid supporter of professional, local police work. He said that he was confident that the country would win the continuing battle against crime. Twice he stated how important it was that local law-enforcement officers take pride in their work. He stressed individual initiative and hard work.

I was very impressed with how quickly the president had developed a rapport with the two men. He then wished them a fast and complete recovery, adding that our country—and Kansas City—owed them much.

"I mentioned to Chief Kelley on the way over here this morning how much he and I owe to men like you. While we get our pictures in the papers, you men are in the trenches every day. The work is always hard—and often dangerous. You deserve our appreciation, and you have it."

This thought, expressed sincerely, made these men feel good about themselves, despite their pain.

This day was probably a high point in both their lives. I know it was in mine.

As we left their room we found that the crowds in the hallway had grown. All hospital decorum had disappeared. People were everywhere, anxious for a glance, a handshake, a smile, a nod, or a wave from Richard Nixon.

The president took it all in stride, without so much as a raised eyebrow, obviously pleased with the crowd's attention . . . and very positive reaction. The plans for escorting the president to *Air Force One* were already in place and the motorcade was waiting. I thanked him profusely. In turn, he thanked me.

"You've given me an opportunity to get a little closer to the people of your city—as well as show my support of the work you and your men are doing. This was a marvelous idea, and I thank you."

He shook my hand, waved to the crowd, and departed for the airport.

I thought at the time: this must be Richard Nixon at his best. He had impressed me as a caring, polished professional. He was on top of his job. Though I have always considered myself an independent voter, at that moment, I was definitely in Richard M. Nixon's corner.

The news media that evening confirmed Ron Ziegler's judgment in going along with my idea. The Kansas City newspapers played up the president's impromptu visit to the medical center, and network television newscasts all mentioned Nixon's bedside visit to the police officers. Ron had to be smiling now.

I saw Richard Nixon again, briefly, in the summer of 1972, during the Republican National Convention, and then not until the late spring of 1973.

On a Saturday afternoon, in June of that year, I received a direct call from Ron Woods of the White House Personnel section. I say "direct call" because it was different from other calls I'd received from the White House. Normally, you hear a pleasant, utterly professional female voice say, "This is the White House calling in Washington, D.C. Is this . . . ?" Then you are told to hold for whoever is placing the call.

Not this time.

"Hello, Mr. Kelley, this is Ron Woods of White House Personnel. The president is forming a commission to study crime in the United States. He would like to consider you as a candidate for that commission."

"By all means," I said. "I'm very flattered." I was also very puzzled by the fact that this kind of call was coming from the man who was in charge of personnel matters at the White House. That didn't seem to fit.

Furthermore, I knew also that there were several crime commissions already under way, and I wondered why the president would form yet another.

I added, "And how will this crime commission differ from some of the others already ongoing?"

Woods was evasive. "I really don't know too much about the others, I'm sorry to say."

"May I ask who else will sit on this particular commission, Mr. Woods? I'm anxious to help but I'm not sure how," I said.

Again he was evasive, suggesting that I was the first man he had called. At once sincerely flattered by the request and confounded by it, I finally said, "Naturally I will give it serious consideration . . . but I'm not sure what this commission will do." I tried to make that sound like a question.

Not responding to it, Woods thanked me and said goodbye.

As I hung up, I thought that the whole thing sounded fishy. The world didn't need one more crime commission.

Later that evening my wife Ruby and I discussed the call. We noted that J. Edgar Hoover had died in May of 1972, thus ending his forty-eight-year career as director of the FBI. The Watergate break-in had taken place almost a month after Hoover's death. In November Nixon scored a landslide re-election victory. Thereafter, his presidency began to unravel as Watergate grew in size and seriousness. Several White House officials resigned. In April the controversial nomination of L. Patrick Gray for permanent FBI director was withdrawn. Acting as director since Hoover's death, Gray had recently become ensnared in the tentacles of Watergate, thereby losing all chance of gaining Senate approval. That was barely a month ago.

"Maybe Nixon wants you to be the next director," Ruby suggested.

"If so, I'm glad he can't check that one out with J. Edgar."

"Seriously, you have some pretty fair credentials for the job."

And she reviewed for me how my resume might be written—a veteran FBI man.

"Don't hit that 'veteran' too hard. I'm barely out of my fifties."

"You'll be sixty-two your next birthday, but we're off the subject. You've got a law degree. You've been a wonderful chief of police in Kansas City, so you have demonstrated leadership and administrative skills. I think you're terrific."

"I do, too. But now *you're* getting us off the subject."

"And you're about as far from being involved in any kind of scandal as anybody in America," she said. "Whatever Pat Gray did wrong, he's forcing the president to go outside of Washington for the next director."

If Ruby was right, I seemed to be threading the needle. "I don't know about being the best candidate for the job," I said. "But you sure make me sound like the safest and dullest they could find."

Sure enough, the White House called a few days later. Again directly. And again it was Ron Woods.

Getting right to the point, he said, "The president wants you to come to Washington to talk to us about the possibility of being nominated as the next director of the FBI. Might this interest you, Chief Kelley?"

I allowed that it might interest me a great deal.

"Can you come to Washington right away?" he asked.

"I'm about to sit down and eat my dinner."

"I'm sorry, sir," he laughed. "I meant tomorrow, if at all possible."

"My schedule is flexible enough to allow that, Mr. Woods."

"Good. Travel and lodging will, of course, be taken care of. Please call me when you get to town."

Thrilled over the possibility of being the nation's number one policeman, but very much in awe of the responsibility, I flew to Washington the next day. I'll never live long enough to forget how it felt to think I might return to the FBI as director, the very position held so long by Mr. Hoover.

Being invited to the White House is no small matter. After arriving in Washington I checked into the Shoreham Hotel. A taxi took me to the White House for my appointment.

At the White House gate my credentials were checked via telephone with Personnel. Then I was ushered into the White

House. I was thrilled but not overwhelmed by this attractive four-story building located on the historic eighteen-acre site selected by George Washington.

For two days I was interviewed by three very capable personnel men. The interviews covered everything in great detail: my boyhood in Fairmount, my college background, my wartime service in the Navy, my career prior to and after the Navy, everything. Or almost everything. I was never asked about my political affiliation or what I would do if I became FBI director. In all, I was quite impressed with the thoroughness of their questioning.

A week later I returned to Washington for a personal meeting with the president to discuss the appointment.

Again I checked into the Personnel Section, waiting there until it was time to see the president. Soon I was escorted to receptionist Shelly Buchanan's office, adjacent to the Oval Office. It was the old one-office-at-a-time game, a Washington favorite that I remembered so well from FBI days. I sat in her office for a few minutes. Then she left, went into the Oval Office, and quickly returned.

"Mr. Kelley, the president will see you now."

As I entered the Oval Office for the first time I was struck by its spartan appearance.

I had seen photos of the Oval Office during Franklin Roosevelt's time. It looked cluttered and busy. The same held true, for the most part, under Truman, with the notable addition to his desk of the famous sign "The Buck Stops Here." I do not recall seeing photos of the Eisenhower Oval Office, but Kennedy's had a very distinctive, nautical decor, along with prints, ship models, and, of course, the famous rocking chair. The Johnson office, always a whirlwind of activity, featured the normal amount of office furnishings plus, I believe, three television sets and a news tickertape.

But the Oval Office I entered that day in the summer of 1973 greatly contrasted with those I had seen in photographs. The room was painted in a rich, warm cream color. The walls were decorated quite sparingly. A painting of George Washington overhung the fireplace, flanked by small candelabra on either side. Several small statues adorned the recessed bookshelves, as did a round needlepoint of the Presidential Seal, which I believe was stitched by one of Nixon's daughters. There were a few additional paintings. The oval-shaped carpeting was a rich blue with the Presidential Seal in bright gold woven into the center. Four chairs and two couches were arranged tastefully by the fireplace. Behind Nixon's desk were attractively curtained windows and six flagpoles, from which hung American flags decorated with military ribbons.

His desk was massive and highly polished, with subdued white-striped chairs on either side. The desk was quite startlingly clean except for a push-button black telephone, a pen set, and an empty "in" box. The only other object on his desk was a legal-sized manila file which probably contained information on me and, perhaps, other matters relating to the FBI.

It was obvious, as I entered, that he had just finished reading the file. He closed it, put it to one side, and stood to greet me, hand extended.

"Hello, Mr. Kelley. It's good to see you again. Thank you for coming to see us here in Washington. Ron Woods tells me that he and his people had a great meeting with you last week. Please have a chair."

During the three years since I had last seen him, the president's face had become much more lined. He was, however, deeply tanned and appeared to be in excellent physical condition.

Coffee was served in china cups. He again demonstrated that ease of conversation I had noticed before. He asked about me and my family, and was quite solicitous of my wife, whose illness had now been diagnosed as cancer.

Having reviewed my record carefully, he felt I was the man needed as director of the FBI.

"Since Edgar died," he said "the FBI has had some problems."

"Until the day he died, he ruled that entire organization with an iron hand," I said, safely.

"Now I need another strong hand to take control again. I personally think some changes are in order."

He felt I was the one to make the necessary changes. He picked up my manila file, opened it for a moment, and then looked at me.

"Mr. Kelley, with twenty-one years of FBI experience, I'm sure that you know how the FBI works, good and bad. You know how strong that organization is. Once you're in the director's chair, however, if you see problems, don't hesitate to clean house."

I thanked him for his confidence in me and said I would appreciate the opportunity to do the job.

"I will nominate you immediately," he said. "First there will be a hearing before the Senate Judiciary Committee."

With Patrick Gray's problems still fresh in his mind, he advised, "Occasionally things get a little rough, but just stand your ground. With your record, you won't have any trouble."

The unfolding Watergate investigation was never mentioned, although surely it was the single most important reality in his life at that time.

The president called for a second cup of coffee, and he again spoke of my wife's health and he promised that she would get the finest medical care in the world. He paused again, then turned and looked toward the entrance to the Rose Garden. He said nothing for perhaps thirty seconds and seemed lost in thought. He was holding a pencil and lightly tapped his teeth with it. Was this the moment when I would be asked for my views on the emerging Watergate scandal . . . as Pat Gray must have been? He said nothing, turned back to me, and smiled. Then he stood, and came around the desk to walk me to the door.

"Thank you for coming to see me, Mr. Kelley. We're looking forward to having you on our team. You'll pass Judiciary with flying colors. I know you'll do a good job."

I thanked him again for his confidence and left.

My hearings before the Senate Judiciary Committee went quite well and, as a result, I was quickly confirmed. The vote was 96-0.

After my confirmation I returned immediately to Kansas City for a series of sendoff luncheons and to prepare for my move to Washington and my new position as head of the FBI. Soon after my return I received a call at home from the White House. The official suggested that, since my wife was quite ill, perhaps it would be best for all concerned to have the swearing-in ceremony as FBI director at an appropriate place in Kansas City. That seemed like an excellent idea to me. The White House official added that the president, the first lady, other members of the immediate Nixon family, and several cabinet and congressional members would be there also.

Then, without the slightest pause, the caller asked, "Would it be a good idea to have the ceremony at your house?" I couldn't believe that I heard him correctly.

"You mean the president would come *here?* To *my* house?"

"Well, yes. That's what the president had in mind." Once again, Richard Nixon at his best.

I told him that my home wasn't nearly large enough for the gathering, but I was extremely grateful for this consideration.

Then, without breaking stride, the caller said, "Well, I see. That's all right. We will take care of all the planning. I'll have a man come out there from the White House. We'll find a suitable site in Kansas City. The president would like to have the ceremony on July 9. How's that work with your schedule?" I told him July 9 sounded perfect.

On the morning of July 9, 1973, *Air Force One* touched down at the new Kansas City International Airport. As usual, all runways were cleared to make way for the president. I had reached the pinnacle of my law-enforcement career. I was thrilled to be the new FBI director under Richard Nixon, and my good will toward the man could not be described.

Several top administration officials accompanied the president, including Attorney General Elliot L. Richardson and acting FBI Director William D. Ruckelshaus. The black presidential limousine with American flags flying was waiting in the motorcade—as usual, with engines running. My wife and I and Mr. and Mrs. Nixon rode together in the large presidential sedan, at a fast motorcade speed. The swearing-in ceremony was to be held in downtown Kansas City, near police headquarters, on the Federal Office Building grounds.

It was a happy day for me, but not everyone shared my high spirits. The president, for one, had taken a terrific battering in the press since I had last seen him. He must surely have known by now that he was in deep, perhaps irreparable, political difficulty. On that day, in fact, former Attorney General John Mitchell was scheduled to begin testimony before the Senate Watergate Committee. There was serious talk of presidential impeachment by the Congress.

Seated in the presidential sedan, I was shocked by the wounds of Watergate that were visible on the president's face. His features were puffy and yet drawn and haggard. His eyes, once clear and sharp, now seemed listless. His whole appearance was, in a word, rumpled.

Mrs. Nixon, although attractive and well tailored, seemed tired and withdrawn. My wife and I had spoken to her when she deplaned and her greeting was cordial. Thereafter, incredibly, she said nothing—not a word to anyone during the motorcade and the walk to the speaker's podium at the ceremony. Almost certainly she was overwhelmed by the ordeal of Watergate. Whatever her thoughts may have been on that day, she kept them to herself.

The president, however, rose to the occasion. While not ebullient, he was charming, and we chatted pleasantly. To Ruby, he was most kind. He sensed my enthusiasm for the day. I took the oath of office at outdoor ceremonies under a bright and, for me at least, glorious sun. The estimated twelve-thousand in attendance heard the president deliver brief remarks. It was his first public appearance in more than a month. Nixon then congratulated my wife and me and, without seeming at all brusque, he left as quickly as he had arrived.

Just seven days after I became director, I (with the rest of the nation) was confronted with some astonishing news about the president.

The existence of a secret, voice-activated tape-recording system in the Oval Office came to light during White House Assistant Alexander Butterfield's testimony before the Select Committee on Presidential Campaign Activities. I, of course, had no idea that anyone had been taped. Like the rest of the nation, I was surprised.

I wondered if our conversations had been taped. I found myself trying to remember what I had said. Had I mentioned Watergate? Had Nixon? I felt very uncomfortable about this and I wished I could have known more.

I did not, however, see the president again for almost six months. Then, late in 1973, I got a call from his secretary. The president wanted to see me. No reason given. Two days later I was in the Oval Office.

My final Oval Office meeting with President Nixon was as bittersweet an experience as I have ever had. On one hand, there was the special magic of being at the very center of power with the president of the United States. On the other hand, the tragedy of Watergate permeated the office. The chief executive was being assailed daily by the press, by the public, by Congress.

The president stood behind his desk and extended his hand. "Mr. Director, I'm glad to see you."

As soon as I sat down at Nixon's right, the president ordered coffee. Almost immediately we were served the hot coffee in elegant white cups and saucers, emblazoned with the Presidential Seal. The blurred image of the china was reflected in the polished surface of the president's desk. Again I noticed that President Nixon's desk was free of papers.

The president again appeared haggard, much more so than in July. The hair once so black was showing more and more flecks of white. With sadness I remembered how vibrant he had looked the first time I had seen him thirteen years ago in Birmingham. I also recalled how fit he had looked just three years ago, during his 1970 visit to Kansas City. He was a man, I felt at the time, completely on top of his job. Now there were deep, dark circles under his eyes. No longer were his movements crisp. No longer was his voice clear and forceful. His previous conversations with me had been at once pleasant and concise, his thinking incisive.

Not so now.

He rambled. Digression followed digression. Distilled, the logic of his conversation went like this: As president, he reserved the right to meet with me directly without going through my immediate superior, the attorney general.

"I did it this way with Edgar, and unless you object, I'll do it this way with you."

Then, abruptly, he asked about my wife and the medical treatment she was getting. I told him that Ruby's progress was halting at best, but with the medical care she was getting, we were hopeful of her eventual recovery. He expressed a few words of encouragement and sipped his coffee. Then the conversation changed once again.

"Other presidents have taped their conversations, you know . . . Kennedy and Johnson did it extensively. Johnson also authorized a number of wiretaps. I even heard that Franklin Roosevelt taped conversations. It's really not a change in White House procedure."

He then defended the general policy of taping presidential conversations. I disliked this turn that the conversation had taken. It made me even more self-conscious about sitting there. Was this meeting being taped? If so, it made me sad to think that later on somebody would hear the president of the United States going on this way.

As the president continued, my amazement grew. There was no apparent purpose or direction to the conversation. I began to wonder if there were elliptical phrases or nuances that I was missing.

I saw a man breaking down under enormous strain. He was facing the possibility of his life's work being shattered, his place in history forever marred.

Long, awkward pauses marked his conversation—sometimes

in the middle of a thought. During some of them, it may have been appropriate for me to interject something, but because of the professional nature of our relationship, I really didn't know what to say. I did have the impression, the apprehension, that perhaps he was indirectly asking for my help, wanting me to do something related to the Watergate investigation.

Although he alluded to the investigation several times, he never expressly mentioned it. It was as if that was something happening out in space. I think it is important to say I was never asked to do anything questionable, let alone unethical or illegal. His mind shifted repeatedly from something somewhere out there to something in the here and now, some object in the room.

As we drank more coffee, he said, "One of the nice things about this job is that they let you use this beautiful china. Ike used to say he never saw anything like this in Kansas."

Then he went back to the subject of Oval Office surveillance.

"There are times, you know, when a president has to determine that telephone tapping is really necessary. Only the president has the total picture, and only he, in the final analysis, can determine when the security of the nation is at stake. Don't you agree, Mr. Director?"

Now I had to say something.

"Wiretaps could conceivably be important in such a matter, but they could only be conducted within the scope of the law," I replied somewhat obliquely.

The president turned in his chair and laid his left arm on his desk. I suddenly noticed something I hadn't seen before: a small statue of Abraham Lincoln on the table behind the president's desk. Perhaps it had always been there and I had never noticed it before, but I had the feeling that Richard Nixon at that time wanted to be very close to any vestige of integrity.

The president grew silent again, as if waiting for me to speak.

It was awkward. I noticed, for the first time, how hushed the Oval Office really was. A fleeting thought almost triggered a question about the Watergate investigation. The moment seemed opportune. But I grew very nervous thinking about it. What would I say? I considered something like: "Mr. President,

I'm the director of the FBI. Is there anything that you would like to tell me?" But I wasn't sure how he'd take that.

Instead, I heard myself making only a bland perfunctory remark: "Mr. President, if there is anything that I can do for you, please let me know."

No matter, though. The statement fell on inattentive ears. His own thoughts were somewhere else at that moment. The president merely smiled halfheartedly, and then slowly arose to signal that the meeting was over.

Suddenly, as he was walking me to the door, Nixon stopped, as if he didn't want me to leave. Again he looked at me as if he needed and wanted my help. Now another awkward silence. I'm certain the president had Watergate on his mind and wanted desperately to say something about it, but no such words were forthcoming.

At last he simply smiled and asked me, "How do you like being at the helm of the FBI?"

"I have my hands full," I replied, "but I feel that we are making good progress in several areas." The most important of which was Watergate, I thought, feeling almost guilty. "I appreciate the opportunity to serve your administration and the country," I added aloud. "You chose me for the job, and I am thankful. It's a great honor."

"You bring honor to the position, Mr. Kelley. I knew you would." Another wan smile.

"Thank you, sir." And I shook his hand and left.

Why we had this meeting in late 1973, I've never known. And I'm rather sure that even if President Nixon knew when he called us together, once we sat down in that room he found it impossible to express his thoughts. In any case, I never saw him again.

What are my conclusions about Richard Milhous Nixon, thirty-seventh president of the United States? As a man, Nixon was a bright, introspective, ambitious loner. As president, he was without question a reasonably capable chief executive, expecially in foreign affairs. Even his severest critics acknowledge his breakthroughs with China and the Soviet Union. What then went wrong with his presidency, and what was in the character of the man that allowed Watergate to happen?

Richard Nixon, as I said in the beginning, is an enigma—always was, I believe. From the earliest he was star-crossed. He was born, in this land of plenty, to a poor family. His family, headed by his Quaker mother, had to struggle to survive. Young Nixon saw a brother die in boyhood. This must have seemed unfair to him. It may have made him bitter at an early age. I picture young Richard Nixon wondering why others had so much more. The phrase, "developing a chip on one's shoulder," is probably correct. Nixon, no doubt, wanted what others had. Why shouldn't he? He resolved, therefore, to work harder than all the others, and to trust very few people. He would prevail—and triumph—on his own. Alone.

Nixon's determination to succeed was, I believe, fueled from an early age, by an overpowering need for possessions, for acceptance, for popularity. The fuel for his drive led, in turn, to his basically amoral attitude. He would accomplish his goals by whatever means necessary. Theodore White's analysis of the Nixon personality is penetrating: In *Breach of Faith* he said of Nixon:

> . . . here was a man who could not, in his waking moments, acknowledge the man he recognized in his own nightmares—the outsider, the loner, the loser.
> Throughout his career, except for a few brief years in 1971 and 1972, that had been his inner role—the outsider, the loser. "They" were against him, always, from the rich boys of Whittier College to the hostile establishment that sneered at his Presidency. . . . Losers play dirty. . . . His ruthlessness, vengefulness, nastiness were the characteristics of a man who has seen himself as underdog for so long that he cannot distinguish between real and fancied enemies, a man who does not really care whom he slashes or hurts when pressed, who cannot accept or understand when or what he has won.

There is no doubt that this "nastiness" permeated the White House and led inevitably to Watergate. The viciousness which he is certainly capable of first manifested itself, in a public way, as early as his 1946 campaign for Congress. That campaign, which he won, was a brawl. He became a determined congressman who spearheaded the Alger Hiss investigation. In 1950, following his hard-nosed, sometimes unethical, campaign against Helen Gahagan Douglas, he moved on to the U.S. Senate. From there to vice president under Eisenhower. But, never, never for all of his efforts, did he become a member of the club, the inner circle. He never became one of "them."

His narrow defeat by John F. Kennedy in 1960 must have been galling to him. But his 1962 California gubernatorial campaign defeat was a humiliation. Did he ever recover from that loss? Has he ever recovered from Watergate?

His brilliance was often seen through his public actions and his accomplishments. Despite this, however, his inherent bitterness apparently led to his own private agony behind the scenes—the enemies list, the paranoia, the vulgarity and profanity made public on the famous tapes, and ultimately the final degradation, the disrespect for the Constitution. But all that I say here I've heard from afar. Personally I never saw this darker side of the man.

My Nixon memories are of the cheering crowds in Birmingham, of a morning ride to Kansas City's Menorah Medical Center, a meeting in Washington when he offered me the directorship of the Federal Bureau of Investigation, and of those defeated eyes looking into mine that day we met without aim or agenda in the Oval Office.

5

The Saturday Night Massacre

The Day of the Firestorm

WITH THE SATURDAY NIGHT MASSACRE, the Watergate scandal became the Watergate tragedy.

For the Nixon presidency, it was the beginning of the end. For the rest of us, it was "the day of the firestorm," as Alexander Haig later termed it. And, one way or another, all of us got burned.

After Saturday night, October 20, 1973, nothing about the administration in office was ever the same again.

For me personally it was a turning point. Until that night, I was hopeful that the Nixon administration could be saved. Even though I, as the man in the FBI director's chair, was responsible for many aspects of the Watergate investigation, I couldn't help but hope that the stupidity of Watergate wouldn't reflect directly on the president's White House staff, and would never reach the Oval Office.

After that night, however, my emotions, and those of my top staff at the Bureau, all shifted into neutral. With that series of callous miscalculations, the very tone of our Bureau staff meetings changed dramatically. The gauntlet having been thrown down, the two sides polarized at once: Nixon supporters wanted the president left alone—no matter what his personal involvement might have been. Nixon haters wanted him impeached and imprisoned, the sooner the better. Most of us simply wanted the drama to be played out, the consequences left to take care of themselves.

123

I had been in office only fourteen days when Watergate began its escalation into something more than a ragtag break-and-entry case better suited for the Keystone Cops than the Federal Bureau of Investigation.

Then on July 23, Archibald Cox, Watergate special prosecutor, asked the grand jury in Washington to issue a subpoena for the tapes, notes, and memoranda regarding nine specific Nixon conversations. The Bureau had the responsibility to conduct whatever investigation might be requested by the special prosecutor's office, headquartered on K Street in Washington. I followed these fast-moving events with the feeling that the action by Cox was aggressive, daring—and logical. My staff and I had no idea, of course, what the White House reaction to the Cox subpoena might be.

We didn't have long to wait. Three days later, the White House flatly rejected the subpoena. They stated that neither tapes, nor notes, nor memos would be forthcoming. "Executive privilege," they said. Period.

Next, Archibald Cox himself pleaded the case before U.S. Federal Judge John J. Sirica, asking the president to show cause why the subpoena was rejected. Cox argued that because there was reason to believe the tapes contained material of sufficient importance to suggest that members of the White House staff— and possibly even the president—were involved in a criminal coverup, the tapes should be made available to the special prosecutor.

"And," Cox further argued, "executive privilege cannot be stretched to hide criminal activity—if such activity exists."

The matter rested in Judge Sirica's court for more than a month while White House attorneys battled lawyers from the special prosecutor's office over all the sidebar issues attendant to the case.

As a lawyer, I was fascinated by the constitutional arguments presented by both sides. Unprecedented legal ground was being covered daily by lawyers whose own emotions were caught up in the furor of Watergate.

And, as director of the FBI, I tracked every event to see how each decision would affect us. Meanwhile, the investigative work of our agents continued without interruption. In fact, requests for additional investigation from both the special prosecutor's office and Senator Sam Ervin's committee actually increased during what should have been a lull period.

I recall those days as being almost more than I could handle. Not only were the times turbulent, but the challenges I personally faced were many, with most related to the management of the FBI.

Because I was so new to my job as Bureau director, I was trying to cope and catch up at the same time. In addition to the daily administrative requirements of the office itself, I was working on far-reaching reforms of FBI management structure, much of which had remained intact and unchanged for nearly fifty years.

Also commanding my attention was a two-page memorandum that was written to me by my predecessor, William D. Ruckelshaus. Titled "Substantive Issues Regarding the Future of the FBI," it identified the topics that Bill Ruckelshaus believed warranted my immediate action—legal/moral considerations involved in investigative techniques like wiretapping, intelligence gathering, income tax return reviews, harassment tactics employed by the FBI, to mention but a few.

In addition, I was busy trying to surround myself with the best executive personnel available to form my new management team. Then, too, there was my concern about the Bureau's relations with the news media. For some time the press, both print and broadcast, had been riding the FBI pretty hard—and frankly, not all the unfavorable publicity had been unjust.

There was more. I was working to resolve Bureau morale problems that had been allowed to fester over the years. This was one that I felt very close to personally, and I intended to bring a halt to the practices and procedures causing so many good men to leave the agency at what should have been the peak of their careers.

Concurrent with the rebuilding of my management team, I

was examining and evaluating FBI operations root and branch—from the essential status of our counterintelligence machinery (more about this in the chapter "Cointelpro" later on) to the overall effectiveness of our fifty-nine field offices nationwide.

Finally, I was attempting to implement another part of my management plan, namely, to make my philosophy known directly to as many FBI people as I could. Time-consuming though it was, with required tours to each headquarter's division, and with follow-up visits to as many of our field offices as time would allow, I was convinced that it was necessary to sell the new FBI point of view to as many of our people as possible.

Because of my new position, I also began receiving growing numbers of speech invitations from criminal justice and law enforcement organizations as well as professional and civic associations nationwide. Aware of the enormous public relations opportunities these speaking engagements presented, I welcomed the chance to tell the story of the new Federal Bureau of Investigation.

Altogether, this was a full plate of responsibilities—without adding to it the most devastating White House scandal in the history of our nation.

Daily, the growing spectre of Watergate darkened even more. Daily, the case consumed more of my time. Daily, the tension mounted between the government's investigative and prosecutorial machinery and the entire administration of Richard Nixon, the man who chose me for the office I now held.

The events that led to Saturday, October 20, 1973, fell out so relentlessly that I began to wonder if the American government itself had lost its balance.

Here is what happened: On August 29, 1973, Judge Sirica ordered that the White House tapes and other materials in question be turned over to him for his personal review. About the same time, Spiro Agnew's sordid past began surfacing. Concurrently, Senator Ervin's Senate committee revealed, each day before a nationwide television audience, new Watergate dirty tricks and illegal acts.

Two men about whom I cared very much were deeply engaged in the growing confrontation with the White House—Attorney General Elliot L. Richardson and Deputy Attorney General William D. Ruckelshaus. Both had been strong White House advocates of my appointment as director, and both had flown to Kansas City for my July swearing-in ceremony. That meant a lot to me.

I shared a unique kinship with Bill Ruckelshaus. He was not only, as deputy attorney general, my associate, but, as acting director of the FBI, he was my immediate predecessor in office. He had been immensely helpful to me during the transition period. As we charted the Watergate investigation, I spoke with him by telephone at least two or three times a week during this entire period. It was obvious that tension had reached fever-pitch throughout the Justice Department. It became clear to us that we were heading toward a showdown with the White House.

I knew, however, that no matter what happened, the integrity of Elliot Richardson and Bill Ruckelshaus would remain intact. I knew I could count on them; I believed they had the same confidence in me.

On September 10, 1973, Judge Sirica's ruling on the tapes was, as expected, carried by the White House to the U.S. Court of Appeals.

Then, less than a month later, the Yom Kippur War exploded with electrifying fury.

As if Watergate at home wasn't enough, the president suddenly had a major international crisis on his hands. On October 9, 1973, three Soviet airborne divisions were put on full alert in support of Russia's Middle East allies against Israel. How much more pressure, I wondered with alarm, could the president stand? Now he faced, potentially, another traumatic confrontation—this time with our most powerful adversary in the world.

Would the president, given his precarious state of mental anguish, be pushed into a miscalculation that could be catastrophic, perhaps even trigger World War III? Surely, I felt, he must be reaching his breaking point. Was there no relief in sight?

The pressure only grew.

On October 12, 1973, the U.S. Court of Appeals affirmed Judge Sirica's order with modifications, and directed the judge to listen to the tapes to determine if they contained discussions that could not be protected by executive privilege.

The following week, amid my heavy travel schedule, I met with my assistants at FBI headquarters to consider what would happen next. By this time most of our field offices were engaged in the Watergate investigation. I was enormously proud of the performance of our agents in gathering the information requested by Special Prosecutor Cox and Senator Ervin. At this point, however, I couldn't imagine how the tension could escalate anymore.

To relieve some of the pressure, on October 19 the president announced a compromise proposal. His idea: Senator John Stennis would listen to the tapes, then review a White House-prepared statement regarding their contents. If Stennis agreed with the statement's accuracy, it (not the tapes) would be given to Cox and the grand jury. As a condition of the compromise, however, the special prosecutor must agree not to pursue further any litigation regarding the White House tapes.

Cox rejected this notion without a moment's hesitation.

The next day, Saturday, October 20, the special prosecutor appeared at a news conference to explain that he would not comply with the president's demand that he (Cox) make no more attempts by judicial process to obtain any tapes or other documents relating to Watergate. Furthermore, he announced his intention to press his investigation until every White House secret was revealed.

I missed all of this.

On October 19 my wife and I flew home to Kansas City for the weekend. The preceding week had been one of those rare times that Ruby had felt well enough to stay with me in Washington. However, it was necessary to take her back to Kansas City for medical consultation. In addition, I needed to get away, if only for a weekend, from the drumfire of events in Washington.

Arriving home early on Friday evening, we spent the next day consulting with several physicians about my wife's illness, which would subsequently be diagnosed as terminal cancer. We returned home early that evening. She and I fixed dinner together, hoping to have a rare evening to ourselves. Let's forget Washington, we said. We will not even turn on the news. It was, however, to be an evening that I will remember for the rest of my life.

Some time before eight the tranquility of the moment was shattered by the ring of the telephone. I lifted the receiver.

"Hello," I said, afraid of what I might hear.

"Mr. Director, this is Alexander Haig." I didn't expect to hear that.

Because the call did not go through the White House switchboard, but came directly from the office of the White House chief of staff, I knew something was up. Besides, Al Haig didn't make a habit of calling me at home—in Washington or in Kansas City.

"What can I do for you this evening, General?" I asked.

"Mr. Director, we've had some difficulties at the Justice Department today. Have you heard?"

"General, I've heard nothing. My wife and I have been out all day. What's happened?"

"Elliot Richardson, William Ruckleshaus, and Archibald Cox are no longer in the government." Haig paused for a moment. "The attorney general has resigned and the deputy attorney general has gone with him. Both resigned for the same reason: Early this evening Archibald Cox was fired as special prosecutor." Haig paused again. Then he went on, "The president is thinking about abolishing the special prosecutor's office. He might want the Justice Department to take over its function." Haig stopped talking.

What could I say?

My heart sank. I almost fell to the floor, but managed, "I see. Those are some fairly significant developments."

"Yes, they certainly are significant, Mr. Director. The president has been concerned about the special prosecutor's office for some time. And, well, he felt he had to do something after Mr. Cox refused to compromise with him on the issue of the tapes."

Haig paused, then added, "In light of what has just happened, we would like you to send some of your people over to protect the special prosecutor's office—and also protect the offices of Elliot Richardson and William Ruckelshaus in the Justice Building. We want to make absolutely certain that nothing in the way of files or materials regarding the investigation leaves those offices."

"We can certainly do that, General, but aren't matters like this ordinarily handled by the United States marshal's office?" I asked.

"Yes, but we would like to have your people do it," Haig insisted. "Possibly, after all the difficulties have subsided and the offices are secure, we can turn it over to the marshal's people. But right now we're concerned that there might be some reason for some people to try to remove materials and files from those offices. We want them secured right away!"

Something about the way Haig said "we" that last time suggested that our conversation had run its course.

"I understand, General. I'll take care of it at once."

I immediately called FBI headquarters in Washington and asked to be put through to Edward S. Miller, deputy associate director. With all that was going on there in Washington, I knew I could count on Ed Miller. Almost instantly Ed was on the line. He spoke first.

"Have you heard the news, Mr. Director?"

I told him I just heard it. From Alexander Haig.

"All regular television programming," he said, "has been interrupted to cover the story. We don't know where it's all going to end. It sounds like everybody in Justice is going to quit—if Nixon doesn't fire them first. The media is having a field day. They're calling it the Saturday Night Massacre." Ed paused a moment, then quickly asked, "Did you say Alexander Haig told you?"

"Yes, I did, Ed. I just got off the phone with General Haig. The White House wants us to immediately secure the office and files of former Special Prosecutor Cox, and also the Justice Department offices of former Attorney General Richardson and former Deputy Attorney General Ruckelshaus. Nothing is to be removed from those offices. Get some of our people over there fast, and then contact Assistant Attorney General Petersen to obtain his understanding and concurrence." (Henry Petersen, in charge of the Criminal Division of the Justice Department, had been in charge of the Watergate investigation before the appointment of the special prosecutor.)

Ed replied, "I'll do it right away."

"Be careful, Ed. Our role in this matter must be handled diplomatically. I don't want the FBI looking like it's trying to protect anybody or cover anything up. At the same time I don't want any bully-boy charges leveled against us. The situation could be very harmful to us."

"I follow you, Mr. Director. We will be tactful and careful. Goodbye."

Miller went into action immediately. At 8:10 P.M. he contacted John J. McDermott, Washington field office special agent-in-charge, and instructed him to begin at once the surveillance requested by the White House. McDermott was informed by Ed that there were not to be restrictions on individuals entering or leaving the offices. Bureau personnel must, however, explain to everyone that the FBI presence had been requested by the White House. No individuals would be permitted to remove any official government documents, and all briefcases and attaché cases would be inspected.

Several minutes later, Miller attempted, through the Justice Department switchboard, to reach Assistant Attorney General Petersen. He was unsuccessful but asked that the Justice Department operator keep trying.

At 8:30 P.M. McDermott instructed Special Agent Angelo J. Lano of the FBI Washington field office to proceed immediately to the Watergate special prosecutor's office on K Street.

By 8:45 P.M. Miller got a call through to Henry Petersen's

home. His daughter told Ed that the assistant attorney general was at his cottage at Dale Beach, Maryland. She advised Miller that she would try to contact her father.

Six minutes later, at 8:51 P.M., McDermott called Ed Miller back at FBI headquarters to report that agents were on their way to the special prosecutor's office and the Justice Department.

At 9:00 P.M., Elliot Richardson called me in Kansas City to brief me on developments as he understood them. We talked for several minutes.

"Clarence, I knew that this situation was explosive," he said. "I talked with Archibald Cox last night at some length about the whole matter. He said that the kind of deal the White House was talking about would be a breach of his independence, and was therefore out of the question. The president had told me to tell Cox that as a condition of turning over the tapes as verified by Stennis, Cox would have to agree not to seek any additional tapes. And, of course, I wasn't about to tell the special prosecutor that."

"What a position you both were in! You couldn't tell Mr. Cox not to do his duty as special prosecutor," I said.

"That's right. Then today's press conference was the last straw. Archibald Cox said, as he had to, that he would continue to pursue the investigation wherever it might lead so long as he was on the job. The president saw Cox's refusal to accept any restriction on his future access to the tapes as an act of insubordination, and that was his excuse for getting Cox fired."

"Did you see the president today?" I asked.

"Yes, I did. It was a strange meeting. He began by referring to the crisis in the Middle East and asked me whether I had considered the possibility that Brezhnev would think that he had lost control of the government. He asked me to delay my resignation. And when I refused, he said, 'I am sorry that you choose to put your purely personal commitments ahead of the national interest.' I told him as calmly as I could manage that it appeared we had different views of the national interest. Except for a few additional words about my regret on leaving an administration in which I was proud to have had a part, that was that. All this took place about 4:30 this afternoon."

"What did you do next?"

"I went directly to the Justice Department and talked with Bill Ruckelshaus and Bob Bork," Richardson replied.

"I understand Bill has resigned also."

"Yes, about 5:00 this afternoon. He left for the same reason I did: He wouldn't dream of telling Archibald Cox to back off. Bob Bork didn't want any part of it either, I can assure you of that. But Bill and I persuaded him that if he didn't fire Cox the president would just keep going down through the department until he found someone who would. Besides, we pointed out, Bob didn't have the same kind of direct commitment to Cox's independence that Bill and I did."

"So it was actually Bob Bork who fired the special prosecutor?"

"Yes."

"Was Alexander Haig there in the Oval Office when you saw the president?"

"No, he wasn't. I saw him just before I saw the president, and he too tried to persuade me to delay my resignation. He was the one who called Bill Ruckelshaus, and then Bob Bork," answered Elliot.

"What's your assessment of the situation now?" I asked.

"Well, right now it looks terrible for the White House. The truth is going to come out one way or another—and it's going to go very badly for the president," he replied.

"Elliot, you and Bill probably more than anybody were instrumental in my becoming director. And now this unbelievable turn of events . . . with the media exploding and people demanding answers. Is there anything I can do for you? You know I feel badly that you're caught in the middle of all this. I hope you agree, however, that the FBI is doing the right thing in carrying out Haig's order tonight."

"I don't think you had any choice," he replied. "Obviously the Watergate files must be protected. And you are the people to do it. I've spent many years in government, and this is the most incredible situation I've ever seen."

The conversation lasted only a few minutes longer. I described to the former attorney general in more detail the action that we were taking. He remained calm, suggesting that I be extremely careful in handling future White House requests. I again expressed my personal regrets and told him that I would stay in touch.

While I was on the telephone with Elliot Richardson, the first FBI agent, Lano, arrived at the special prosecutor's office. He identified himself to the special prosecutor's assistants and the approximately twenty-five other staff memebers still at work.

The agent explained to the somewhat incredulous staffers why he was there and the nature of his orders. The office was to be closed; nothing was to be removed.

At 9:15 P.M. I called Ed Miller at FBI headquarters and told him I had spoken with Richardson and had received his assessment of the Watergate investigation as it stood now. I then asked Ed for an update. It was clear to me that the situation, although still frantic, was coming under some control. Within fifteen minutes McDermott and four agents had arrived as backup to agent Lano. Concurrently, agents had arrived at the Justice Department to seal off the offices of Elliot Richardson and Bill Ruckelshaus.

Miller had also called Henry Petersen's daughter the second time. He was told that Petersen was on his way back to Washington and should arrive home within the hour.

The instant Ed Miller was off the phone with Petersen's daughter, he received an urgent call from George Quinn of the FBI External Affairs division, our public relations arm. Quinn had been called by the *New York Times*.

"They want to know what is happening," Quinn said. "Why is the office of Special Prosecutor Cox sealed off? What was the story at the Justice Department? Why are the offices of Elliot Richardson and William Ruckelshaus under tight security?

Who ordered all of this? And what is the FBI doing in the middle of it?"

Quinn needed instructions on what to tell the *Times* and needed them right away. The press was in an uproar, understandably so.

At 9:50 P.M. Ed Miller called me in Kansas City for advice. We talked for several minutes. We knew that every newspaper, TV, and radio newsperson would soon be screaming for information.

"Mr. Director, we're caught in the middle here. We have to tell them something. Shall we mention Haig's call to you?"

After thinking it over, I told Ed: "Contact Jerry Warren in the White House press office. We're following Alexander Haig's instructions. Now the White House owes us an answer. What should we tell the *Times*? What should we tell them *all*?"

Ed called the White House right away. He told Warren what kind of media heat the Bureau was getting. Warren replied that he would have to discuss the matter with some appropriate officials. The Bureau would be called back as soon as possible.

Ed Miller later told me he figured he was in for a long Saturday night wait.

To Ed's amazement, barely ten minutes later the deputy press secretary returned his call. The FBI was to answer all media inquiries as follows: "The FBI has sealed off the offices of the special prosecutor, the attorney general, and the deputy attorney general on orders of the White House." Because that was the extent of our involvement, that should be the extent of our comment.

The White House deputy then said, "If the news media has further questions for the FBI, the Bureau should refer them to the White House press secretary's office."

Miller reviewed with me what the White House spokesman had said. I didn't take long to mull it over.

"What else could—or should—we say, Ed? There's really nothing for us to add. It's the truth, and it is exactly as much as I want said." I, therefore, approved the White House secretary's suggestion. And, to myself, I had to thank Al Haig for his quick support on this one. I was certain the word came from Haig.

Ed relayed my approval to George Quinn, who then called the media, gave them our story, and told them to contact the White House for any further information.

While this frantic telephoning was in progress, our agents completed their deployment at both the special prosecutor's office and the Justice Department.

Henry S. Ruth, Jr., deputy special prosecutor, told Agent Lano at the scene that two of the file cabinets located there contained extremely sensitive Watergate investigative information. "If that stuff ever gets out," Ruth told Lano, "somebody could get in a lot of trouble. It's that hot," he added.

"Are you serious?" Lano asked him.

"Very serious. These two cabinets must not be opened." Ruth said, pointing at the two. "I think they're why you're here."

Lano told Ruth that this incredible bit of news should be given directly to the Justice Department, preferably to Assistant Attorney General Petersen. At 10:30 P.M. Ed Miller spoke with our agents at both locations—Justice, and the special prosecutor's office—to confirm that there were no problems. That's when he heard, for the first time, of the two "hot" cabinets.

Three minutes later, at 10:33, Henry Petersen arrived at his home in Washington and immediately called Ed Miller at FBI headquarters. He was briefed on the tumultuous events of the past two-and-a-half hours. It was suggested to Petersen that it would certainly be in the best interests of the FBI for the Justice Department to make arrangements, as soon as possible, for United States marshals to relieve the FBI of this particular assignment since the FBI men were professional investigators, not security guards. Ed mentioned the delicacy of the two cabinets. It was exactly the sort of situation that called for U.S. marshals—not the FBI. Petersen immediately agreed. He said that he would discuss the matter with acting Attorney General Bork the next morning.

By 11:00 P.M. Henry Ruth of the prosecutor's office had also been in contact with Petersen about the files that contained the sensitive Watergate information.

About that same time I received a second call from Alexander Haig, again a direct call. The general said that reports had reached him at the White House that there had been some "over-reaction" by FBI agents assigned to secure documents at the Cox, Richardson, and Ruckelshaus offices. It had been a long day, and at this point I didn't want to hear about somebody's hurt feelings.

"Could you please be more specific, General?"

"We've had some complaints that some people were unable to go into their offices to get their belongings."

"Well, General, those are the instructions I gave to my agents. I told them not to allow anything to be taken out of those offices."

"Well, that's a little bit discriminatory. I don't know whether we can do that or not," Haig said.

"General, you wanted us to secure those offices. We secured them. I know of no way that we can determine on our own exactly what can be properly taken out. I'm sorry if we locked up somebody's umbrella. But I've instructed FBI people to secure those offices."

"Well, I see." He paused. Then said, "Thank you, Mr. Director," and hung up.

He must have agreed with me because he didn't call back that evening.

Nevertheless, I did call Ed Miller in Washington to relate my conversation with Haig. "Try to find out what Al Haig's hearing. I think he's supportive of us, and I think he knows we're being cooperative."

Then I repeated my earlier caution. "I don't want any news stories about the FBI discriminating or overreacting to anything. Ed, we have to walk right down the middle of the road on this one."

Ed immediately called John McDermott at the scene and asked for details. John stated that any "discriminatory" allegations were completely unfounded. He emphasized that individuals at all three locations were free to come and go as they pleased. However, as instructed, agents were not allowing the removal of any official documents, memoranda, or similar papers.

But in the middle of the Saturday night of the Massacre there was a touch of comic relief.

At about the same time I was talking to Al Haig about locking up somebody's umbrella, we did have a near donnybrook—fortunately our only one. A deputy in the special prosecutor's office refused to permit Agent Lano to inspect a briefcase he was carrying out of the building. Lano reached for the valise.

Lano insisted that he must inspect the case, orders from Al Haig. The two men tugged at the case, tipping it back and forth.

The man insisted that the FBI had no authority to inspect his personal belongings—Haig or no Haig. Another tug at the case. Another tip.

"Such a search is in violation of my constitutional rights," he insisted. "If you search my briefcase without my permission, I will press charges at once!" Tug. Tip.

Tempers flared momentarily and there was another sharp exchange of words as the two had a final tug-of-war over the briefcase, with still more tipping back and forth. At last the deputy yielded. And at last Agent Lano had an opportunity to inspect the briefcase. Its dangerous contents: the morning newspaper, two very heavy law books . . . and a mashed peanut butter and jelly sandwich.

Bemused, Lano returned the briefcase to a thoroughly irritated deputy who departed without further discussion.

It was almost midnight when Assistant Director Miller called me for the last time that Saturday night. He confirmed that the situation was well in hand and that, aside from one unfortunate peanut butter and jelly sandwich, there had been no casualties, certainly nothing that would make headlines the next morning.

After that last call I went into the kitchen and told Ruby where matters now stood. It had been a frantic Saturday night. I had updated her after each call. She knew I was upset. Our relaxing weekend had gone up in smoke. I then went into our living room and sat down to think about the whole Watergate affair, with the lives of so many people thrown into turmoil this way. For some reason, I recalled an incident that had taken place in Kansas City while I was chief of police.

There had been a shooting in a local tavern and we received an emergency call at police headquarters. Four police officers responded to the call. After arriving at the tavern, two uniformed officers went in the front door and the other two, plainclothes detectives, went in the back. Then, pandemonium. The man with the gun was at the tavern's bandstand and when he saw the police, he began shooting. All four of our officers shot back—at the same time. One of our plainclothesmen was killed instantly. Incredibly, nobody else was killed and, as suddenly as it started, the shooting stopped. The assailant was quickly taken into custody and charged with first-degree murder. The story given to the news media by the Kansas City Police Department said that one of our detectives had been killed in the line of duty. His assailant, we reported, was now in custody, awaiting trial. It was clearly an open and shut case—so we thought. Two days later I learned that the bullet which had killed our detective came from the gun of one of the uniformed officers. The man in the tavern who had started this whole affair was guilty of several crimes, but innocent of murder.

As chief of police, I was concerned about the best way to handle this. Through an honest error, we had given an inaccurate news report to the media and, consequently, misinformed the people of Kansas City. How could we correct the matter? I knew there was only one answer: Tell the truth. But what was the best way to do it? Would the public image of the Kansas City Police Department really be damaged if we simply told the truth? The public, I thought, surely must know that a policeman would be capable of this human error.

After considering various options, I called a press conference to air all the details. Members of the news media filed into my office. After they sat down, I explained to them that the police department had made a mistake and, as chief of police, I was responsible. We had jumped to a conclusion about the recent homicide and had now discovered our error. Further, I had asked them to come over so that I could provide them with a news release that would correctly detail the homicide. We were sorry for the mistake. They were professional journalists and, to a person, appreciated our honesty. Only a few had questions. Apart from the tragedy of losing a fine police officer, the mistake was, by and large, forgotten.

That incident prompted me to wonder about the president. Hadn't he been in like circumstances? Wouldn't it have been so much easier for him at the beginning simply to step forward and say, "We made a mistake, and I am responsible." Think of the aggravation that could have been avoided. I, like many Americans, had been more than willing to give him every benefit of the doubt.

But now, after this Saturday night, for me at least, it was all too late. And it was too revealing. The president had indeed something to hide on those White House tapes. To me, it was as simple as that. Richard Nixon was an immensely capable man. But this was so stupid. I was heartsick.

Judge Sirica later said, "Of all the incredible events during the Watergate affair, that Saturday's were the most unbelievable."

At 11:30 the next morning, General Haig called me to say that the surveillances at Richardson's and Ruckelshaus's offices could be discontinued, and that U.S. marshals would replace FBI agents at the special prosecutor's office.

Before hanging up, Haig said that he personally appreciated the cooperation he'd gotten from the FBI ". . . and I applaud the way your people handled the entire matter, Mr. Director. It was a hot potato that I handed you last night, but we all felt more comfortable knowing the FBI was involved. Thank you."

I then called Ed Miller and told him to prepare for the termination of our operations at the offices of the former attorney general and the formery deputy attorney general. FBI surveillance of Cox's office would end at 12:30 P.M. when the assignment would be turned over to the U.S. Marshal's office.

As the FBI's involvement came to a close, I asked myself: Did I follow the proper course of action?

That FBI agents were so ordered into service on that infamous evening caused many persons to question whether we were right in doing what Alexander Haig had asked. Had the FBI been misused for political purposes? I was convinced that we had acted properly. Further, I did not—and do not—believe anybody misused us for their own political ends. But I also knew that in an atmosphere of growing suspicion of the entire Nixon Administration, I had to be most cautious in judging the legality of any future White House requests.

I spent a sleepless night on October 20 and was extremely tired on the plane trip back to Washington the next night. Anxiety pursued me. My wife was far too ill to travel back to Washington with me and that greatly saddened me. My FBI responsibilities and my plans for improving the Bureau weighed heavily on my mind. And, of course, closing in was the Watergate scandal. Would the Nixon presidency survive? Would the presidency itself survive?

In a free society like ours, the citizens must have faith in, and respect for, the institutions of government. All three of our separate-but-equal branches of government must have the public trust. Otherwise, our system of government won't work. As one of the three cornerstones of our republic, the office of the president within the executive branch is especially dependent on public confidence. If the presidency cannot command the respect and voluntary cooperation of the citizenry, its continuity and prestige will be threatened. The image and the security of the office had been badly shattered since 1960. In the first presidential term of the decade, John F. Kennedy was shot and killed. In the second term of the decade, Lyndon Johnson, by the end of his term, could not travel safely anywhere in the country: so great was the violence of anti-Vietnam hysteria. Now it looked as if the third president in a row, Richard Nixon, would not only be unable to serve for two uninterrupted terms of office, but in this case might actually be put in jail for his transgressions.

As I flew into Washington's National Airport, I recall wondering just how all of this would end. What had Watergate done to the fabric of our society? Who or what could pull it all together?

6

The Lessons of Watergate

A View from the Director's Chair

THIS IS NOT ANOTHER Watergate exposé.

It is neither a full nor a definitive chronicle of any part of Watergate. It's not even meant to be a sketchy account of what happened. In great depth many scholars, researchers, reporters, and historians have already described—and tried to explain—the stormy, day-by-day events of that episode. And there will be more Watergate books in even greater detail in all the days to come.

What follows here is how I saw it, how it affected me, and the way it influenced what I was trying to do as director of the FBI.

I will tell you what I thought, what I think we (in law enforcement) thought, and what I perceived to be the changing mood of the people around me during those tumultuous two years from 1972 to 1974.

How could Richard Nixon have avoided the final Watergate showdown—once the break-in happened? Once they were caught, how could the president have gotten them out of that mess? Did Nixon deliberately order the break-in? Unconsciously, did he *wish* it? Finally, what impact—if any—did Watergate have on the FBI?

It is a fascinating, tragic-comic story.

When the burglary at the Democratic National Committee headquarters took place on June 17, 1972, I was the chief of police of Kansas City, Missouri. The affair, which got minimal

143

press coverage in the beginning, seemed so ludicrous as to defy belief. I could not—and even today cannot—comprehend how the rich, powerful, successful incumbent Republican party came to the conclusion that it needed inside information on the Democratic party's campaign strategies. I cannot imagine what the Committee to Re-Elect the President expected to find that could conceivably help a cause that didn't need any help. The polls at the time indicated that President Nixon was in a very strong re-election position. No Democratic candidate was even close to him.

In June of 1972 there should have been no reason for worry by the Committee to Re-Elect.

But apparently there was.

In my office at police headquarters in Kansas City we discussed the episode with amused fascination. As police officers, we deemed the break-in to be the work of the rankest of amateurs. That black masking tape placed over those door latches in the Watergate complex was one example of their amateur trappings. In fact, from where we sat it looked more like a Pink Panther comedy than a routine burglary. I knew from my lengthy career in law enforcement that the ex-CIA or ex-FBI men who were tangled in that web had to be hoping none of their old friends were watching.

Beyond any other consideration, however, was the basic and stunning incredibility of the White House being involved in anything like this. How by any logical thought process could anybody connect the two? We were half-convinced that this whole thing must be a misunderstanding; the news media must be playing a joke on us.

Unfortunately it was all too true. In fact the truth was even more grotesque than most early reports suggested.

What, I've been asked in jest, could the Watergate planners have done to ensure their success?

The answer to that is simple enough. Anyone who wanted to break into the Democratic Party's National Committee headquarters should merely have gone out and hired a handful of journeymen thieves. Two would have been enough; maybe one.

It would have been an easy task for a mediocre criminal to enter the headquarters, accomplish his objectives (whatever those were), and get away without being caught.

The events that followed the burglary are now common knowledge.

The FBI moved into the investigation the very next day. And, as we now know, from the beginning President Nixon was involved in the coverup. The president and his chief of staff, H.R. Haldeman, discussed the incident—and what to do about it—on June 23, just six days after the fact. The attempted break-in was but one of many sinister activities of the Nixon Administration, dating back to 1969. As Judge John J. Sirica said: "Only a few people in Washington that summer (1972) knew that the break-in was really just one act in a long series of White House-inspired attempts to circumvent the law."

Curiously, although the media covered the break-in when it happened, not much attention was given to it during the 1972 presidential campaign. In fact, publicity was minimal until John Dean's testimony was televised. Dean's revelations, which began in the spring of 1973 in the Senate Caucus Room before the Senate Select Committee on Presidential Campaign Activities, blew the lid off Watergate. Several top White House officials resigned. Acting FBI Director L. Patrick Gray left at this time. In announcing his resignation on April 27, Gray cited "serious allegations concerning certain acts of my own during the ongoing Watergate investigation" and declared that the FBI had "been in no way involved in any of those personal acts or judgments." Following this, missing FBI wiretaps were discovered by the new acting FBI Director William Ruckelshaus in the White House offices vacated by John Ehrlichman.

By the time I became director of the FBI in July of 1973, Watergate had emerged as a full-blown scandal and certainly the leading item of national concern.

At a news conference held in Washington on June 27, 1973, following the Senate's confirmation of my nomination as director, I responded to a question regarding the Watergate investigation stating: "I know nothing about it at this point, and I can only say that I will become acquainted with it after I come into office." Little did I know just how quickly I would become acquainted with all of it.

I accepted the post of FBI director certain that Watergate would grow in scope. After taking office, I immediately concerned myself with the breadth, direction, and mechanics of the Watergate investigation, satisfying myself that it was being conducted in a prompt, thorough, and impartial manner by FBI personnel who could not have been a party to the coverup.

The investigation, as it developed from summer 1973 on, was a joint effort of three government entities. The first was the special prosecutor's office, established by Attorney General Elliot L. Richardson to look into the Watergate scandal. The second was the Senate Select Committee on Presidential Campaign Activities, chaired by Senator Sam Ervin, widely acknowledged to be the leading expert in the Senate on the Constitution. And last was the FBI investigation itself, conducted at the request of the U.S. Department of Justice. Information was frequently exchanged between these three groups. In the beginning, most of the work done by the FBI was handled by our Washington field office.

Since the FBI was the largest investigative arm of the United States government, I wanted our efforts to be well coordinated with those of the special prosecutor's office and of the Senate Committee. The working relationship we developed was a good one. Here, in its simplest form, is how it operated:

The special prosecutor's office would send us several queries each week requesting Watergate investigative work on certain matters. Tagged to each communication was a statement that said, in effect, if any other information developed beyond the specific request, please explore it fully. So each request had its own built-in and also open-ended set of instructions. Reports of our findings in each situation were sent directly to the special prosecutor's office. We also conducted investigations for the Senate Committee which, at this time, employed about sixty lawyers who would also send us weekly requests for investigative work.

No FBI reports were sent to the attorney general unless

approved by the special prosecutor. This approval pertained only to matters of official concern to the Criminal Division of the Justice Department. Furthermore, we agreed that any attorney in the special prosecutor's office could deal directly with individual FBI agents, and further, that all work requests from the special prosecutor would be expedited. This unprecedented arrangement was made necessary by the highly unusual circumstances of the time.

From these early beginnings in July 1973 events moved—as I've outlined in the previous chapter—with lightning speed until the fateful night of October 20 when Special Prosecutor Cox was fired, and Attorney General Richardson and Deputy Attorney General Ruckelshaus resigned.

Following October 20 we were faced with a new challenge: Was the president of the United States involved in a felony? This man had been elected to the office held by George Washington, Thomas Jefferson, Abraham Lincoln, Franklin Roosevelt, and John F. Kennedy. Could it be, the world wondered, that the president of the United States, the most powerful leader in the Western world, perhaps in the entire world, faced the ignominious prospect of imprisonment? Though it seemed inconceivable to me, it was my responsibility to find out the answer to this question. The awesomeness of my task almost overwhelmed me. It was my duty to gather and assemble all the facts relating to Watergate and deliver them to the proper authorities, who would, I was certain, press the investigation to an ultimate conclusion.

On November 1, acting Attorney General Bork announced that Leon Jaworski would succeed Archibald Cox as Watergate special prosecutor.

I immediately liked and respected Leon Jaworski.

Jaworksi was the quintessential lawyer. A tough Texan, an experienced and distinguished attorney, Leon Jaworski was ever candid, above board, and a hard worker. We lunched together about once a week to discuss and plan the forthcoming events. When we occasionally saw each other at social functions, talk invariably turned to how we could work better as a team. I found him always a gracious, even courtly, human being. I'm confident that we trusted and respected each other. I know we worked long and hard toward our common goal during those months together: the investigation of every aspect of Watergate.

On November 21 White House attorneys told U.S. District Judge Sirica that a key portion of one of the subpoenaed White House tapes (originally subpoenaed by Archibald Cox) was blank—the famous eighteen-and-a-half-minute gap. Sirica made the matter public the same day. Rose Mary Woods subsequently testified in U.S. District Court before Judge Sirica that she had accidentally erased it. We were told that President Nixon was perhaps the most mechanically inept man in the world, and could not possibly have erased the tape himself. Nevertheless, we at the FBI did look into the matter carefully and concluded that the erasure was deliberate. Thus, it became a question of who was not telling the truth.

At a press conference on January 17, 1974, held in Phoenix, I noted that the Watergate investigation continued to gain tremendous momentum and the workload of the entire FBI was very substantially Watergate-related. In fact, at this time nearly all of our fifty-nine field offices were looking into all the facets of the break-in and scandal. Prosecutive action had been taken against eighteen persons and corporations. Twelve had already been sentenced, and additional court proceedings were still pending. With no letup in sight, I expected that the Watergate special prosecution force would continue weekly to send us requests for more work.

The pressure on the White House increased inexorably.

On March 1 and again on March 7, 1974, grand juries returned the long-awaited indictments of seven former White House officials and campaign aides of President Nixon. All were charged with conspiring to obstruct justice. President Nixon was named an unindicted co-conspirator by the grand jury, although that information was held secret.

Among those indicted were H.R. Haldeman, assistant to the

president and White House chief of staff; John D. Ehrlichman, assistant to the president for domestic affairs; and John N. Mitchell, former attorney general and campaign director of the Committee to Re-Elect the President.

On April 29 the president appeared on national television to announce that he would supply the House Judiciary Committee with 1,254 pages of edited transcripts of subpoenaed conversations he had held with key aides regarding Watergate. He would, further, make this information public.

Although the amount of material released was vast, it did not include eleven of the most condemnatory of forty-two specific conversations subpoenaed. Also, supplementary notes and Dictabelts under subpoena were withheld. The most important missing tapes were a recording made on June 20, 1972, three days after the Watergate burglary, in which the president and H.R. Haldeman discussed the arrests (part of this tape was obliterated by Ms. Woods), and the June 23 tape, in which the president and Haldeman devised a plan to have the CIA impede the FBI investigation of Watergate.

The tapes shocked the nation.

Much of the material contained the basest of profane language. The subject matter could not have been more sordid. The discussions revolved around overt perjury; how and where to spend "hush money"; thwarting congressional probes by any manner of dirty tricks; violating grand-jury secrecy; and every possible way to manipulate—and even deceive—the Watergate prosecutor and FBI investigators.

The summer of 1974 was unforgettable.

And by that midsummer nerves were raw at FBI headquarters. The media, dogged in its pursuit and coverage of the rapidly developing Watergate events, seemed to want a breakthrough story almost every hour. The American news media, consisting of some remarkably hardworking and capable reporters and journalists, simply refused to let go of the Watergate story. It appeared to me that the working press, the government's investigative and prosecutorial machinery, and of course, U.S. Judge John J. Sirica were indeed setting the stage so that justice could be done. Thus, as that hot summer wore on, the tension grew. President Nixon and his White House aides attempted to fend off each and every Watergate probe, whether from Congress, the FBI, the media, or the special prosecutor's office.

The evidence and data we had compiled at the FBI was massive, representing thousands of hours of investigative work. But it wasn't enough.

Congress, the investigators, and the prosecutors still demanded a "smoking gun."

With pressure for impeachment growing more intense each day, everybody wanted the same thing: final—and damning— tapes and documents to clinch the case.

Finally, as ultimately it must, the matter reached the highest court in the land.

On July 24, 1974, the vital question of the special prosecutor's access to the final Watergate tapes and other documents had been laid before the Supreme Court. It was an historic confrontation and time almost stood still as the nation watched.

The matter involved two cases—Case No. 73-1766, United States vs. Richard M. Nixon, and cross-petition Case No. 73-1834, Richard M. Nixon vs. the United States.

The White House defense team based their defense primarily on the claim of "executive privilege"—the nearly sacrosanct right of the White House to conduct its affairs in complete privacy and secrecy.

On the other hand, the Supreme Court was being asked by government prosecutors to uphold Judge Sirica's August 29, 1973, order that specific White House tapes in question be given to him for review by the United States District Court for the District of Columbia. The government argued that the claim of executive privilege was subordinate to the need for evidence in this criminal trial.

There were indeed, the Supreme Court granted, certain executive privileges of secrecy implicit in the office of the presidency itself. But in this matter, the court held, the claim of executive privilege was simply too broad. Moreover, a clear need existed for relevant evidence in what was, in fact, a criminal proceeding.

In 1942, I was assigned to the FBI Training Center in Quantico, Virginia, as a firearms instructor. During this assignment I had a close-up look at the various facets of J. Edgar Hoover's personality.

I left the Bureau to become chief of police of Kansas City, Missouri. I took the oath of office on August 28, 1961.

My years in Kansas City as chief of police were, in many ways, among the most rewarding of my life.

These pictures were taken on April 9, 1968, near Twelfth and Locust in downtown Kansas City. Racial riots broke out in reaction to the assassination of Dr. Martin Luther King, Jr. Kansas City, along with the rest of the nation, was torn by the violence and tragic loss of life. Police used tear gas cannisters to disperse rioters.

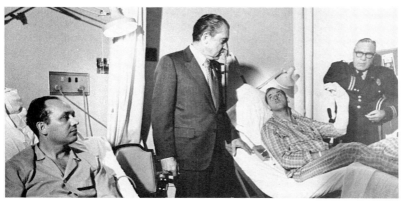

President Richard Nixon, during a stopover in Kansas City in 1970, made a hospital visit to wounded Kansas City Police Officers Charles T. Robinson and Kenneth M. Fleming.

I inspected the scene of a bombing on East Twelfth Street in downtown Kansas City on April 16, 1970. Officers Robinson and Fleming were severely injured in this bombing.

The last time I saw J. Edgar Hoover was from across the table at a White House conference in June of 1971. The consensus was that he seemed to be in good health—I detected no signs of physical deterioration.

Upon my arrival as the new FBI director, President Nixon commented: "We are looking forward to having you on our team." His team fell apart shortly after that. But I was very grateful for the support of Attorney General Elliot Richardson, pictured here with us.

On July 9, 1973, I took the oath of office as the new FBI director before a crowd of about 12,000 in downtown Kansas City. President Nixon made arrangements to have the ceremony in Kansas City.

The second administration I worked under was that of President Gerald R. Ford. He became president on August 9, 1974, shortly after a fallen Nixon left the White House. I found Ford very likable and a solid individual.

The court wasted little time.

On that same July 24 it delivered a sledgehammer blow to the Nixon presidency. The Court ruled, by 8-0, against the White House. President Nixon must provide "forthwith" sixty-four tapes of White House conversations subpoenaed by Leon Jaworski for the pending Watergate coverup trial of former presidential aides.

It was all downhill from there.

Less than a week later, on July 27, by a vote of 27-11 the House Judiciary Committee approved its first article of impeachment, charging President Nixon with obstruction of justice in attempting to cover up Watergate. That day the committee also charged Nixon with abuse of presidential power. The next day he was charged with illegally defying congressional subpoenas.

On August 5, 1974, after twenty-five months of deceit and deception, the president released the transcripts of three conversations on June 23, 1972. At the same time he admitted a "serious act of omission" in his previous accounts of the Watergate coverup: he had indeed ordered a halt to the FBI's probe of the break-in of Democratic National Committee headquarters in the Watergate Building. The information was quickly made public. The effect was devastating.

The release of the remaining subpoenaed transcripts (the smoking-gun tapes) was almost anticlimactic. The Nixon presidency was over. I didn't think that he would resign as quickly as he did, but it was apparent the president had to leave, either forcibly or voluntarily. Wisely, he chose to leave voluntarily.

On August 9, 1974, Richard M. Nixon resigned as president of the United States and Vice President Gerald R. Ford was sworn in as his successor.

More than a decade has now passed.

My term in the director's chair provided me with a vantage point for close-up observation of Watergate. Some of my reflections on Watergate may be questioned, but I believe they are sound.

The obvious question is: How did this idiotic, then tragic, affair happen in the first place? The answer is plain enough: The president placed himself above the law. He created a climate of moral permissiveness and outright disregard for the law (dating back to the beginning of his first term, the spring of 1969, when he first set up those wiretaps). Then he surrounded himself with sycophants, who by definition cannot serve honorably. When these two prime ingredients were mixed together the Oval Office became a breeding ground for nefarious activities. The conversations within the Oval Office during those years reflected this. They were, at best, coarse and offensive. At worst, they were criminal.

Despite his arrogance, I believe Richard Nixon was in many ways childishly simplistic.

The fatal Watergate order was probably indirect.

I believe that one day the president simply made an offhanded remark, such as, "I wonder what information the Democrats have," or, "We need to get into the damned Democratic headquarters to find out what they are thinking." And a White House aide or flunky from the re-election committee simply took it from there. All the way to Watergate.

Did anything good come from the Watergate nightmare? At this point, let me be very subjective. As far as the FBI is concerned, the answer is a resounding yes.

In fact, I believe that Watergate served as a much needed cleansing agent for the Bureau and helped me initiate long overdue reforms within the organization.

In the late sixties and early seventies the FBI had become involved in some questionable activities. Suddenly, Watergate made the "good old days" history. For most of its organizational life the Bureau had largely been free of public criticism and, to almost the same extent, free of media criticism until the late 1960s. But Watergate revealed that the Bureau had to change some of its practices, such as some of its borderline Cointelpro-type investigations.

A second impetus for change was from the top. I became FBI

director in July 1973, close to the time that Watergate began to grow into a scandal of massive dimensions. I undertook to change my policies, and to correct abuses in FBI conduct. In all, the process took three years to complete. It would have taken longer without the catharsis of Watergate.

At every level of government an examination of conscience was suddenly much in order.

Therefore, my staff and I conducted lengthy and thorough studies of every phase of Bureau activities, responsibilities, management structure, philosophy, and general organizational strategy. We wanted a Bureau that would be more efficient, more responsible, and more professional and that would operate well within the law. Our analysis was not completed until summer 1976. Accordingly, at that time I announced what was believed to be the most far-reaching restructuring of the FBI in its history.

The most important change was the transfer of responsibility for investigating domestic radical and terrorist groups from our Intelligence Division to our General Investigations branch, which operated under more restrictive guidelines. As a result, our domestic intelligence probes dropped from twenty-two thousand annually to four thousand, a decline of almost 82 percent in three years.

In addition, investigations that dealt primarily with internal subversion, including attempts to overthrow the United States government, would be moved to the General Investigations Division "for the express purpose that they be managed like all other criminal cases in that division." The General Investigations Division would confine itself to investigating actual violations of the law rather than spying on persons merely suspected of planning to break the law.

Our Intelligence Division would continue to handle cases involving foreign governments or groups. These cases included espionage and terrorism. We also revitalized our foreign intelligence programs and consolidated our Internal Inspection Service with our Office of Planning and Evaluation.

I placed new emphasis on participatory management. Subordinates and co-workers were encouraged to express their ideas and develop their own expertise as far as their individual talents allowed. This represented a radical change of management philosophy not unanimously accepted by those who grew up during the J. Edgar Hoover years.

Last, I established the Office of Internal Professional Responsibility to investigate charges of misconduct by our personnel.

I acknowledged publicly and unequivocally that the Bureau had made mistakes in the past. Our house was not entirely in order. Many of the problems had been brought to the surface by Watergate. But they were, in large measure, corrected by the changes instituted.

The efforts of the FBI in the Watergate investigation were prodigious. At the height of the special prosecutor's intensive operation, from 1973 to 1975, agents from almost all of our fifty-nine field offices, as well as agents assigned to several FBI posts abroad, conducted more than 2,600 interviews at the special prosecutor's request. Our lengthy and, I believe, comprehensive written reports made up a large portion of the special prosecutor's files. Also, the services of our laboratory and our Identification Division were made available to the special prosecutor's office for examination of fingerprints, documents, and even polygraphs. I believe we fulfilled every request for investigative work that we received, and can recall no request from the special prosecutor's office or Senator Ervin's committee that we felt was unreasonable. Moreover, FBI personnel did ultimately transcribe the sixty-four subpoenaed White House tapes.

I am still frequently asked about other aspects of Watergate.

For example, the subject of "Deep Throat" occasionally arises in conversation. Deep Throat was, supposedly, a well-placed government official who secretly supplied *Washington Post* reporter Bob Woodward with confidential, "deep background" information about Watergate and its coverup. In my opinion, Deep Throat was somebody's publicity stunt. He did not exist— not as one person. Deep Throat was a group of informants.

Not long ago many people thought Deep Throat might have been my old friend Mark Felt, a former high-ranking FBI official who at one time was considered for the director's position and who resigned just before I became director. This is nonsense. No one person, no one informant, could have had access to as much confidential information on such a broad scale as Deep Throat supposedly had.

What about the Nixon administration wiretaps?

An ongoing controversy has developed concerning the use of wiretaps to stop news leaks. As we now know, the use of unethical wiretaps in the spring of 1969 was the first step in the Nixon administration's doomed journey to Watergate. Clearly, the administration should have explored alternatives to wiretapping to stop leaks of sensitive information to the news media. As Theodore White has written: "What is interesting about the wiretap and surveillance system setup in May, 1969, is the quality of inevitability of the historic 'glide'—the glide that Nixon's men took, unconsciously in the beginning and then very consciously and maliciously, across the line of law."

Ironically, the wiretaps weren't really effective. The identity of those in the Nixon administration who provided news leaks in 1969 was never determined. In my law-enforcement career I've discovered one interesting thing about wiretaps. Individuals rarely discuss sensitive, secret, or classified information on the telephone. They are afraid that they may be wiretapped. Wiretapping, I believe, can be productive in certain situations, such as kidnapping, but in the case of the Nixon wiretaps, the whole effort was less than fruitless. It was counterproductive.

Was there something else that the Nixon Administration could have done to stop the news leaks? One alternative was never tried but should have been. Each time I visited the president, I was struck by the immense mystique of the Oval Office. It is practically impossible to walk into that room and not be overwhelmed by the sense of history that pervades it. The president could have taken advantage of this aura to solve the problem of leaks in 1969 as they related to the administration's secret diplomatic and military efforts to end the Vietnam War.

Is it naive to think that by calling newspeople and politicians alike into that office and simply *asking* them to stop the news leaks that this would end the leaks? Maybe it *is* naive to think Richard Nixon could have done this, and maybe it would have taken a great amount of time, but I think the effort would have been worthwhile.

Based on my experience as an FBI agent and as a chief of police, I would have urged the president not to wiretap certain suspected government officials and journalists but, rather, to summon each of them into the Oval Office, individually or in small groups, over a period of several days. Then, exploiting the mystique of the Oval Office he could have appealed directly to each individual's sense of national interest and patriotism, saying something like this:

"Our men in Vietnam deserve our full support; right or wrong, the war is there, and it must be fought. American boys are being killed every day. Leaking information of this type is actually hurting efforts we are making to protect our men, to save their lives and the lives of our allies, and to extricate ourselves from this terrible war. I am asking you on behalf of the United States not to release information to the public that will undermine our cause."

Would any reasonable man or woman have refused this direct request from the commander-in-chief? I doubt it. But that method was never even tried, and that's a pity. It might have deflected the Nixon Administration from its long, sad journey to Watergate.

Finally, let me say that I think there was another option open to the president which would have spared him, and the nation, the disgrace of August 1974. If only, in the summer of 1972, he would have either called a national press conference or given a nationwide speech on television and straightforwardly acknowledged that "a mistake has been made. Here are the facts, and the matter is being corrected." Perhaps the tragedy of Richard Nixon is that he never could have played it so straight. Perhaps, caught between the banality of "Checkers" and the venality of "your president isn't a crook," a candid statement like this never could have passed his lips.

At that point in time—the early 1970s—the people of this country, sick of being lied to, would have found delightfully refreshing a politician who confessed genuine remorse and pledged to do better next time. The president could have defused the issue and won the support of the American people. He could have, but he didn't. It wasn't in his makeup. So we had Watergate.

7

Cointelpro

Countersubversion vs. the Constitution

IT ALL BEGAN in a most illegal way.

On the night of March 8, 1971, a group calling itself the Citizens Committee to Investigate the Federal Bureau of Investigation burglarized the FBI's small Philadelphia resident agency in Media, Pennsylvania. A case of break-and-entry and theft. A serious felony under the law.

They stole more than one-thousand highly sensitive FBI internal documents. A flagrant violation of federal law. Nearly all were related to the FBI domestic counterintelligence programs known within the Bureau as "Cointelpro."

Within days, copies of about twenty of these documents were sent anonymously to two members of Congress, Senator George S. McGovern of South Dakota, and Representative Parren J. Mitchell of Maryland, both Democrats. Also, these documents were sent to selected prominent newspapers, including the *New York Times,* the *Washington Post,* and the *Los Angeles Times.*

Because of the highly confidential nature of the stolen materials, and because several of the Cointelpro operations were actively being pursued at the time, Attorney General John N. Mitchell issued an urgent appeal to the newspapers to withhold, in the national interest, publication of any of the FBI data.

At first, the *New York Times* and the *Los Angeles Times* honored the request. The *Washington Post,* however, published parts of the documents, withholding individual names and locations. The

New York and Los Angeles newspapers immediately followed suit.

In my view, these documents were not only obtained illegally, but were published entirely out of context. Thus they represented a moral transgression on the part of the Citizens Committee, as well as a criminal act.

Although the Cointelpro documents covered a wide range of Bureau investigative activities, the Committee (showing editorial skills as well as criminal aptitude) chose to release only those few memos that depicted the Bureau's more questionable methods of internal surveillance on the many activist groups that flourished during the years 1956-1971, especially during the 1960s.

One published memo, for instance, directed that FBI agents investigate and monitor groups organized to meet the demands of black activist students.

Another FBI memo encouraged agents to pose as student or graduate "backers" and penetrate and infiltrate various student dissident organizations.

A third memo discussed recruiting college-student informers, between the ages of eighteen and twenty-one, to report campus extremists to the FBI. Operating within a network of other informants at their college—the network including college staff personnel, postal employees, and local police, all feigning to be supporters of the cause—the students would then give this information to the FBI. The Bureau would then do its utmost to embarrass the extremists.

All in all, not an attractive view of the internal thinking—and proceedings—of the Bureau at that time. But the armed violence of some on-campus militants wasn't very pretty either. The Citizens Committee, of course, chose to ignore these rebellious activities that made the FBI's presence on campuses necessary in the first place.

As a member of the FBI at this time I remember hearing that most Bureau people found these on-campus assignments to be distasteful, justified only by the extreme measures taken by some college leftist groups. Throughout this entire period, the FBI's extensive efforts were intended only to keep in balance—"neutralize"—the seething unrest in colleges and college towns throughout the land.

Other released memoranda revealed a subtle shift in FBI surveillance of racial groups from the post-World War II period through the early 1970s.

For example, in the early years of the civil rights demonstrations, the Bureau looked for foreign (Communist) influences within the movement. After the traumatic urban violence of the 1960s, however, the Bureau realized that the civil rights movement was under no foreign influence whatsoever.

Also, as the published documents revealed, the Bureau maintained confidential intelligence files on the Ku Klux Klan, the Socialist Workers Party, the Black Panthers—and almost every other organization that the FBI thought could threaten public tranquility or the security of the government. These files, carefully maintained and enlarged over a period of several years, came to form a sizable portion of the Bureau's data bank in Washington.

Cointelpro-like programs were born of a real need at the beginning of World War II. Since 1940, with few exceptions, the United States government has used the FBI to thwart the internal subversive efforts of hostile foreign powers. During the war, of course, the enemy was Germany and Japan.

Following the war, the enemy became communism. Communism, the Communist International Movement, the Communist Party in the U.S.A., Communist espionage. The names are all too familiar: Gerhart Eisler, Elizabeth Bentley, Rudolf Abel, Klaus Fuchs, Harry Gold, the Rosenbergs.

Through the entire Cold War period—until this very day—the FBI represented America's chief internal agency in countering intelligence and espionage threats from hostile foreign, primarily Communist, governments. Designed to block or short-circuit an enemy's source of information, to deceive the enemy, to prevent sabotage, and to gather political and military information about the enemies of the United States, FBI counterintelligence skills moved with the greatest of ease from Communist subversion to Klan activities in Mississippi. As the intelligence activities of foreign powers grew more ambitious, the scope of the Bureau's counterintelligence activities widened. The FBI studied, monitored, even infiltrated, numerous elements in American society, from the extreme left to, in time, the far right. Eventually, the FBI began to investigate groups and organizations wholly unrelated to an international Communist conspiracy, or the actions of any hostile foreign power. This broadening of FBI responsibility, evolving from the espionage requirements of World War II and the Cold War period, 1945-1956, led ultimately to the Cointelpro activities that the Citizens Committee found so abhorrent.

Even though I was an FBI special agent during the early years of Cointelpro, 1956-1961, I was not personally involved in any Cointelpro programs. Thus the methodologies of these programs were unknown to me.

The details—and the full significance—of Cointelpro first came to my attention when I became director of the FBI in July of 1973. For me, it was quite an eye-opening experience. As I studied this wide-ranging FBI pursuit, evaluating grievances against it, I saw the clear need for moderating some Cointelpro techniques. What might have been allowable during the Second World War, or the Atomic Energy War immediately thereafter, wasn't necessarily tolerable in the Age of Aquarius. The times of 1973 were, after all, colored by the flower children. As bad as Kent State was, it couldn't compare with Hiroshima.

I began immediately to recommend strong corrective courses of action for the Bureau. Our programs needed moderation, and I took steps in that direction. It was a delicate and sensitive matter, this pulling back. Viewed by some within the Bureau as a compromise with "anarchists," it caused some hard feelings during my entire term as director of the FBI. But first I wanted to look closely at some history.

The FBI's first official Cointelpro was directed, as might be expected, at the Communist Party, USA.

The CPUSA-Cointelpro lasted from August 28, 1956, until the spring of 1971. Many reasons justified its existence. First, the Bureau learned that, as a result of extensive counterespionage operations during World War II, international spying directed against the security of the United States was widespread—and not all threats came from our wartime enemies: Los Alamos co-workers Klaus Fuchs and David Greenglass were not stealing atomic secrets for the Japanese or Germans.

With the war won, the FBI turned its attention to the Communist International Movement (the Comintern), and the support it was getting from CPUSA.

J. Edgar Hoover believed that it was his obligation to meet the Communist threat wherever it existed. Hoover and other high-ranking FBI officials were convinced that traditional law-enforcement techniques available to the FBI prevented them from eliminating the subversive activities of radical organizations.

As a result, the FBI took off the gloves.

In the interest of national security and to more successfully wage its war against communism on American soil, the FBI began to systematically destroy CPUSA. But not without official sanction. Hoover knew the Washington rules too well to overlook that.

The approval obtained by Hoover at the National Security Council meeting on March 8, 1956, attended by top officials of the Eisenhower Administration, including the attorney general and President Eisenhower himself, allowed the FBI to initiate a series of extremely "ambitious" counterintelligence programs—the actual prototypes of Cointelpro.

Indeed at this particular meeting Mr. Hoover presented in some detail the new FBI methodologies to be utilized in destroying CPUSA. These included: surreptitious entry, safe-cracking, the photographing of private documents, telephone "surveillance" (tapping), mail "monitoring" (opening), meeting disruption, infiltration of CPUSA itself, and a variety of other techniques, all questionable, even at their mildest. There was no objection by those in attendance to the use of any of these tricks by the FBI in domestic counterintelligence programs.

I later reviewed all of these programs in careful detail from the vantage point of the director's chair in 1973. I was not very pleased with what I learned. But what I would have thought in 1956, at the height of the KGB-FBI conflict, I'm not sure. With the Russians paying little heed to Marquis of Queensberry rules, how gentlemanly could the FBI afford to be?

What is certain is that those who undertook these counter-intelligence programs did so based on what they perceived to be the best interest of the United States. I cannot fault them for that. Most of my studies of earlier Cointelpros were done in the serenity of my Washington apartment during the quiet evenings in the late summer and early fall of 1973. Reading then of what was done earlier, I winced at such hard-hitting tactics, so close to being below the belt. Again, however, I was far removed from the Cold War at its hottest.

As I read, one thing became very clear: The methods worked.

In addition to the tactics discussed at the NSC meeting in March of 1956, some of the other wartime-inspired counter-intelligence efforts later used against the Communists (and others) included: electronic surveillance (bugging), derogatory (sometimes even *true*) individual background exposés, the use of informants to create controversy within organizations, planting news stories (of dubious accuracy) with sympathetic media, tat-tling on unfriendly opposition, preventing Constitutionally-al-lowable meetings from being held—and even encouraging street warfare among rival factions. One of the most successful tricks was to get Fascist groups to enter into brick-throwing fights with the Communists.

Just as the FBI perfected these methods of combatting radical political organizations, the times began to change. Suddenly, the Communists and the Fascists were gone, replaced by freedom-now-activists and dorm-crashers. And just as suddenly, the tech-niques for combatting the crimes were, at least, overzealous.

Or so I came to believe as I studied my Cointelpro history in the refuge of a quieter time.

The Bureau's principal effort in the CPUSA Cointelpro was to monitor, analyze, infiltrate, and ultimately destroy the American Communist Party. There were, in all, 1,388 actions approved and implemented against the CPUSA from 1956 to 1971.

These efforts devastated the American Communist Party. All Cointelpros were coordinated and controlled at FBI headquarters and the operations were limited to twelve FBI field offices. In its CPUSA Cointelpro the Bureau was able, through a fifteen-year program of careful informant development, to penetrate and neutralize the American Communist Party activities at virtually every level of party organization.

Some of these operations were quite imaginative; others, extremely rough around the edges. For example, the FBI anonymously sent Jewish Communist Party members anti-Semitic articles that had appeared in Soviet newspapers, as well as American news articles on the harsh treatment of Soviet Jews.

Communist Party attempts to infiltrate mass organizations in America were consistently neutralized by the Bureau. FBI agents nearly always knew, well in advance, of Communist Party infiltration targets, targets as diverse in purpose and membership as the NAACP is to the United Farm Workers. When a Communist Party member infiltrated an organization, an FBI agent usually approached the club's leader with the startling information that a known Communist had joined that organization. This by itself was in most cases disruptive enough to eliminate potential subversive activity by the Communists.

If more provocative action seemed needed, the FBI might plant in several local papers an article informing one and all that known Communists were infiltrating an organization, naming names and giving specific infiltration goals in certain instances.

Other successful techniques used by the FBI against the CPUSA included packing Communist Party rallies and meetings with vocal and obnoxious anti-Communists, sending invitations to Communist Party functions that would never take place, provoking last-minute cancellations of rental halls for party functions, and providing reporters with hostile questions for Communists they planned to interview.

One incident, quite serious at the time, seems amusing in retrospect.

A Communist Party official planned to hold a secret two-week training seminar for area youths in a midwestern city. The FBI, however, arranged a greeting on his arrival at the local airport by, of all people, a news reporter and film crew. The Communist quite simply blew his top, angrily pushed the reporter away and, amazingly, swung his briefcase at the film crew—as it was shooting the entire melee. The incident was, of course, featured live on local television news broadcasts. So much for the secrecy (and the success) of that training program.

The documents revealed other areas of attack against the Communist Party, such as the use of informants to capitalize on areas of inherent conflict within the party. (One such example was the traumatic Khrushchev denunciation of Stalin.) Additionally, FBI infiltrators in the Socialistic Workers Party spurred its members into open attacks against CPUSA. The ideological gulf between pure socialism and the ugly reality of communism gave FBI undercover agents numerous opportunities to needle their "fellow Marxists" into action in conflict with Stalinist goals. Also, the Internal Revenue Service was called into the fray against underground CPUSA members. Under hot pursuit by the IRS one usually has little time for involvement in any kind of extracurricular activity, let alone the complex tricks demanded by covert political intrigues. How does one go about overthrowing the government of the United States when the IRS won't get off your back?

In some cases school teachers became special Cointelpro targets because the Bureau knew that they were in a unique position to influence the thinking of young people. In one situation a high school teacher became a direct Cointelpro target because he had invited radical antidraft speakers to the school. The Bureau responded by sending anonymous letters about the teacher—and especially his speakers—to local newspapers, the board of education, and the high school administration office.

Almost 60 percent of all Cointelpro actions were directed against the U.S. Communist Party. By the early 1970s the party's membership declined from an estimated eighty thousand members to about three thousand very visible, very observable Marxists. By any standard, this was a hugely successful counterintelligence action. There was no longer any need to be unduly concerned about the Communist Party, U.S.A.

Next came the "SWP" Cointelpro.

The second Cointelpro, begun on October 12, 1961, was directed against the Socialist Workers Party in the United States. This was, by comparison, a small Cointelpro effort, with only forty-six actions directed against Socialist Workers' targets and their subsidiary group, the Young Socialist Alliance. The Socialist Workers Party had a history of being extremely vocal in their support of socialism, an ideology then viewed as being nearly as dangerous to the security of the United States as communism. In fact, the SWP was initially targeted by the Bureau because of its rhetoric.

Additionally, as I discovered, the memorandum originating Bureau involvement in the project outlined various SWP political strategies which included such activities as supporting socialist candidates for public office. It outlined, as well, the support of "such causes as Castro's Cuba and integration problems arising in the South." The American people should be alerted to the fact that "the SWP is not just another socialist group but follows the revolutionary principles of Marx, Lenin, and Engels as interpreted by Leon Trotsky."

In one SWP–Cointelpro action anonymous letters were sent by the Bureau to the parents of two students at a Midwest college (who were not members of either SWP or the Young Socialists Alliance) participating in a hunger strike to protest the war in Vietnam. These students were targeted by the Bureau because the fast was sponsored by the Young Socialist Alliance. The Bureau letters warned parents that further participation in this hunger strike by their sons could seriously damage both their health and academic standing. The letters urged the parents to protest to the college administrators that such activities not be allowed to take place on campus.

Protests were made. When the college threatened expulsion of the fasters, the hunger strike was called off at once.

The Bureau was also concerned about a developing alliance between the Socialist Workers Party and "black power" organizations. Thus, in this instance, information was anonymously circulated to key officials within the fundamentally religious Muslim mosques which outlined the basic atheism of the SWP. Such activity, of course, did disrupt the relationship between the SWP and this particular black organization, comprised of followers of the late Malcolm X.

In time, the SWP–Cointelpro just ran out of a reason for being. By the late 1960s, the ideology of Marx, Lenin, and Engels—"as interpreted by Leon Trotsky"—no longer had much appeal. Woodstock seemed like a much better idea to a lot of people—young and old.

The White Hate Cointelpro was launched by the FBI on September 2, 1964—its primary target the Ku Klux Klan. Operations were originally launched against seventeen Klan groups and nine other so-called "white hate" organizations, including the National States Rights Party and the American Nazi Party.

An early J. Edgar Hoover memorandum on the Ku Klux Klan probably best described the activities of the White Hate Cointelpro:

"We conduct intelligence investigations with the view toward infiltrating the Ku Klux Klan with informants—neutralizing it as a terrorist organization, and deterring violence."

Again, as with the leftist groups, the operations were extremely effective—as well as heavy-handed. This Cointelpro lasted seven years, until 1971. By that time the Bureau had demonstrated its extraordinary ability to infiltrate, expose, and disrupt fanatic organizations, whatever their convictions, wherever their origins.

In the White Hate effort, various techniques were used against the KKK. For example, the FBI once created a fictional Klan-like organization, comprised of FBI agents and paid informants. This new "Klan" actually competed with the traditional Klan, the United Klans of America, for new members, and in the process neutralized many of the Klan's terrorist activities.

In this context, a 1967 Bureau Cointelpro memorandum understated it thus:

> We have found that by the removal of top Klan officers (by) provoking scandal within the state Klan organization through our informants, the Klan in a particular area can be rendered ineffective.

In one situation the Bureau learned that a certain Klan organization was raising operating funds through a rather clever kick-back scheme. A member of this Klan group was selling insurance policies to other Klan members. He would regularly deposit a sizable portion of the premiums in the Klan treasury. The Bureau learned of this activity through an informant and, anonymously, informed the insurance company of this Klan fundraising activity. The insurance company immediately cancelled all of the policies held by Klan members, eliminating a significant source of income used to finance Klan activities. The fact the FBI was involved was never revealed.

Another tactic used by the FBI was to anonymously distribute embarrassing personal information about selected Klan officials to the local press and the officials' immediate families. The impact can be well imagined. In other cases, fictional letters were sent anonymously by the Bureau to Klan members to create friction and discord within the Klan. I have considerable misgivings about this technique; nevertheless, I will share an actual anonymous letter that the FBI sent (names and locations changed) to the wife of a Grand Dragon of the United Klans of America from (allegedly) a "God-fearing klanswoman."

> My Dear Mrs. (A),
>
> I write this letter to you only after a long period of praying to God. I must cleanse my soul of these

thoughts. I certainly do not want to create problems inside a family but I owe a duty to the klans and its principles as well as to my own menfolk who have cast their divine lot with the klans.

Your husband came to our state about a year ago and my menfolk blindly followed his leadership, believing him to be the savior of this country. They never believed the stories that he stole money from the klans in South Carolina or that he is now making over $25,000 a year. They never believed the stories that your house in Louisiana has a new refrigerator, washer, dryer and yet one year ago, was threadbare. They refuse to believe that your husband now owns three cars and a truck, including the new white car. But I believe all these things and I can forgive them for a man wants to do for his family in the best way he can.

I don't have any of these things and I don't grudge you any of them neither, but your husband has been committing the greatest of sins of our Lord for many years. He has taken the flesh of another unto himself.

Yes, Mrs. A, he has been committing adultery. My menfolk say they don't believe this but I think they do. I feel like crying. I saw her with my own eyes. They call her Jewel. Her last name is something like Smithers. I know this. I saw her strut around at a rally with her lustfilled eyes and smart-aleck figure.

I cannot stand for this. I will not let my husband and two brothers stand side by side with your husband and this woman in the glorious robes of the klan. I am typing this because I am going to send copies to Mr. Johnson and some of the klans leaders that I have faith in. I will not stop until your husband is driven from this community and back into the flesh-pots from wherein he came.

I am a loyal klanswoman and a good churchgoer. I feel this problem affects the future of our great country. I hope I do not cause you harm by this and if you believe in the Good Book as I do, you may soon receive your husband back into the fold. I pray for you and your beautiful little children and only wish I could tell you who I am. I will soon, but I am afraid my own men would be harmed if I do.

A God-fearing klanswoman

Let me repeat: the above letter was written by the FBI and mailed by the FBI to the wife of one Klan leader. Though it contains enough facts for the recipient to believe it was all factual, the essence of it is a complete fabrication. Had I been director at the time I would have studied this type of activity very closely. Nevertheless, from my current vantage point, I understand why this type of activity was used.

The Bureau also regularly sent the names of police patrolmen and officers who were Klan members to their governors and, if they lived in the South, to their mayors. In all, the 289 separate actions implemented against the White Hate groups were successful in reducing lynching, murder, and other ugly activities perpetrated by them.

The Cointelpro against the Black Nationalist Hate Groups began on August 25, 1967, in response to the racial violence of the time. Pressure for the FBI to take action came from President Johnson, Congress, media representatives, and the general public. The major cities of America were literally being set on fire. This crescendo of arson, violence, and looting in our cities reached its peak in 1967. During the first three-quarters of that year race riots erupted in more than sixty American cities, almost a hundred people were killed, and well over three thousand injured. Violence continued into 1968 and thirty-nine more died in riots.

Cointelpro targeted organizations like the Student Nonviolent Coordinating Committee (SNCC), the Black Panthers, and the Congress of Racial Equality (CORE). Well over half of the FBI's fifty-nine field officers were involved in this Cointelpro and almost 400 separate actions were launched against black activist groups. The Bureau's directive instructed agents to "expose, disrupt, misdirect, discredit, or otherwise neutralize the activities of black nationalist hate-type organizations. . . ."

Many methods were used.

One of the most popular techniques used by the Bureau was the classic "snitch-jacket"; that is, neturalizing a target group by labeling its key individuals as informants, even though they were not. In one snitch-jacket operation in California, four Black Panthers and their leader were arrested and jailed. Shortly afterward, the four members were released but the leader was not. He was being held in protective custody, it was explained. The local FBI field office then circulated the rumor that the Black Panther leader was cooperating with the police. This, to be sure, was untrue but it nevertheless destroyed the reputation of that Panther leader.

On another occasion, the Bureau learned that a Black Panther official, who had been brought into custody on numerous charges, was also suspected of being an FBI informant (which he was not). Nevertheless, the Bureau anonymously sent letters to other Panther members saying that the man was indeed an informant. His career as a Panther ended then and there.

Almost one-third of the Black Nationalist Hate Group Cointelpro activities were designed to weaken individual groups by setting organizations against each other. For example, in Chicago, anonymous and extremely antagonistic letters written by the FBI were circulated among rival gangs. This technique created an atmosphere in which black groups vented their hostility against each other instead of against society at large.

In time, the Bureau also became concerned about potential alliances between black groups and other nonblack hostile radical organizations. For example, one potential alliance that worried authorities was a possible union between the Black Panthers and the Students for a Democratic Society. The Bureau again used the anonymous letter technique in which FBI-created communications were sent to each group to cause friction. Here is a portion of one such letter (as released by the Church Committee):

Dear Brothers and Sisters.

Since when do us Blacks have to swallow the dictates of the honky SDS? Doing this only hinders the Party

progress in gaining Black control over Black people.
We've been --- over by the white facist pigs and the
Man's control over our destiny. We're sick and tired of
being severely brutalized, denied our rights and treated
like animals by the white pigs. We say to hell with the
SDS and its honky intellectual approaches which only
perpetuate control of Black people by the honkies.

From the beginning until the end of the Black Nationalist
Cointelpro, the FBI effort was to penetrate, disrupt, and neutralize black-hate activities. A total of 362 separate actions were
implemented with, in some cases, an extraordinary degree of
success. Clearly, the FBI was getting good at this sort of thing.

The last of the original group of Cointelpros was the New Left
program, which began October 28, 1968, and lasted until April
27, 1971. The FBI launched the Cointelpro–New Left primarily
to stem the tide of extreme New Left violence across America. As
I said in 1973 in a press release from the director's office:

> In the late 1960s, a hard-core revolutionary movement which
> came to be known as the New Left set out, in its own words,
> to bring the government to its knees through the use of force
> and violence. What started as New Left movement chanting
> of Marxist-Leninist slogans in the early years of their
> "revolution" developed into violent contempt, not only for
> government and government officials, but for every
> responsible American citizen. During these years, there were
> over three hundred arsons or attempted arsons, fourteen
> destructive bombings, nine persons killed, and almost six
> hundred injured on our college campuses alone. In the
> school year 1968-69, damage on college campuses exceeded
> $3 million and in the next year mounted to an excess of $9.5
> million.

Cointelpro–New Left targets included the Students for a
Democratic Society, the excessively violent splinter group
Weather Underground, and the Maoist Progressive Labor party.
As in the case of the other Cointelpros, the FBI utilized standard
counterintelligence techniques, infiltrating leftist groups, dis-

rupting their organizations—all in attempts to neutralize their effectiveness.

In an FBI memo to various field offices concerning the Cointelpro–New Left the following twelve suggestions were listed:

1. Preparing leaflets designed to discredit student demonstrators, using photographs of New Left leadership at the respective universities. "Naturally, the most obnoxious pictures should be used";
2. Instigating "personal conflicts or animosities" between New Left leaders;
3. Creating the impressions that leaders are "informants for the Bureau or other law enforcement agencies";
4. Sending articles from student newspapers or the "underground press" which show the depravity of the New Left to university officials, donors, legislators, and parents. "Articles showing advocation of the use of narcotics and free sex are ideal";
5. Having members arrested on marijuana charges;
6. Sending anonymous letters about a student's activities not only to parents, but also to neighbors, and the parents' employers. "This could have the effect of forcing the parents to take action";
7. Sending anonymous letters or leaflets describing the activities and associations of New Left faculty members and graduate assistants to university officials, legislators, Boards of Regents, and the press. "These letters should be signed 'A Concerned Alumni,' or 'A Concerned Taxpayer'";
8. Using "cooperative press" contacts: to emphasize that the "disruptive elements" constitute a "minority" of the students. "The press should demand an immediate referendum on the issue in question";
9. Exploiting the "hostility" among the SDS and other New Left groups toward the SWP, YSA, and Progressive Labor Party;
10. Using "friendly news media" and law enforcement officials to disrupt New Left coffeehouses near military bases which are attempting to "influence members of the Armed Forces";

11. Using cartoons, photographs, and anonymous letters to "ridicule" the New Left; and
12. Using "misinformation" to "confuse and disrupt" New Left activities, such as by notifying members that events have been cancelled.

One Cointelpro targeted a professor at Arizona State University who had been actively involved in promoting campus antiwar/antidraft demonstrations. FBI agents contacted the directors of a foundation that was a major supplier of funds to the university in a successful effort to discredit the professor. He was subsequently fired.

On another occasion, the FBI mailed anonymous exposé letters about a leftist college professor to local news media, government officials, and the board of regents.

In 1967 the "East Village Other" organization planned to "bomb" the Pentagon with flowers during a rally in Washington, D.C. In preparation for the demonstration the group ran a newspaper ad seeking a pilot who would fly the bombing mission over the Pentagon. The ad was answered in secret by the FBI New York field office, promising that a fully qualified licensed pilot would be available. The pretext was maintained right up until the group's leader showed up at the airport with 200 pounds of flowers. There was, of course, no one available to fly the plane and no flower shower for the Pentagon that day.

In one usage of the Cointelpro "disinformation" technique the Chicago FBI field office duplicated blank forms, prepared by the National Mobilization Committee to End the War in Vietnam, soliciting housing for demonstrators coming to Chicago for the Democratic National Convention. The Chicago FBI office filled out over 200 of these forms with fictitious names and addresses and sent them to the NMC, which in turn gave them to demonstrators who made "long and useless journeys to locate these addresses." The NMC then discarded all replies received on the housing forms rather than have out-of-town demonstrators try to locate nonexistent addresses. If the NMC ever suspected the FBI of being involved here, no mention of it ever got back to me.

The FBI also attempted to prevent New Left target groups

from meeting. Frequently used techniques included contacting the owner of meeting facilities to have him refuse to rent to the group; attempting to have a group's charter revoked; using the media to disrupt a "closed" meeting by arriving unannounced; and attempting to persuade funding sponsors to withdraw their support.

In 1969 a group of midwestern college students, known to be SDS members, planned to go to Washington to disrupt the inauguration of Richard Nixon. The FBI learned of their plans through student informants and made a series of anonymous, boycott-threatening telephone calls to the bus company that the SDS planned to use for their trip. In addition, to further confuse things, FBI agents called student organizers regarding bus information. The FBI callers, posing as representatives from the bus company, gave erroneous information to the organizers regarding routes, costs, departure, destination times, etc. The Bureau also distributed leaflets on campus listing contradictory and incorrect information concerning the group's travel plans. Not surprisingly, the trip never materialized. These actions were successful, as were most of the nearly 300 separate Cointelpro actions against New Left organizations that took place from 1968 to 1971.

When I became FBI director in 1973 no Cointelpro operation had been used for more than two years, probably because of the Pennsylvania office burglary—and deepening concern within the Bureau over total public disclosure of the program. But as of 1973 the public and media had seen only the tip of the iceberg. In fact, all that was then known by the public was the information in the approximately twenty documents released to the press by the Citizens Commission to Investigate the FBI after the Media, Pennsylvania, burglary.

I knew, given the tenacity of the American press, this state of affairs would not last long.

I was right. It didn't.

On March 20, 1972, almost a year-and-a-half before I became director, NBC-TV news correspondent Carl Stern had written to Attorney General Richard G. Kleindienst asking for copies of specific FBI documents and papers relating to "Cointelpro–New Left." His request was made under the provisions of the Freedom of Information Act (Title 5, U.S. Code, Section 552). His request was refused. The refusal was based on certain exemptions in the act as interpreted by the Department of Justice: confidential files of an FBI agent, unofficial defense data, and confidential interagency correspondence.

Carl Stern decided to take the matter to court.

In early 1973 he filed suit in the United States District Court for the District of Columbia, appealing the Justice Department ruling.

Stern sought two documents. The first was a letter dated May 10, 1968, addressed to a field official from FBI headquarters in Washington, officially authorizing the "Cointelpro–New Left" action. The second, a communication from headquarters to all field offices, canceled all existing Cointelpro operations as of April 28, 1971.

The release of the two documents could, I felt, have damaged the FBI. Their disclosure would not have been in the national interest. My strong feelings against disclosure were based on my career-long beliefs about successful law-enforcement operations and proper investigative and intelligence procedures in a free society.

First, a reliable system of confidential informants must be developed and protected. Without that network, law enforcement in a free society would grind to a halt.

Second, confidential information must remain confidential. It is well and good for philosophers and political scientists to theorize about a totally open and free society, with a totally free exchange of any and all ideas and information. The problem is, such a society could never work—outside the mind of Plato. A free society like ours, peopled with human beings that are imperfect, indeed often criminal, must take the necessary steps to protect itself. The Cointelpros, despite some disturbing "improvisational" characteristics, were designed by the FBI to protect the stability of our nation, and to promote its general welfare through an unfortunately unavoidable secret battle with those who would promote anarchy and violence.

Notwithstanding, on July 16, 1973, seven days after I was in office, we delivered, in response to the district court's request, copies of the two documents in question to United States District Judge Barrington D. Parker. The judge decided that the documents should be given to Stern, and on December 6, 1973, the requested Cointelpro documents were given to the NBC-TV reporter.

The day before, December 5, I issued a special precautionary memo to all special agents-in-charge nationwide. I mentioned the anticipated publicity surrounding the developing Cointelpro disclosures and how they might elicit concern over possible violation of individual liberties. FBI employees, I emphasized, were to refrain from engaging in investigative activity that could abridge in any way the rights guaranteed citizens by the Constitution. Neither were they to conduct themselves in any way that might result in defaming the character, reputation, integrity, or dignity of any citizen or organization.

Two days later, I authorized a national press release on the Cointelpro operations and the social upheavals that had made them necessary. I stressed that at a time of national crisis the government would have been derelict in its duty had it not taken every legal measure to protect the fabric of our society. The FBI has the responsibility of investigating allegations of criminal violations and of gathering intelligence regarding threats to our nation.

On the same day, December 7, I received from Carl Stern a personal letter in which he requested additional Cointelpro documents, including:

> Whatever documents authorized and defined the programs Cointelpro-Espionage; Cointelpro-Disruption of White-Hate Groups; Cointelpro-Communist Party, USA; Counterintelligence and Special Operations; Cointelpro-Black Extremists; Socialist Workers Party-Disruption Program. Whatever documents directed changes in the programs.

Whatever documents authorized a counterintelligence action
of any kind after 4/28/71.

Also that day, reporter Fred Graham of CBS News requested
access to documents relating to Cointelpro–New Left and to all
documents relating to any other Cointelpro programs.

I answered Carl Stern's letter on December 26, 1973, informing him that the documents he requested were in our confidential
investigatory files and were for law enforcement purposes.
Therefore, they were exempt from public disclosure according to
the provisions of Title 5, United States Code, Section 552 (b) (7).
Stern could, I said, appeal my decision through judicial review
or by writing directly to the attorney general.

He did the latter.

Attorney General William B. Saxbe agreed on March 6,
1974, to supply "part, but not all," of the requested materials.

Stern received a document from our Cointelpro files dealing
with white-hate groups, two documents on black extremists, one
regarding the Socialist Workers Party, and three memoranda
under the general classification "Counterintelligence and Special Operations." Individual names and places were deleted
from the released materials and a number of classified secret
papers were not released. One day later, seven additional Cointelpro documents were given to Carl Stern under the Freedom of
Information Act. The following day Fred Graham was provided
with the same material.

In the meantime, Saxbe advised me by letter that President
Ford had requested information about FBI counterintelligence
programs.

Saxbe had therefore asked Assistant Attorney General Henry
Petersen to create an interdepartmental committee to review all
FBI files, documents, and papers relating to all Cointelpro oper-
ations. The committee was comprised of four attorneys from the
Criminal Division of the Department of Justice and three repre-
sentatives from the Federal Bureau of Investigation selected by
me. I chose Inspector Thomas Smith, and Special Agents James
Williamson and Edward Pistey.

The committee was at work before the end of January. The members reviewed document summaries compiled directly from the FBI Cointelpro control files. The identities and affiliations of the various Cointelpro targets were deleted from the study.

About the time the Petersen Committee was beginning its work, I received a lengthy inquiry from Senator Sam J. Ervin, Jr., chairman of the Subcommittee on Constitutional Rights, Senate Committee on the Judiciary.

Senator Ervin's letter read: "This subcommittee will conduct an inquiry into FBI domestic surveillance activities and (would need) detailed information on the so-called Cointelpro operations." His letter contained almost eighty specific questions.

Immediately after his letter arrived, I received a direct call from the senator. His southern accent was unmistakable.

"Mr. Kelley, I wanted to follow up my letter of the eighth. As you know, my committee is interested in looking into the Cointelpro operations," the senator said.

"Thank you for calling, Senator," I replied. "I have your letter in front of me right now."

"We need your assistance, sir. I hope my request for information won't place too great a burden on the FBI," he said.

"I will study your letter, Senator, and prepare my reply by this afternoon. Will that be acceptable?"

"That will be helpful, very helpful. We just want to understand, Mr. Kelley, the policy reasons for developing those programs in the first place, how they operated, and some other matters."

"As you know, Senator, these programs are already under review by the Justice Department." I said.

"I understand that, Mr. Kelley, and I assume that we will receive a copy of their final report. However, my subcommittee wanted to look into the matter also, perhaps in greater detail. I'm sure you understand."

"A discussion of this sort, the discussion of sensitive intelligence issues in an open forum is frankly of concern to me, Senator," I replied.

"I understand your concern, Mr. Kelley, and I share it. But my subcommittee must know more about this. Anything you can do to help us will certainly be appreciated. Please get back to me as soon as possible."

"We will take care of it right away, Senator," I said.

Following this conversation I studied the senator's letter, weighing all of its ramifications, before drafting my reply.

In my response, I told the senator that the FBI was unable to comply with the subcommittee's request. I felt there were compelling reasons why the Cointelpro operations should not be discussed in a public forum. The confidentiality of our original investigative data as well as our network of informants must be protected.

I explained that, in my opinion, classified secret information is implicitly exempt from disclosure under the Freedom of Information Act. The public disclosure of the specific techniques and operations used to counter any subversive intelligence activity in the United States could cause catastrophic damage to the future effectiveness of our countersubversion efforts. And exposing the identities of our private sources and double agents would actually jeopardize their lives.

But I felt a spirit of compromise was in order.

"Could we consider having the Cointelpros brought up in executive session of the Senate Oversight Committee on the FBI?" I asked. I also supplied the senator with copies of the Cointelpro documents that had been previously released under the Freedom of Information Act.

Senator Ervin understood my concerns, and agreed to this compromise.

Assistant Attorney General Petersen's report on FBI counterintelligence activities arrived on my desk on May 21, 1974.

The report said that members of organizations targeted by Cointelpro *might,* in a few instances, have been deprived of their rights under the First Amendment to the Constitution.

To its credit, the committee took into account several important factors.

First, many Cointelpros were developed in response to public demand that the FBI contain and neutralize the radical forces of social upheaval in the 1960s.

Second, each program had been approved in advance by J. Edgar Hoover.

In June, Saxbe and I briefed the FBI Oversight Subcommittee (a subcommittee of the Senate Judiciary Committee) on many aspects of the Cointelpros. In accordance with my agreement with Senator Ervin, it was held in a closed executive session. About the same time, the comptroller general of the United States asked for Cointelpro data as did Peter Rodino, chairman of the House Judiciary Committee. Specifically, Congressman Rodino asked that the House Subcommittee on Civil Rights be briefed on the Cointelpro operations. However, for various reasons, we were not able to act on these requests until fall.

On June 20, 1974, Saxbe and I attended the graduation of the ninety-seventh class of the FBI Academy at Quantico, Virginia. Saxbe was the commencement speaker. In his speech to the graduates he referred to the Cointelpro programs and said that it was his personal conviction that the Federal Bureau of Investigation set up these programs in the first place because of deep concern for the security of the United States. He did go on, however, to say that problems arise when intelligence-gathering techniques cross over into the questionable arena of disruption tactics.

"The dirty tricks are over," Saxbe said. "Law enforcement at every level must operate within the letter of the law."

Following the FBI graduation speech I found myself devoting more time to matters related to the Watergate investigation. Thus, even though Cointelpro was being discussed in Congress, in certain departments in the executive branch, and in the news media, I was not deeply involved again until the fall.

I, along with several members of the Petersen Committee, had believed that the final report was not to be released to the public. In October, however, I learned that Saxbe had decided he should release the findings of the Petersen report to the press.

I immediately called a meeting on November 7, 1974, with my seventeen highest assistants—our executive committee, the top management of the FBI. We discussed our position and possible courses of action in light of the imminent disclosure of more Cointelpro documents.

Our management team unanimously felt that there should be no additional release of Cointelpro documents and papers under the Freedom of Information Act. Those materials were unquestionably investigatory data and, as a result, exempt from release. We would deny future requests for Cointelpro documents under the Freedom of Information Act—and let the courts decide the issue. Judicial review would determine whether the documents were indeed privileged by virtue of their investigatory nature. We believed that the courts would rule in our favor. If not, we would cooperate.

Four days later a Cointelpro meeting was held in the office of Congressman Rodino. It was attended by Saxbe (who called the meeting), Peter Rodino, Edward Hutchinson (the ranking minority member of the House Judiciary Committee), several other government officials, and me.

The meeting was not stormy, but strong feelings were certainly expressed. First, Saxbe read aloud the entire Petersen report. Then, he voiced his own opinion about disclosure: "The Cointelpro matter has been discussed at some length with the Senate's FBI Oversight Committee. I've also reviewed the departmental analysis of Cointelpro with the committee. I've discussed Cointelpro and the analysis with Senator Ervin privately. He is a strong proponent of Freedom of Information but opposes the release of the Cointelpro report," Saxbe said.

One of the congressmen asked, "How do the rest of the Senate committee members feel about releasing the Cointelpro report to the public?"

"They are all opposed to the release of the report; they also oppose the appointment of a special prosecutor to investigate the matter," Saxbe replied.

"What is your position, Mr. Saxbe?" Rodino asked.

"I really don't see how we can avoid releasing the report to the public. First of all, we have the matter of the college professor at Arizona State who was fired from his job because of an anonymous letter sent by the FBI. The professor has filed suit and has been given back pay, his job back, and he has requested, under Freedom of Information, the FBI background file on him. I don't see how we can turn him down."

Further, the attorney general expressed his opinion that the FBI had "gone beyond the letter of the law" in its Cointelpro programs, and, as far as he could determine, "no attorney general had been aware of the programs when they were in operation."

I then addressed the group. First I pointed out that "Mr. Saxbe has gotten his historical facts wrong. Attorneys general going back to the first Eisenhower Administration were aware of—and approved—the basic Cointelpro activities," I said.

"In fact, presidential directives for aggressive counterintelligence programs similar to Cointelpro actually date back to the Roosevelt presidency at the opening of the Second World War," I added.

I mentioned the important National Security Council meeting held on March 8, 1956, when J. Edgar Hoover proposed a number of very specific Cointelpro methodologies to a group that included not only Attorney General Herbert Brownell but also President Eisenhower.

"The most critical issue of all," I suggested, "was not who knew and approved of Cointelpro practices, but what harm a full public disclosure would do at this time. Full disclosure would doubtless affect the overall operation of the FBI. Not only would it undermine our credibility with the American people, but such disclosure might well result in an inability to develop and use informants. Speaking of informants," I said, "a number of good, innocent citizens who had been associated with Cointelpros in the past would now suffer undo hardships—if their involvement were to become public knowledge."

I paused to let that sink in—especially with William Saxbe. I knew the issue of protecting the innocent was always important to him.

"Those involved in Cointelpro activities did what they believed to be in the best interest of the country at that time," I said. "And to try to defend Cointelpro operations of the past in today's world will probably make matters worse," I said.

I concluded by stating my opinion that the matters under discussion were in our investigative files and thereby excluded from disclosure under the Freedom of Information Act.

Saxbe countered by saying that various communications about Cointelpro actions were not purely investigative—and were therefore subject to release.

"And I'd like to point out that President Ford favors disclosure, and that certain members of the press already know of at least a portion of Cointelpro," Saxbe continued. "Besides, it will be only a matter of time before the whole Cointelpro story is revealed."

As the meeting closed, I thought to myself that this conjecture on his part entirely missed the point. And I wondered who had briefed Gerald Ford on the implications of full disclosure in this instance.

On November 18, 1974, Saxbe held his long-awaited press conference. He released a summary of the Petersen report, which I was glad to see had been sharply edited to remove sensitive information that might jeopardize national security. In a very moderate statement that accompanied the release, Saxbe said that there were seven basic Cointelpros—five domestic programs and two foreign. The Cointelpro operations had been ongoing between 1956 and 1971. During that time, the Petersen Committee found, 3,247 counterintelligence proposals had been made to FBI leaders. Of those, 2,370 had been implemented. In less than 500 of these were the results quantifiable. Measurable or not, in almost every instance the programs were successful in countering sabotage, espionage, and subversion.

Moreover, the great majority of the cases utilized practices and techniques that were entirely legitimate. In only 1 percent of all Cointelpro activities and techniques, Saxbe continued, could it be even argued that the FBI had acted improperly or illegally. Nevertheless he felt that certain tactics "must be considered to be abhorrent in a free society such as ours." All the programs had now been canceled, he stated in conclusion.

Though the attorney general didn't give me much to argue with, I released to the press a lengthy statement strongly supporting the activities of the FBI.

My release explained that since taking office as Bureau director on July 9, 1973, I had made a study of the same FBI counterintelligence programs.

"The FBI's intent," I noted, "was to prevent dangerous acts against individuals, organizations, and institutions—public and private—across the United States. FBI employees in these programs had acted in good faith and within the bounds of what was expected of them by the president, the attorney general, Congress, and, I believe, a majority of the American people."

I reminded those who now criticized the FBI that the United States Capitol building had been bombed; explosions had rocked countless other buildings in our cities. Rioters led by revolutionary extremists had laid siege to military, industrial, and educational facilities. Random killings, atrocities, and other violence had sent shock waves from Maine to California.

I gave specific examples: a bombing at the University of Wisconsin; Chicago's "four days of rage"; racial riots in virtually every city; the murders of Robert F. Kennedy and Martin L. King, Jr.; the horror show outside the Democratic Convention site in Chicago in 1968; and the antiwar violence on campuses. In most cases, the victims of these illegal acts were citizens who looked to the FBI and other law enforcement agencies to protect *their* lives, *their* property, and *their* civil rights.

On November 20, two days after the Saxbe press conference, amid heavy media coverage, Deputy Attorney General Lawrence Silberman, Henry Petersen, and I testified before the Subcommittee on Civil Rights and Constitutional Rights of the House Judiciary Committee.

I assured the subcommittee that the Cointelpro programs had been discontinued, but I again defended those in the FBI who implemented and conducted the programs.

"Should questions arise in the future about similar programs," I said, "I would consult with the attorney general before implementation."

I was in a tight spot.

As the relatively new FBI director, I needed the loyalty of the entire organization. To gain its loyalty, it was important that I defend the Bureau strongly, but without belligerence. I also had to demonstrate that the FBI was a prudent, honorable organization—not only the nation's leading investigative agency but also a responsible branch of government operating professionally—and within the law of the land.

Many of the questions from the House subcommittee were incisive. Others, obviously designed for public consumption, were acrimonious. Exchanges were often sharp. In the end, we did agree on the need for a joint congressional committee of oversight to monitor domestic counterintelligence activities, which supported the position I had taken all along.

In the same month, November of 1974, Attorney General Saxbe requested that Assistant Attorney General Stanley Pottinger of the Justice Department's Civil Rights Division conduct a review of Cointelpro activities to determine if in fact civil rights violations had occurred.

On January 3, 1975, Pottinger's conclusions were announced: There was no basis for any criminal charges against those involved in the Cointelpro operations.

Later in January, the Senate created the Select Committee on Intelligence Activities. It was authorized to investigate "the extent, if any, to which illegal, improper, or unethical activities were engaged in . . . in carrying out any intelligence or surveillance activities by or on behalf of any agency of the federal government." The Bureau fully cooperated with the committee for the next two years of hearings.

Edward Levi became attorney general on February 7, 1975, replacing William Saxbe, who had resigned to become an ambassador to India.

About two months later I presented Levi with some surprising news. We discovered, after an exhaustive search of our investigative files, five more counterintelligence programs. I brought the information to Levi, who in turn told Peter Rodino. Instead of seven, we were now dealing with twelve Cointelpros, although the newly discovered ones were much narrower in scope than the others. One was directed toward radical Puerto Rican independence groups, two concerned organized crime and the Communist Party, and the remaining two were classified secret foreign intelligence programs.

There was to be more testimony before Congress.

On December 10, 1975, I testified before the Senate Select Committee on Intelligence Activities. I cited measures invoked during my term as director to prevent a recurrence of the possible errors and abuses of the Cointelpro programs.

I also emphasized "the urgent need for a legislative charter from the Congress defining our intelligence jurisdiction."

Less than two months later we were involved in yet another senate inquiry.

I appeared before the Senate Committee on Government Operations on January 26, 1976. I testified that for many months the FBI had undergone a most exhaustive review of its intelligence operations. We were in regular contact with Attorney General Levi regarding counterintelligence activities. Access to our sensitive information must remain limited, I emphasized.

I asked the senators if they thought our country would benefit from continuing such heavy direct congressional access to FBI information. Or would it be better served by requiring all FBI directors to be accountable to an oversight committee through sworn testimony? I said that in my opinion the Congress and the FBI would best fulfill their separate responsibilities by the latter means.

As we seek to define the proper degree of oversight of Bureau operations, the FBI's administrative burdens must be considered. I pointed out that, in responding to requests of the two select committees, our headquarters' staff alone had expended 3,976 days of agent personnel and 1,964 days of clerical personnel from April through December 1975—this represented manpower diverted from FBI investigative duties. The cost was about $640,500. Additionally, the cost of conducting background investigations of committee staff members had reached $393,699. Many requests from Congress were duplicates. Though we tried to respond accurately in each instance, it was an expensive, time-consuming operation. We felt that the interests of the American people would be best served by Congress consolidating its oversight functions in one joint committee.

On April 1, 1976, Attorney General Levi announced the creation of a special review committee within the Department of Justice to contact persons who may have been personally harmed by improper and questionably legal Cointelpro actions. They would be notified that they had been subjects of Cointelpro activities. Notification would be limited to those who the Justice Department thought had in some way been wrongfully harmed by Cointelpro action.

The final report of the Senate's Select Committee on Intelligence was submitted April 23, 1976. It was exhaustive and, I thought, overwhelmingly inconclusive. Following twenty years of Cointelpro operations, hearings, examinations and introspections, we had a report that said of Cointelpro: "The notification program of Cointelpro victims was a positive step."

For well over two years, I reflected at the time, controversy over Cointelpro had gone on, with seemingly no end in sight. In an effort to bring the controversy to a close (and to end recriminations against the FBI for a very small number of questionable activities during a time long past), I addressed the issue directly in a speech at Westminster College in Fulton, Missouri, on May 8, 1976:

> During most of my tenure as director of the FBI, I have been compelled to devote much of my time attempting to reconstruct and then to explain activities that occurred years ago.
> Some of those activities were clearly wrong and quite indefensible. We most certainly must never allow them to be

repeated. It is true that many of the activities being condemned were, considering the times in which they occurred, the violent sixties, good-faith efforts to prevent bloodshed and wanton destruction of property. . . .

After my speech, the controversy abated.

Two months later, on August 11, 1976, I transferred domestic intelligence investigations to the General Investigative Division, where they would be managed like all other criminal cases in that division. The transfer included our investigations of the Communist Party, USA, the Socialist Workers Party, and all other domestic security investigations. Under the guidelines governing FBI activities, all such domestic security investigations would be required to be reviewed periodically by the attorney general. Under the Freedom of Information Act, on November 21, 1977, I released some 52,000 pages related to the twelve Cointelpros—our entire file. Though I had personal misgivings about releasing all of this data, I believe that, in all fairness, the Act was a wise piece of legislation and prudent for the times.

Cointelpro activities raise an interesting philosophical question: Can we conduct an effective countersubversion effort in our country without endangering our constitutional liberties in the process?

My answer is yes.

The preponderance of historical evidence and the ultimate results suggest that, by and large, what the Bureau did was right for the time and, without question, in the best interests of the United States. Constitutional liberties were not trampled. Though abuse may have existed, I believe it was minimal. And though minimal, it was not illegal in any instance.

On the other hand, I know from firsthand experience that the abuse heaped on the FBI was considerable. And therein lies something of a paradox. During the fifteen years of Cointelpro, the FBI handled an average of about 700,000 investigative matters a year. This, then, amounts to about 10.5 million investigations for the period. To put the Cointelpro into perspective, consider that there were only 2,370 Cointelpro actions taken by the FBI during these 15 years. This means that Cointelpro represented .002 percent of the Bureau's workload during the years 1956-1971. Thus, the program that generated some of the most vituperative tirades against the FBI, encompassed a mere two-tenths of one percent of FBI investigative operations!

But please do not misunderstand me.

To insure protection of our constitutional freedoms, I believe that the investigative arm of the government must be accountable to the citizens at large. How can this be best implemented? In my opinion the most practical and most effective way to accomplish this is through a plan of prudent joint congressional hearings, in closed sessions, with the director providing sworn testimony to a Congress representing the American people.

8

The Hearst Kidnapping

The First Political Kidnapping in American History

IN JUNE 1973 a bizarre organization which came to be known to the world as the Symbionese Liberation Army held its first meeting in the San Francisco Bay Area.

The agenda for that initial meeting is unknown to us, but we do know that at another SLA session later that summer the idea of a political kidnapping was first voiced—and one of the candidates for abduction was the daughter of millionaire publisher, Randolph A. Hearst.

But I'm way ahead of myself.

The SLA was born within the California prison system, the offspring of a do-good coterie of white liberals—mostly women—and a band of black prison inmates. This ill-defined group, calling itself the Black Cultural Association, had been formed to provide cultural programs (art, music, literature), educational-vocational training, and prerelease guidance for the prisoners.

In the beginning, the BCA was directed by a succession of prison inmates, each of whom guided and led the group according to the dictates of his own whim.

Then came Donald D. DeFreeze, a prison escapee who was a hardened, habitual criminal with a chain of convictions including armed robbery, assault, and possession of stolen property. Whatever DeFreeze's societal shortcomings, however, he didn't lack for leadership skills or the determination to use those skills to his own ends.

Thus, the genesis of the SLA came directly from the Black Cultural Association. DeFreeze, a black, became the leader of the SLA, which was comprised mainly of white extremists.

While keeping one eye alert for the authorities who were after him, DeFreeze proceeded to formalize the group. Under his leadership the SLA organizing committee was formed.

Its members and their titles included: Nancy Ling Perry, "field commander," a white woman living in the Berkeley area who was known to be heavily into drugs, and who dated only black men; William Wolfe, "treasurer and chief of information," a white radical from a well-to-do family; Thero Wheeler and Russell Little, "lieutenant field commanders." Wheeler, a black militant, and Little, a white anarchist, spellbound by Donald DeFreeze's rhetoric, both believed that only through the SLA could they help forge a new American society. In addition, the committee included black prison veterans Clifford Jefferson, LeRoy Sparks, and James Holiday—"board members."

Among other original deputies were such now-familiar names as William and Emily Harris, graduates of Indiana University; Angela Atwood, also an Indiana graduate, a resident of Berkeley, and girlfriend of an SLA member; Joe Remiro, a local extremist; Camilla Hall, a lesbian from the University of Minnesota; and Hall's good friend, Patricia Soltysik.

The people of the Bay Area first heard of the Symbionese Liberation Army on August 21, 1973, when the band sent its first communiqué to all media in the area. In it the SLA issued a "Declaration of War," stating as its ultimate goal: "the destruction of the capitalist state." It also announced its intention to secure state control of industry by the people, to form communes across the country, and not suprisingly, to eliminate all prison systems.

Their first act of violence was brutal and savage.

The SLA targeted several officials in the Oakland public school system for death by execution. Then, late on the night of November 6, Oakland Superintendent of Schools, Dr. Marcus

Foster, and his assistant, Robert Blackburn, were gunned down in a parking lot near the Oakland school administration building. Dr. Foster was killed and Blackburn was seriously wounded by cyanide-tipped bullets fired by members of the SLA who were hidden in ambush. Foster and Blackburn, it was announced by the SLA, had been found guilty by "a people's court" for the most heinous of crimes: proposing the introduction of police guards and ID badges into the Oakland school system, measures that the two administrators felt would help control delinquency within the schools.

Seventeen hours later, the SLA sent a letter to the *San Francisco Chronicle* claiming responsibility for the shooting of Foster and Blackburn. The letter spelled out the nature of the "crimes" committed by these two dedicated public officials, and pledged that this retribution was just the beginning.

Because the FBI had no jurisdictional involvement in the crime, and there was no SLA history to be passed along to us, no information on the group or the homicide reached my attention at FBI headquarters in Washington.

We later discovered that Donald DeFreeze, by labeling Dr. Foster as a "turncoat brother," had, in effect, assumed that the murder of this distinguished educator would somehow generate unreasonable violence by the police against all black people in the Bay Area. This action, the SLA believed, would mobilize the area's—and then the nation's—black people to join the SLA in coast-to-coast guerrilla warfare against the United States government. Thus the SLA gave new meaning to the phrase "lunatic fringe."

For the next few months the Oakland police investigated the Foster-Blackburn shooting, as well as the mysterious SLA. By the end of 1973 the investigation had reached a dead end. The members of the Symbionese Liberation Army had gone underground, leaving not a trace. There seemed to be no way to locate them, much less apprehend them.

Then suddenly, at 1:30 in the morning on January 10, 1974, came a dramatic break in the case. In nearby Concord, an alert citizen, concerned about a van circling the same block several times, called the police. Arriving on the scene, two officers stopped the van for a routine investigation. SLA member Joseph Remiro drew a gun and began shooting at the officers, who returned his fire, injuring Russell Little. Both men were taken into custody and, in due time, charged with illegal possession of firearms, assaulting an officer of the law, and resisting arrest. They were eventually sent to prison.

The local police discovered that the van was carrying a library of SLA literature, political manifestos, revolutionary propaganda, and hit lists. More importantly, they found the Foster homicide weapon, a .38-calibre German-made automatic pistol. This evidence immediately led the police to SLA headquarters at 1560 Sutherland Court, in Clayton, only two blocks from the site of the January 10 shooting.

The police were almost too late. Upon arriving, they found the Concord headquarters going up in smoke.

Nancy Ling Perry had set fire to the two-bedroom ranch house as the group fled. The blaze was, however, extinguished quickly enough to save much SLA propaganda, membership lists, scrapbooks, charts, and personal effects. This information provided the Contra Costa County sheriff's deputies and other authorities with background data on most SLA members, and the addresses of other SLA hideouts, including Bill and Emily Harris's apartment in Oakland. Police immediately raided those hideouts but again too late. Having heard that the police were closing in, the inhabitants fled.

At the end of January, with East Bay authorities continuing to investigate the Marcus Foster murder, the case was still primarily local.

That changed within the week.

On February 4, 1974, the Symbionese Liberation Army gained front-page notoriety around the world. This radical group, with its ominous-sounding name, kidnapped Patricia Campbell Hearst from her apartment near the University of California campus in Berkeley.

And at last the FBI became aware of the SLA.

The next day, all activities and available history on the SLA landed on my desk in Washington. The Hearst kidnapping quickly developed into one of the most unusual cases ever to confront the Bureau. (As for public interest, only a few other cases—the Lindbergh kidnapping, the Rosenberg espionage trial, and the Kennedy assassination—aroused such a magnitude of attention.)

The entire Patty Hearst ordeal symbolized many contradictions, stresses, and extremes of society then in turmoil in the United States—rich and poor, conservative and revolutionary, victim and aggressor. In this case, over time, the distinction between aggressor and victim became cloudy, then contradictory. During the next nineteen months this investigation was to take many turns that defied understanding—or rational explanation.

The initial report was simple enough.

On the night of February 4, 1974, the FBI was notified that there had been a kidnapping at 2603 Benvenue Street, a modern fourplex apartment building south of the Cal-Berkeley campus. Patricia Hearst, daughter of newspaper magnate Randolph Hearst, had been abducted from her apartment at approximately 9:20 P.M. by a group of men and women, black and white. Shots were fired. The apparently blindfolded Patty Hearst was thrown into the trunk of a white convertible and the abductors sped away. Her fiancé, Steven Weed, a twenty-three-year-old Princeton graduate, beaten during the abduction, was left behind.

The Bureau became involved immediately as the investigative departments of the San Francisco FBI field office and the Oakland and Berkeley police departments mobilized. By next morning, February 5, authorities assumed that the kidnapping might be the work of the SLA. The FBI and local police began compiling a list of suspects.

When the telex bulletin on the Hearst kidnapping arrived on my desk that morning I was stunned to read that a member of one of the nation's most powerful, wealthy, and socially prominent families had actually been attacked, captured, and carried away screaming in the night. Seriously underestimating the SLA, we at FBI headquarters initially thought that we would find Patty quickly. She was too well-known to be kept hidden. Our informants would know who she was—and where she was.

Personally, I was unfamiliar with the SLA before that morning, and at first I was unconvinced that this band of "Study-group Liberals" could be involved in anything like the Hearst kidnapping. However, reports from our San Francisco office insisted that this small band of militant leftists was most probably involved. Certainly, both the boldness and brutality of the crime bore the SLA stamp, our Bay Area people said.

Coincidentally, Mr. and Mrs. Randolph Hearst were in Washington at the time of the kidnapping. At about 10:30 A.M. my secretary buzzed me on my private line. She announced that Randolph Hearst was calling to speak personally with me.

I picked up the phone. "Hello, Mr. Hearst, this is Clarence Kelley."

"Hello, Mr. Kelley, I wanted to speak to you directly," Hearst said. "I'm sure you are aware that my daughter has been kidnapped."

"Yes, as a matter of fact Assistant Director Gebhardt and I are discussing the matter right now. I'm so sorry that this has happened. I know that you and Mrs. Hearst must be deeply worried."

"Yes, we are. We are thunderstruck, Mr. Kelley. May I have your assurance that everything possible will be done?"

"Absolutely. Indeed, you have my word that the FBI will do everything possible on this. We are in the process of making plans to pursue the matter to the fullest extent of the law. Charles W. Bates, our special agent-in-charge of the San Francisco office, will personally head up the investigation and we have some excellent people out there to assist him."

"Mrs. Hearst and I will be returning to California within the next two hours. Should we go directly to the FBI office in San Francisco?" he asked.

"No, Mr. Hearst, that won't be necessary. Our people and the local police will be in touch with you later this afternoon. Mr. Bates will be your direct contact with the FBI. Here in Washington, Robert Gebhardt will be working directly with me. He will also be our regular liaison on this matter with the San Francisco field office. I want you to know, Mr. Hearst, that we will do everything in our power to return your daughter to you as quickly as possible. But our first priority will always be her safety and well-being."

"Thank you for saying that, Mr. Kelley. We want our daughter home, of course. We are worried sick about her safety."

Hearst was very calm, but in obvious anguish over what happened. As a father and as the FBI director I felt a dual obligation to the Hearsts. There was very little I could tell him at this time, except that we would give the matter our full and urgent attention. And assure him that we would keep Patty's well-being foremost in mind.

"Your daughter's safety, I promise you, Mr. Hearst, will always be the Bureau's first concern," I repeated.

Thus our conversation ended—and my personal commitment to Randolph Hearst began.

I felt that we were fortunate to have Charles Bates in San Francisco to handle the investigation. He had an excellent record with the Bureau, was a career man, and had served as J. Edgar Hoover's special liaison with Scotland Yard in England. He had also served as assistant director of the FBI General Investigations Division. In this capacity he had, by and large, supervised the Bureau's investigation of the Watergate break-in. Following that, he was transferred, at his request, to our San Francisco office.

Interestingly enough, Bates was also in Washington at the time of the kidnapping. We had met the day before to discuss other FBI matters. When news of the abduction reached headquarters, he left for San Francisco almost immediately.

It wasn't long before all suspicions about the SLA involvement in this case were confirmed by the SLA itself.

In a letter to a Berkeley radio station, the Symbionese Liberation Army claimed responsibility for the abduction. As proof of its claim the SLA enclosed one of Randolph Hearst's credit cards. The extremists declared that Patty Hearst's father, Randolph A. Hearst, president and editor of the *San Francisco Examiner*, was a "corporate enemy of the people." They proclaimed that Patty Hearst had been "arrested" and taken into "protective custody." If necessary, they added, she faced "execution."

The letter was explicit. "Should any attempt be made to rescue the prisoner or arrest or harm any SLA members, the prisoner will be executed."

By now I was well-aware of the short but violent history of the SLA. I believed the threat was real.

On February 12 an SLA tape recording arrived at a local radio station. The Symbionese terrorists announced a spectacular—and, to our chagrin, untraceable—ransom demand. The Hearsts were to provide seventy-dollars-worth of food for every needy person, man, woman and child, in the entire state of California. Depending on how you defined "needy," experts estimated that this could amount to as much as $300 million worth of food.

The tape featured Donald DeFreeze, spokesman for the group, identifying himself as "General Field Marshal Cinque." Patty Hearst, whose voice also was on the tape, said she was "a prisoner of war" but was "okay." The food distribution plan, Cinque said, would be deemed by the SLA an "act of good faith" on the part of the Hearsts.

The militants also demanded that the radio, along with television and the newspapers, publicize their SLA emblem, the philosophy of the organization, and the "selflessness" of their demands.

This emphasis on philosophy and psychology made me very nervous.

Clearly, the Hearst kidnapping was taking an ominous turn that most of us had never seen before. Indeed, it was something new in the twentieth century history of our country: a political kidnapping with no demand for ransom in the traditional sense.

The SLA was using Patricia Hearst as a propaganda weapon, a hostage whose life was in mortal danger. To what end they were doing this had not yet been made clear to me. What did the SLA *really* want from all of this? I wondered if they themselves knew at this point.

Writer Shana Alexander has suggested that by the time Patty Hearst was kidnapped, "the SLA members were either on their way to or had become suicidal psychopaths."

The question I didn't know then and don't know today was: How far along this road were they? They suddenly were playing a very go-slow game with those of us who were working to free Patty Hearst (if we could just find her). If they knew what they wanted, why didn't they come out and say so? If they didn't know, and this is what I feared most strongly, we were in for a long and painful ordeal before events worked themselves out.

Where had all my early optimism for a quick arrest gone?

Randolph Hearst again responded immediately to this new SLA demand.

Within twenty-four hours Hearst appeared on TV to announce that he would do everything within his power to comply with SLA demands. Hearst added, pleading for time, that in order to meet the SLA orders, "there were some serious logistical problems that had to be surmounted." He promised "a meaningful counteroffer soon."

By now, Charles Bates had set up a functional command post at the Hearst household. Two FBI agents were in constant attendance at the Hearst mansion in Hillsborough, a San Francisco suburb, to take hundreds of phone calls, check leads and extortion attempts, monitor police-band radios, and ensure the security of the Hearst home itself. The news media were there day and night. Bates visited the Hearst home every day to review the overall status of the investigation and to communicate face-to-face with the FBI agents on duty.

During the first several weeks of the case I reviewed developments daily. Though Assistant Director Gebhardt continued to be my main liaison with the San Francisco office, I personally spoke with Charles Bates by telephone at least once a week for the first several months of the investigation. These were frustrating conversations for both of us. The absence of even one solid lead was almost unbelievable in a case like this. But the fact of the matter was that the SLA had gone underground, and none of our many informants could—or would—give us any information concerning their whereabouts.

On February 16 another SLA tape was sent to the radio station. Its contents left us with very mixed feelings. On the one hand, the extreme demands of the first tape now seemed somewhat tempered.

"A sincere effort by Mr. Hearst in complying with our orders would now be acceptable," the SLA reported.

All hope given us by this mild concession, however, was dimmed by the message delivered by Patty Hearst.

In a voice sounding stronger and clearer than ever, she mentioned the FBI in a context that gave me great concern. She expressed growing suspicions that "the FBI would come busting in on me." She went on to say that "this act of war on the part of the FBI will result in many deaths." This was SLA talk at its most basic, and made several of us wonder exactly where it was coming from. At the time, we assumed that Patty was reading these words with a gun at her head. We later came to believe that this was the first indication that the SLA was successfully brainwashing Patty Hearst.

Soon thereafter a representative of the Hearst Foundation came to see me in Washington. We spoke for more than an hour in my office. I briefed him on the progress of the investigation, then nearly two weeks old. He wanted to know if I believed the SLA's ransom demands should continue to be dealt with. That, I emphasize here, is an extraordinarily difficult question for any law enforcement officer. The key issue is: Will paying ransom in effect be a surrender to the kidnappers, and will it ultimately bring back the victim?

In responding to the representative of the Hearst Foundation, I couldn't honestly say, "If you pay this ransom, Patty Hearst will be released unharmed." On the other hand, I also couldn't tell him to forget the ransom demands, because I believed there was a reasonable likelihood that she would be killed. Ultimately this is a decision that can be made only by the victim's parents. I could only assure the Hearst representative that we at the FBI were working around the clock on the case as we continued to aim for an early, safe release of Patty Hearst.

"Please reaffirm to Mr. Hearst my commitment to him," I said. "We all sympathize with the Hearsts. We are family men first, law enforcement officers second. His daughter's well-being is our first priority."

On February 18, Randolph Hearst announced the details of a $2 million food giveaway plan which he felt would meet the ransom orders of the SLA. The program was to be called People In Need (PIN).

On the following day, another SLA tape was delivered. It called the Hearst plan a "few crumbs" and demanded that an additional $4 million be given away within twenty-four hours. A logistical impossibility. Reason had again vanished.

Two days later I was in Los Angeles where I held a press conference. I announced that the Hearst investigation would continue under the direction of Charles W. Bates. I also stressed that the feelings of the Hearst family with regard to the unusual ransom demands would, of course, be honored by the Bureau. Questions from reporters were often pointed, almost hostile. They reflected, I'm sure, the public's rapidly growing impatience with the investigation.

For example, one reporter asked, "Why is it that in this particular kidnapping, the Hearst affair, the FBI seems to be so powerless?"

Skirting the political implications of this crime, I said the FBI's activities in any kidnapping were primarily designed to produce the safe return of the victim—and we were committed to that concern in this case.

On February 22 Randolph Hearst said that the latest SLA ransom demand was "simply beyond my financial capability" and the matter was now "out of my hands." He stated that the Hearst Corporation, however, would put up the additional $4 million that the SLA had asked for ($2 million immediately and $2 million in January 1975), but only if Patty was released unharmed.

People In Need was a travesty from the very beginning.

The first food giveaway got under way in Oakland, with unruly crowds and near-riot conditions. The same was true at other food giveaways held at distribution points in the cities around the Bay Area, including Palo Alto and Richmond as well as in San Francisco. In the second giveaway, on February 28, between 25,000 and 30,000 bags of food were distributed, many of which, we learned later, the "needy" immediately resold for one-third to one-quarter of their retail value.

I, of course, continued to monitor the Hearst investigation from FBI headquarters in Washington. We developed a loose, informal working group, which included Bob Gebhardt and a few other assistants at the highest levels of the Bureau. Much day-to-day work was involved, including reports and dispatches to review on a regular basis. Rumors of Patty Hearst sightings abounded. There were numerous extortion attempts from other extremist groups and even cases of individual blackmailers.

Because the SLA kidnappers were not demanding a ransom for themselves, the Hearst case, now clearly political in nature, became more difficult to solve with each passing week. All efforts notwithstanding, we seemed to be losing ground.

The question continued to pursue me: What did the SLA really want? After working on the case for several weeks, I concluded that they had several objectives in mind.

First, there was the brainwashing. What wasn't clear to me at first, but became obvious as the weeks passed, was the fact that the militants wanted to show our society that they could capture and brainwash a member of the white upper class. Second, they most certainly saw Patty Hearst as a valuable asset in bargaining for the release of jailed SLA members, particularly Joseph Remiro and Russell Little. Third, in its wilder imaginings, the SLA came to believe that through its activities "on behalf of the poor" it could somehow trigger a nationwide revolution against the traditional United States power structure, and perhaps even the government itself. These objectives were entirely political, and none gave the FBI anything to work with. None pointed to the whereabouts of the kidnappers or the kidnapped.

We now know that during those early weeks of the kidnapping, Patty was carefully imprisoned in the SLA's Daly City, California, hideout. This city south of San Francisco, a "middle-class" American suburb, would not seem to be the most ideal location for hiding the most media-visible kidnap victim in forty years. But the SLA made it work by keeping Patty hidden—and by intimidating into silence every informant who might have helped the police. We now know that a number of Bay Area underground members knew where the SLA hideout was located, but both sympathy with the SLA's "cause" and fear of retribution from SLA adherents kept any in-the-know informants from coming forward.

Certainly, we later learned, the treatment of Patty Hearst was insanely savage. She was locked away, blindfolded and tied, in a two-foot-by-six-foot windowless closet for a period of almost eight weeks. She was brutalized and terrorized to the point of delirium. Her captors were themselves past the edge of sanity. (Pathological indeed, we later learned, was the SLA's hatred of the FBI and the Bureau leadership.)

And with the barbarism came the propaganda. Slowly, over many weeks, the SLA subjected Patty to a brainwash of ruthless, mind-altering Marxist-Maoist ideology. In addition to the political theory and terror, Patty also heard incessant diatribes concerning the FBI, and the dangers it represented. The real possibility that the FBI would, at any time, storm the SLA hideout and kill them all (including—and especially—Patty Hearst) was apparently discussed daily.

Through it all, the People In Need dole continued.

On March 5, 1974, food valued at $300,000 was distributed to the poor in the third installment of the PIN giveaway program. Though the handouts continued to get wide media coverage, at FBI headquarters in Washington all hope that this program would bring about the release of Patty Hearst was given up. Whether PIN was doing any good at all was a moot question. The one thing we couldn't begin to guess at was whether PIN was keeping Patty alive—or even making life more bearable for her.

The next day SLA prisoners Remiro and Little, at San Quentin, sent a letter to a radio station requesting permission to appear at a live press conference to outline a plan they thought would secure the release of Patty Hearst. The fourth installment of the PIN program took place on March 8. By now the value of food distributed under this program had passed the $1 million mark.

Then the SLA delivered its most hostile tape yet, to three Bay Area radio stations.

Patty herself charged her father with "offering only crumbs to the poor." The Symbionese Liberation Army demanded a new and expanded food giveaway program.

SLA leader Cinque urged "all oppressed people to arm themselves and wage war against U.S. corporations."

I personally found the duality of these two messages to be very disturbing. We were entering a new phase in the political struggle. Patty Hearst was actually becoming a spokeswoman for the "help-the-oppressed" crusade, while Donald DeFreeze was now turning his attention to the challenge of becoming "Field Commander Cinque," military leader of the down-trodden masses. At this juncture there was no way to guess how all of this would end.

Another voice on the March 9 tape said Patty Hearst would henceforth be allowed to communicate with her family only after arrangements were made for Russell Little and Joseph Remiro to speak on live television to their SLA comrades and to the public concerning the conditions of their confinement.

Making no mention at all of PIN, the SLA directed several damning remarks at the FBI, most of them delivered by Patty herself. At one point she asserted that "only the FBI and certain people in the government stood to gain anything by my death."

Patty also said that "the news media has been assisting the FBI in what is now an overt attempt to set me up for execution." Finally, she stated, "The SLA are not the ones who are harming me. It's the FBI!"

I was dumbfounded.

The polemics of this tape were nonsense. Yet that nonsense made only more disturbing the inescapable fact that, after many weeks of the most determined investigation, we had no idea where to find Patty Hearst. As the SLA must have known it would, the image of the Bureau was taking a battering over this whole matter. I agonized with my associates at Bureau headquarters over the latest information from San Francisco; we sought new approaches and fresh thinking. We needed all of the innovation we could muster. Because Patty's captors were part of a loose-knit underground network of American society, it was impossible to develop leads of any value.

Moreover, Patty Hearst herself was becoming more and more an integral part of the SLA. Based on all the evidence available to us, she was giving more cooperation to her captors than to those of us who sought to free her. In our frustration it was all we could do to refrain from directing our anger at the kidnap victim. The fact is, we didn't know where to turn, or what to think.

All this while the public outcry for action grew. The press, in its own frustration with the case, had turned on us.

In an effort to bring some balance to the story, and tell our side, I accepted an invitation to attend a *Newsweek* editorial luncheon in late March.

I told the editors that the Bureau had been, over the years, remarkably successful in solving kidnapping cases. I said that I would like to see the press devote more space to the fact that the overwhelming majority of kidnappings are solved by the FBI with the safe return of the victim and the recovery of most of the ransom money. More publicity, I said, should be focused on the actual sentences handed down to the kidnappers by our courts. For example, in the past few years seventy-one convictions had been returned against kidnappers in federal courts. These convictions resulted in twelve terms of life imprisonment and other sentences totaling nearly eight-hundred years. But I knew, as I spoke, that none of these cases involved anything like the Symbionese Liberation Army . . . or a victim named Hearst.

Seven weeks into the investigation, the case began taking on a host of bizarre aspects—extortion attempts by the noninvolved, made-up sightings of Patty by publicity seekers, and, typical of any case with high media attention, contact with a strange assortment of unorthodox, unbalanced characters.

Because of this, time was squandered. An example was the hours we spent at the Bubble Machine.

Following up on a tip, one of our agents accompanied a member of the Hearst family to a carwash in downtown San Francisco called the Bubble Machine. A source had informed our agents that he had "genuine inside information that would lead to the release of Patty Hearst."

To obtain this information, however, a member of the Hearst family must visit, at a prearranged time, the Bubble Machine carwash and have his automobile cleaned. Our agents shadowed Patty's brother, Willie Hearst, as he went to the spot at the specified time and drove his car through the machine. Several heart-pounding minutes passed. Finally, the source appeared in the Bubble Machine parking lot. Our agents also appeared, ready for action. The informant, however, turned out to be a troublesome screwball who, in addition to having no information at all, caused our men, as well as the Hearst family, much needless aggravation. Regrettably, many similar episodes occurred draining the energy—and diverting the attention—of our agents and other law-enforcement personnel.

The Patty Hearst kidnapping investigation, by now coded *Hearnap*, utilized every investigative resource known to the FBI: police dogs, terrorist experts, kidnapping experts, and even a psychic, who on one particular day presided over a prolonged séance. The psychic's psychiatrist was there, as were authorities, who dutifully transcribed everything the psychic muttered. Randolph Hearst attended, but accurately perceiving the psychic's babblings to be a worthless waste of everybody's time, he fell sound asleep. And everyone else should have! The information was not worth the paper it was written on.

The PIN program officially ended on March 25, 1974, with a massive distribution of food at seventeen Bay Area sites.

That same day Berkeley radio station KPFA received a letter from SLA prisoners Remiro and Little. The two complained of the conditions of their confinement and their lack of access to the public. They apparently wanted a nationwide television audience before which they could air their beliefs. Then, just before the close of the message, came the stunning announcement. The two expressed their hope that Patty Hearst would be released unharmed!

This was followed five days later by another surprise plea from another unexpected quarter. Randolph Hearst made public the contents of a letter he had received from Clifford Jefferson, the former member of the original SLA board of directors, and two other inmates of the California prison system. "In the best interest of the poor and oppressed," Jefferson wrote, "we urge the immediate release of Patty Hearst."

I wondered how Field Marshal Cinque viewed these two very clear breaks in the ranks.

We know now that our agents had several times come close to foiling the efforts of the SLA and perhaps capturing the entire group during these amazingly long months early in 1974. For example, authorities had somehow overlooked Patty Hearst's name on the SLA hit list, which was found after the raid on the SLA Concord hideout in January, several weeks before the kidnapping.

We also narrowly missed capturing SLA member Camilla Hall in February when a Bank of America clerk failed to notice an FBI "hold" tab on her bank account. As a result, she freely withdrew all of her cash, closing her account at the Bank of America branch office, all within sight of the FBI office in Berkeley.

Astonishingly, a secretary with the FBI field office in San Francisco, responding to a newspaper advertisement, innocently purchased a Volkswagen van, not knowing it was one of the vehicles the SLA had used the night of the Patty Hearst abduction. Thus it happened that the very same VW van that was the object of one of our most intensive searches was being parked for weeks by one of our own employees in the garage of the FBI office building.

Additionally, one of the SLA hideouts turned out to be less than fifteen blocks from FBI headquarters in the Federal Building in San Francisco. Several local police stations were even closer to the SLA hideout.

On April 2, 1974, a very weary Randolph Hearst issued yet another press release in which he outlined revised ransom terms—significant additional contributions to the PIN program. This offer, similar to the one made on February 22, now had a deadline of May 3. Again Hearst stated that no payment would be made unless Patty's release was assured by the SLA.

On the same day another message was delivered to the underground newspaper, *Phoenix*. In it the SLA promised that an announcement about the release of Patty Hearst was imminent. We later learned that this false alarm was "all in fun." The SLA outlaws were, to their great amusement, toying with the feelings of the Hearst family, and the millions of interested U.S. citizens concerned about Patty's safety.

Next, we received word from the SLA which strained human comprehension. On April 3, the newest SLA tape was delivered to the media. When I got the telex transcript at my desk in Washington, I could hardly believe my eyes.

First, Patty Hearst announced that from now on her name was to be "Tania." She had now joined the SLA to fight for oppressed peoples everywhere. Never could she return to the life she had led before, she said.

Next, she vilified her parents and her fiancé, Steven Weed, because they had not arranged for the release of SLA prisoners Remiro and Little. The PIN program, she declared, was nothing more than a sham. Saving the best for last, she said she was fully aware that *the FBI wanted to kill her!*

Then SLA leader DeFreeze-Cinque named three former SLA members who he believed were FBI informants. They would be shot on sight, he vowed.

My associates and I reviewed this communication at Bureau headquarters in stunned silence. Not only was this the most demoralizing tape of all, but it seemed to underscore one of our worst fears. Patty had now progressed far beyond being the spokeswoman for PIN; she now spoke of fighting for the oppressed, and DeFreeze was preparing for armed violence.

How long, I wondered, before this troop would surface—and under what conditions would they appear?

Little did I know at the time that gunfire was less than two weeks away.

On April 15, at 9:40 in the morning, following a well-coordinated plan, SLA members entered the Sunset branch of the Hibernia Bank in San Francisco, armed with sawed-off carbines, heavily clothed, and disguised. Patricia Soltysik carried a handgun and gathered the money. They got away with more than $10,000. The undertaking took less than five minutes. Two innocent bystanders were seriously wounded as SLA members fired wildly and indiscriminately during their getaway.

And a clean getaway it was. Police had dozens of reports on the cars they used—all reports in conflict with each other. And no one seemed to have any good idea which direction they took as they left the scene. Unbelievable as it sounds now, the SLA had surfaced, had robbed a bank within the city limits of San Francisco, shot two innocent people, and disappeared without leaving a trace.

The early information I received at headquarters was fragmentary. I immediately opened intensive communication between the San Francisco field office and Washington. It lasted all day and into the night. Most of it concerned the whereabouts of Patty Hearst—and the vanishing act pulled off by DeFreeze and his mob. By the end of the day, however, our information supported eyewitness reports: cameras activated during the holdup confirmed that Patricia Hearst was an armed participant in the bank robbery.

A federal warrant for Patty's arrest as a material witness was sworn out on April 16. Arrest warrants on bank robbery charges were also issued for four SLA members: Donald DeFreeze, Patricia Soltysik, Camilla Hall, and Nancy Ling Perry. Four other SLA individuals involved were not immediately identified.

The robbery had three purposes, Patty subsequently said: "To obtain money to finance the revolution; to prove that I had really joined the ranks of the SLA; and to demonstrate that SLA soldiers were daring and fearless in their attacks on a capitalistic society."

A few days later, in an interview with the *Los Angeles Times*, I said: "Despite heavy Bureau investigative activity, we still don't know where Patty Hearst is hiding out." That admission hurt, but we had indeed turned the entire Bay Area upside down, with no luck.

Five days later, on still another SLA tape, Patty emphasized that she was a proud, willing participant in the Hibernia Bank robbery, and in a voice filled with arrogance and hate she said she planned to continue as an active member of the Symbionese Liberation Army.

Patty Hearst must have been living an emotional nightmare. As the investigation continued it repeatedly occurred to me that she was trapped in a classic and terrifying double bind, caught in a crossfire between her captor-comrades and those who claimed they wanted only to set her free. A ghastly conflict of rights and wrongs must have haunted her day by day.

We now know that despite my public statements that the FBI didn't have any idea where Patty was, the SLA felt that we were on its heels most of the time, more because of our vigorous presence in the Bay Area than because of any knowledge of its whereabouts. The Symbionese Liberation Army felt compelled to move from the house in suburban Concord to a Daly City apartment. Then, after the Hibernia bank robbery, they moved again. First to a small one-room house in the Hunters Point district of San Francisco, and then finally, to Los Angeles.

On May 2 our agents, working with local police, found the

abandoned Golden Gate Avenue apartment. The next day the Hearst Corporation's $4 million offer for the release of Patty expired and was withdrawn.

Six days later, May 8, the Hearst family itself offered a $50,000 reward for the safe return of their daughter. On the same day, the Symbionese Liberation Army—with a total of nine members, including Patty Hearst—made its secret move from the San Francisco area to the Los Angeles area.

The move to southern California marked the beginning of the end for the original SLA.

On May 9, in response to hundreds of requests from the press, law enforcement personnel nationwide, and the general public, I held the first national news conference ever conducted by an FBI director. I wanted the public to know that, despite the fact that the Hearst case had not been solved, our agents were working on it and, ultimately, she would be found. Many probing questions were fired at me.

For example, a reporter simply queried, "Why is it so hard for the Bureau to solve this case?" An answer:

> We have been working steadily on this investigation for three months. Our very best people are on the case, both in Washington and in California. However, the SLA is, to put it mildly, an unusual group. Human life means nothing to them. And they're certainly not motivated by money. They make no ransom demands for money for themselves. Thus, the SLA kidnapping is completely different from every normal kidnap I've ever dealt with. And without the customary ransom handover, we are denied one of the traditional opportunities for capturing the group.

In addition, I said, the SLA was fanatically devoted to a revolutionary cause that, however misguided, had become their reason for existence. The members were a tightly structured cadre, and obviously many more of a kindred philosophy supported them directly or indirectly. Many of their supporters or "fellow travelers" lived in the quasi underground.

"This subculture, the FBI knows, is practically impossible to penetrate unless we resort to violating people's constitutional rights. Leads, the lifeblood of an investigation of this type, are not voluntarily forthcoming," I stated.

I ended by saying that, though I was then stumped, Patty Hearst's safe return—or capture—continues to be the first priority with the FBI. "I am certain we will find her. At best the FBI can control her recovery. And I am determined to give the highest priority to her safety."

What I didn't say at the time was that with all of their moving about, the SLA had created a trail—and we were on it.

On May 16, 1974, the pace began to quicken.

My secretary brought a telex dispatch to me: the presence of the SLA in Los Angeles was now confirmed.

A sales clerk at a sporting goods store in Inglewood caught William Harris shoplifting an ammunition belt. As Harris and his wife, Emily, struggled to free themselves from store personnel in front of the establishment, Patty Hearst, stationed in a getaway van across the street, demanded that the SLA members be released. She then opened fire with an automatic rifle. Though no one was hit, she frightened the store personnel sufficiently for the three SLA members to make a successful getaway.

Another telex soon followed, and then another. The SLA getaway van was found abandoned on a Los Angeles street.

Parking tickets found by police inside the abandoned vehicle indicated that the van had been illegally parked at 833 West 84 Street in Los Angeles. Our agents, working closely with the Los Angeles police, concluded that this might well be the location of the current SLA hideout.

Tension mounted as we continued to monitor the urgent communications from our Los Angeles field office.

The small rundown bungalow at 833 West 84 Street was surrounded and stormed by a heavily armed Los Angeles Police Department SWAT team. Too late. The inhabitants had fled just minutes before. I was immediately informed at FBI headquarters of these developments. I was frustrated and disappointed, but encouraged that we were still hot on their trail. Once again, by the narrowest of margins, we had missed nabbing this maddeningly elusive group. However, all was not lost. The search in Los Angeles again intensified. Again we knew we were not far behind them.

Just one tip would do it.

The next day, May 17, a resident of the Eighty-fourth Street area in Los Angeles gave our agents that tip. The FBI now moved to investigate a new possible SLA hideout at 1466 East 54 Street.

The Symbionese were surrounded.

My elation, however, was tempered by the fact that I knew the FBI had no control over this situation.

The SLA enclave was besieged by an army of heavily armed Los Angeles Police Department law-enforcement personnel, including teams of ten SWAT sharpshooters, and more than six hundred police officers. Two helicopters and more than three hundred police vehicles were at hand. Police issued at least a dozen surrender warnings on loudspeakers. No response came from the house. Then, for the next few minutes, silence—in Los Angeles and in my office in Washington—which had now become a working command post. My desk was covered with urgent dispatches and telexes from our Los Angeles office. All the reports read the same: members of the SLA were in that house. Exactly who and exactly how many members was uncertain.

News of the developing situation in Los Angeles caught the attention of just about everyone at headquarters.

I had been informed minute by minute as developments unfolded. We knew things had come down to a virtual standoff, and almost certainly there would be a gunfight.

I pondered the tense situation, then decided that the FBI was no longer needed here. The matter could and should be handled by the Los Angeles Police Department. The contingent of local officers was sufficient—in numbers and arms—to handle an invasion, let alone less than a dozen SLA members.

Holding my breath and whispering a prayer, I ordered our

men to pull out. Withdraw and under no circumstances should the FBI enter into an exchange of gunfire. As my order was being carried out, there was another pause.

Then all the fires of hell descended on that little house on Fifty-fourth Street.

It started with police shooting several tear-gas canisters into the house. The SLA responded with heavy automatic weapons fire. A ferocious firefight then raged for more than an hour. The firing by law-enforcement officers into the house was done by two Los Angeles SWAT teams. While it lasted, the SLA-LAPD shootout was an all-out battle with a barrage from both sides of more than eight thousand rounds of ammunition. What's more, the battle was shown live on nationwide television.

We watched in amazement and horror as this tragedy was acted out before our very eyes. Finally the house burst into flames, but the firing from both sides continued at a furious pace.

Slowly the shooting subsided. Those inside the house, by their own choice, perished.

The charred remains of two men and four women were found in the rubble. Only with difficulty were they identified—Donald David (Cinque) DeFreeze, Nancy Ling (Fahizah) Perry, Patricia (Zoya) Soltysik, Angela (Gelina) Atwood, William (Cujo) Wolfe, and Camilla (Gabi) Hall. At the time, I still didn't know whether Patty Hearst was in the house.

After the shooting we did, of course, ascertain that Patty Hearst and William and Emily Harris had not been in the house. Following the episode at the sporting goods store the day before, the three had become separated from the main SLA group and were unable to locate the new hideout on Fifty-fourth Street. This fortunate happenstance saved their lives.

In point of fact, Patty and her two companions watched the spectacular shootout on television in their motel room in Anaheim, not far from Disneyland.

Patty and the Harrises were in total shock.

After witnessing the death of their six comrades, the three remaining SLA members lingered for a few days in their Anaheim motel. Then, in panic, fearing capture, and heavily disguised to avoid detection, they drove to San Francisco, on to Oakland, and, finally, to an empty apartment in Berkeley.

In the meantime, the Los Angeles district attorney announced that warrants had been issued charging Patty Hearst, William Harris, and Emily Harris with kidnapping, armed robbery, assault to commit murder, and violation of the national firearms act. The Harrises were also charged separately with kidnapping. Bond was recommended at $1.5 million each.

After the death of SLA leader Donald DeFreeze, William Harris assumed the dubious distinction of SLA chief. Though Harris was every bit as radical and diabolical as his predecessor, he did not have the leadership skills of DeFreeze. At the time that Harris took over as SLA head, however, we really didn't know how badly the group had been crippled.

In any event, our pursuit continued.

By late May and early June, about two hundred police and FBI investigators were searching for Hearst and the Harrises. Many investigators were working twelve-hours-on, twelve-hours-off, seven days a week. It was probably the largest single manhunt ever conducted by the FBI. One researcher estimated, and I believe correctly, that by July 1974 at least five thousand people had been questioned about the kidnapping with virtually no information of real value obtained. Admittedly, this was a law-enforcement frustration of sizable dimensions.

Patty Hearst was indicted by a federal grand jury for armed bank robbery and for use of a firearm in the commission of a felony. The indictment was handed down on June 6, 1974.

The next day, a radio station in Van Nuys received an SLA tape in which Patty, again calling herself Tania, said the six dead SLA members were her "beautiful brothers and sisters."

"My comrades did not die in vain," she pledged.

Moreover, she proclaimed that she herself had died in that fire and was "reborn." She also stated that she had loved Cujo (William Wolfe).

It was the final SLA tape.

After its return to Berkeley, the decimated SLA seemed to vanish from the face of the earth. And yet, somehow, Patty and her "comrades," plus leftist sympathizers of every hue, were at once everywhere and nowhere. It is now known that about forty people helped, or participated in, the Harris-Hearst odyssey across the nation.

Patty and her friends made their way east to a secluded farmhouse near Scranton, Pennsylvania. Then across the Delaware River to a remote location in upstate New York near the town of Jeffersonville, and finally back into Pennsylvania. In early fall 1974 they again headed west, going first to Las Vegas, then on to Sacramento. During that summer our people were close on their trail; reports regularly reached my desk for review. Patty remained, however, like quicksilver—slipping through our fingers on several occasions.

On October 31, 1974, Randolph Hearst withdrew his offer of a $50,000 reward for the return of his daughter. And on November 18 *Argosy* magazine offered a $5,000 reward for information leading to the arrest of Patty. In December SLA prisoners Joseph Remiro and Russell Little requested a change of venue in their Marcus Foster murder trial, from Sacramento to Los Angeles. The request was denied.

Ten days before Christmas 1974, Randolph and Catherine Hearst announced that they would move from their twenty-two-room mansion in Hillsborough to an apartment in San Francisco.

In a public letter to their daughter, Mrs. Hearst explained, "Dad and I find it too painful to continue living here, with so many memories of you." Again as both a parent and FBI director, my sympathy went out to the Hearsts. The pain they were suffering over the sordid affair had to be unbearable.

During this period, the SLA had begun recruiting new members to fill the void left by the six deaths in the firestorm in Los Angeles. Jim Kilgore, Steve Soliah, Kathy Soliah, Wendy Yoshimura, and others, are now part of the permanent record of Symbionese Liberation Army activists.

And the SLA continued its many illegal activities.

As usual, each SLA sortie was well planned, and each demonstrated an utter disregard for human life. Only its internal strife hindered more nefarious actions. William Harris, as expected, was having trouble controlling his "army." Nevertheless, the group remained active in 1975.

The SLA successfully stole cash from an Oakland post office, then bombed the Emeryville, California, police station and the Marin County Civic Center. It planned to assist SLA captives Joseph Remiro and Russell Little in escaping from jail, but apparently concluded that its organization was not capable of such an undertaking. Undaunted, Remiro and Little did attempt to break out on their own, coming within an eyelash of succeeding.

The new SLA also robbed the Guild Savings and Loan in Sacramento, and the Crocker National Bank in Carmichael. In the second robbery Emily Harris shot a bank customer to death.

On June 9, 1975, SLA members Little and Remiro were convicted of the 1973 murder of Oakland School Superintendent Marcus Foster and the attempted killing of Robert Blackburn.

Ultimately, the search for Patty Hearst ended where it began—in the San Francisco Bay Area.

In the final analysis, Patty Hearst and William and Emily Harris were found because of the relentless efforts of our agents working in close contact with state and local authorities. The enormity of the effort practically defies comprehension. Over a period of nineteen months, our agents studied and shadowed the wide-ranging network of sympathizers related in some way to the SLA. These individuals, all of whom were close to the SLA, or were part of it, provided assistance or sanctuary to its members. Their value to us was, of course, nil. The complex of events leading to Patty Hearst's rescue (or capture) involved thousands upon thousands of investigative manhours from coast to coast.

On September 18, 1975, the end came. And quickly. It was late morning when my phone rang.

"Mr. Kelley, Charles Bates is on the line from San Francisco," said my secretary.

"Mr. Director, we have some good intelligence developing on Hearnap. I don't want to overpromise but this may be it. Will you be at headquarters for the rest of the day?" he asked.

"I'll be here all day," I replied. "We've got to be careful, we don't want any mishaps now. Please be very careful."

"Yes, sir, I understand. We know that they are armed so we will have to be cautious," he said.

"This looks like good work, Charles. Everyone here is watching this situation. Please keep me fully informed," I said.

Thereafter, updated information reached me every fifteen minutes or so.

At last the final call came through. Patricia Campbell Hearst had been taken into custody, alive and apparently well.

Patty Hearst and Wendy Yoshimura were arrested at 625 Morse Avenue in San Francisco at 2:30 P.M. by Inspector Tim Casey of the San Francisco police and FBI Agent Tom Padden. Moments later William and Emily Harris were arrested at 288 Precita Avenue, about a mile away. The long-awaited news was flashed nationwide and around the world by wire services. The capture was the instant lead story for every newspaper from Maine to California.

At FBI headquarters we were jubilant: We had Patty Hearst . . . and we had her alive. My thoughts immediately went to Mr. and Mrs. Randolph Hearst.

Patty Hearst's sensational abduction was followed by an equally sensational trial, the transcript of which generated over 4,500 pages. The trial began on January 27, 1976, and lasted until March 19. She was sentenced on April 12, 1976, and the long courtroom proceedings made headlines on a regular basis. As we expected, Patty was convicted, her conviction was upheld, and she went to prison. In early 1979, she was granted a pardon by the president of the United States, Jimmy Carter.

Hearnap was one of the most dramatic events during my tenure in the director's chair. It was, by any standard, one of the most astounding affairs of the 1970s. Since leaving the Bureau, I have had the time to distance myself from the very confusing and always frustrating events of the abduction.

The investigation, difficult as it is for me to imagine from this vantage point, took a full nineteen months, ranking it as one of the longest in American history. The publicity probably reached the point of overkill . . . or so it seemed to those of us in the FBI. The episode was, of course, unspeakably tragic for all involved. For the young woman and her family, the scars will always be there. For the victims of the SLA violence, we can only pray.

For a beleagured U.S. government it was one tragedy treading on the heels of another: the Patty Hearst kidnapping and Watergate overlapped for six full months during 1974.

As a result, faith in government, particularly in the executive branch, was at a low ebb.

I, too, felt the pressure.

The often-asked question was, "What's the matter with the FBI? Why can't you find that girl?" Not suprisingly, polls showed that the public's confidence in the FBI, as well as everything else in Washington, slipped precipitously.

Hearnap was very costly in many ways—in human emotion and American dollars.

In fact the Hearst kidnapping case earned the dubious honor of being the most expensive kidnapping in American history. The FBI investigation itself cost the U.S. taxpayer, conservatively, $5 million in salaries. The San Francisco field office alone interviewed over twenty-seven thousand individuals. We can only guess at the cost to state and local governments. For example, the May 17, 1974, gun battle on Fifty-fourth Street in Los Angeles alone cost the city almost $70,000 in salaries, equipment, and ammunition.

What went wrong?

I've asked myself the question: Why did it take the FBI so long to apprehend Patty and the SLA? How did that extremely radical, dangerously unbalanced group succeed in evading a nationwide FBI search for nineteen months, and in thwarting the efforts of thousands of FBI agents and police officers to find them? How did they avoid recognition by millions of Americans?

My first conclusion: There were no informants.

Absolutely no leads reached the Bureau from those fringe elements in our society who knew, really knew, where the various SLA hideouts were located. None.

Second, Patty Hearst made no attempt to escape. Early on, this prolonged the investigation. And later, when she actually joined the SLA, declaring her hostility toward the law enforcement teams trying to rescue her, she dealt a severe psychological blow to us all. It's easy to understand the Los Angeles Police Department's own determination to have it out with this SLA menace. Cornered, Donald DeFreeze allowed no compromise. It was either you or DeFreeze until death decided the match. In fact, from the beginning, this was the point of view of the entire SLA. And those were the people Patty Hearst had joined, lived with, and fought for.

Yet, on reflection, one must sympathize with this young woman; she suffered a terrifying ordeal. She was forcibly carried off in the night and within hours thrown into that small closet. There, blindfolded, she was confined for about eight weeks. The actual depth of her personal, prolonged terror can scarcely be imagined. Under fire, she was psychologically reconditioned and brainwashed. She became convinced the FBI would kill her once we found her. Thus, as I mentioned earlier, her ordeal was doubly hideous. She simultaneously feared her captors and also those who would rescue her.

Thirdly—and I must say this again—the Hearst abduction was entirely different from any other kidnapping I had ever experienced. A political kidnapping, it was unique in modern American history. No ransom was demanded for personal gain—heretofore the underlying motive for the crime of kidnapping. As attorneys rely on precedents to make judgments and anticipate the future, so law-enforcement officials rely much on past experience to plan an investigation. But, we at the FBI had never faced this type of kidnapping. Thus, no casebooks could be followed; no precedents had been set. Generally, the kind of ransom demanded by ordinary criminals provides vital clues for solving most abduction cases. In Hearnap, however, there was no ransom in the traditional sense.

Finally, in light of the fact that the investigation took so long, I have reflected on the question: Should I have changed the investigation or the people working on it at some point? Perhaps, but I think not.

Of course, in retrospect, dozens of problems might well have been handled differently. However, I feel, under the unique circumstances of the Hearst case, that we at the FBI did as good a job as could be humanly expected. Special Agent-in-Charge Charles Bates, Special Agents Lawrence Lawler and Monte Hall, and their investigative staffs, were dedicated public servants who performed above and beyond the call of duty. I was fortunate, as well, to have an excellent group of people working with me in Washington.

Lastly, I personally feel good about the fact that we brought Patricia Hearst back into society. I feel that I kept my word given to a distraught father in a telephone conversation on the morning of February 5, 1974, back in the very beginning.

At the time, the Bureau was subjected to much criticism because we didn't solve the Patricia Hearst kidnapping sooner. Without going back over all the difficulties—and unprecedented challenges—faced by the Bureau during these gruelling nineteen months, I can say that we considered and balanced many factors. Initially we sought to find and recover Patty Hearst, then we worked to "neutralize" and capture her and the SLA tribe she so loyally adhered to.

Given the opportunity to do it over, I would do it just as I did then. I would hand the responsibility to Charles Bates, confident that his experience and skill on the spot in San Francisco represented our best opportunity to rapidly solve this case. All the frustrations faced by Charles Bates in the Bay Area would have been multiplied a thousandfold by an effort headquartered in Washington. Practically speaking, the three-hour time difference alone would have hampered our efforts. Late at night and very early in the morning we would have lost control altogether.

I am not at all critical of the Los Angeles Police Department. They brought the matter to a standstill, and dealt with Donald DeFreeze on the only terms he could understand. The SLA was a fanatical, gun-crazed gang holed up on Fifty-fourth Street. The life of every law enforcement officer in sight was in the greatest jeopardy.

Critics after-the-fact always have many answers. I have heard it said that "the SLA should have been allowed to walk out of there alive." Those critics should have been there when the LAPD instructed them to walk out. Field Commander Cinque was there to kill, not to walk.

Some may wonder how J. Edgar Hoover would have managed the Hearst case. It never crossed my mind to ask myself what the former director would have done. In a situation such as this, one's own experience, intuition, and courage must sustain him. There is no time for looking around—or back. There is no value in wondering what somebody else might have done. However, because I did so often feel that I was in concert with the philosophy of J. Edgar Hoover, I was comfortable that my actions, my decisions, were in accord with the most noble traditions of the FBI.

I believe that the FBI responded to the needs of the moment as they appeared before us during the entire Hearst case. The early frustrations, followed by the heartbreak of Patty's evolution from kidnap victim to armed fugitive, accompanied by the realities of the political nature of this case, tested the skills and emotions of all our people.

The FBI people in San Francisco, Los Angeles, and Washington were dedicated to apprehending Patricia Hearst and her SLA captors-associates. I congratulate them for their accomplishments in ending this SLA menace regardless of the time it took. As well, I express my gratitude to the police departments in San Francisco and Los Angeles for the perseverance and bravery during those long months.

Thank God we have such people.

9

Wounded Knee

The FBI's Trial by Combat

IT WAS THE INDIAN RAID of the century—the twentieth century.

On the night of November 3, 1972, members of the militant American Indian Movement invaded, occupied, and for nearly a week, ransacked the Bureau of Indian Affairs building in Washington, D.C. Then, sometime during the night of November 8, they slipped away.

Shortly thereafter they reappeared, more than a thousand miles to the west. In Sioux reservations in western Nebraska and South Dakota, AIM members took part in a series of violent head-on confrontations with police, officials of the Bureau of Indian Affairs, and other governmental authorities.

These alarming and rapidly escalating clashes moved the Justice Department to instruct the Federal Bureau of Investigation to conduct an immediate and complete inquiry into possible AIM violations of federal laws. Accordingly, about twenty-five FBI agents had begun their investigations when news of the next Indian raid stunned the world.

In a surprise move on February 27, 1973, members of AIM seized the village of Wounded Knee, South Dakota.

Led by Russell Means and Dennis Banks, they held the town for seventy-one tense and traumatic days that mesmerized the media from beginning to end. Finally, on May 8, they surrendered to authorities.

The siege of this tiny, historic village demonstrated the bitterness, hopelessness, and frustration of most of the nation's 800,000 native American Indians. In addition, before the Wounded Knee seizure, there had been a hotly contested control-of-power election within the Oglala Sioux tribe. The Indians had become bitterly divided politically, and, I believe, Wounded Knee represented a show of strength by the younger and more aggressive men of the tribe, particularly the AIM faction headed by Means and Banks.

Certainly this is true: the site chosen for this showdown with the United States government could not have been more symbolic. Wounded Knee has always been engraved onto the collective memory of native Americans.

At Wounded Knee, near the Badlands of South Dakota, was fought the final major battle of the American Indian Wars. On December 29, 1890, elements of the U.S. Seventh Cavalry captured, then shot and killed, some two hundred Sioux—men, women, and children. They later buried the Indians in a mass grave beside Wounded Knee Creek.

Long after the 1890 massacre, claims of deliberate provocation were made by each side. Who knows the merits of these claims? All we can know today is that the Wounded Knee massacre has its own niche in American history, a ghastly and tragic ending to a chronicle of nearly three hundred years of armed conflict between the red native American and the white immigrant.

Even though the American Indian movement, founded in 1958, had become increasingly radical in confrontations with local, state, and federal authorities, the nation was shocked by AIM's takeover at Wounded Knee. Moreover, as we learned quickly, militant Indians within the Wounded Knee village were fiercely antagonistic, heavily armed, and willing and anxious to use their weapons.

The FBI's Minneapolis Special Agent-in-Charge Joseph H. Trimbach, was in an area near the Pine Ridge Indian Reservation with about six other FBI agents the night the seizure took place. When news reached him, Trimbach immediately ordered twenty additional agents located about one hundred miles away in Rapid City to hurry to the scene. On arrival, they set up roadblocks with the aid of U.S. marshals and Bureau of Indian Affairs' police. The first roadblocks were not intended as much to keep fleeing rebels from escaping as to protect tourists and curiosity-seekers who were flocking to the area. Within forty-eight hours FBI agents from other field offices arrived, bringing the number of agents to about 150.

The Wounded Knee siege was long, volatile, and, in some cases, deadly. Sharp firefights, some involving massive amounts of ammunition, erupted on both sides.

By the end of the occupation in May 1973, more than a thousand arrests had been made and, at least for the time being, a tense situation was defused.

When I became FBI director in midsummer 1973, I was extensively briefed on the relationship of the Bureau with American Indians in general and AIM in particular. I studied FBI background files and concluded that the American Indian situation looked like a time bomb ready to go off at any moment. American Indians, according to the U.S. Census Bureau, were, by any socioeconomic scale, the poorest minority group in the United States.

In an age of self-determination and equality-now, the Indian condition in this country was ready to explode—and Wounded Knee was clearly the spark that could make it happen.

Tension began to build anew between AIM and virtually any form of traditional governmental authority—in South Dakota and Nebraska—throughout the summer and fall of 1973. I was regularly advised of developments at Wounded Knee by telex communications from the field, in staff meetings, and by telephone calls from our agents at field offices in the area. My role during this time was primarily to monitor the potential explosiveness of the situation and stay on top of status reports as they arrived.

Preparation for the criminal trials of the participants in the illegal seizure began in the early summer. By late September

1973 it was apparent to me that the massive litigation very likely would constitute a major civil rights case (and showcase) for the American Indian Movement.

In all, as a result of our investigation, well over one hundred federal indictments were returned against AIM leaders and supporters for acts of protests and violations of law in the Wounded Knee occupation. The principal defendants were Russell Means, Dennis Banks, Carter Camp, Vincent Bellecourt, Pedro Bissonette, and Stan Holder. They faced federal charges that included rioting, arson, assaulting federal officers, and conspiracy.

As I followed this situation from Bureau headquarters in Washington, I noted that there had been clashes between American Indians and practically every form of legitimate governmental authority.

Most of the conflict occurred on the Pine Ridge Indian Reservation, encompassing not only Wounded Knee but a sizeable corner of southwest South Dakota. Pine Ridge is the second largest Indian reservation in the country and is about twice the size of Delaware.

In attempting to investigate these acts of violence, law enforcement personnel, including the FBI, were constantly being harrassed and their investigations hampered. By threats of bodily harm, witnesses to this unlawful interference were actively discouraged from relaying their information to investigators. Nevertheless, despite considerable difficulties and pressure, our agents gathered evidence for the upcoming Wounded Knee trials in an orderly and professional manner. And they served federal warrants on dissidents and investigated each new act of violence at Pine Ridge.

On September 26, 1973, Joseph Trimbach informed me by telephone that a federal fugitive warrant was issued for AIM leader Dennis Banks on the assumption that he would attempt to flee the Wounded Knee prosecution.

Then, three weeks later, Pedro Bissonette was shot and killed by a Bureau of Indian Affairs official who was seeking to serve him with a federal fugitive warrant.

Receiving a request to investigate the matter from the U.S. attorney's office in Sioux Falls, I instructed our men to take whatever steps necessary to nail down the facts on this latest violence at Pine Ridge.

The tension at the reservation escalated when, at a press conference in Minneapolis on October 19, 1973, AIM leader Russell Means said that Bissonette's death was another instance "in the federal government's conspiracy to assassinate the leadership of AIM."

This wild rhetoric, without any basis in fact, further inflamed Indian relations with the FBI.

In addition he and other AIM sympathizers "will converge on Pine Ridge" to deal with those he called "the murderers" of Bissonette.

The range of FBI responsibilities is, even in the best of times, vast. Though the Bureau, during my direction, maintained fifty-nine field offices throughout the United States, the number of personnel employed was, by any standard, small. Each agent, every employee, must meet the highest level of performance and conduct. The supply of high-caliber persons is by no means inexhaustible.

The complexity and scope of the Wounded Knee drama nearly exceeded our resources, placing demands upon us in many ways more serious than Watergate. Many of our people worked to the point of exhaustion. During the occupation our men were placed in a military combat situation, a role they were never trained for.

Moreover, the manpower requirements necessary to handle both the Wounded Knee occupation and the FBI's follow-up investigation were so great that we were forced to bring in people from other FBI offices across the country. The paperwork associated with Wounded Knee filled more than 5,000 FBI investigative data folders, which contained over 250,000 entries of information and evidence.

Two separate trials followed in the aftermath of Wounded Knee.

First, Dennis Banks and Russell Means were to be tried in what came to be known as the "leadership case" scheduled for January 8, 1974, in St. Paul.

Second, more than one hundred other Wounded Knee defendants were included in the so-called "nonleadership case" scheduled to be held on February 4 in Sioux Falls, South Dakota. The FBI supplied the investigative data to prosecutors for both trials.

The leadership trial was long and rambunctious. Opening arguments began on January 8.

AIM's defense attorneys were activist lawyers William Kunstler and Mark Lane. Both were highly controversial. Kunstler had gained notoriety as the fiery defender of the militant Chicago Seven group. Lane, a self-styled "investigator" of the JFK assassination, had written a best-selling book suggesting that the slaying of the president was the result of a Mafia plot.

Their defense strategy seemed based on two points.

The first was that the village of Wounded Knee was "reclaimed" only as a last resort by members of the American Indian Movement to dramatize to the nation the desperate need for far-reaching Bureau of Indian Affairs policy reform.

The second was more convoluted, but nonetheless clever enough. To wit: AIM leaders could not be guilty of seizing anything because they were merely repossessing land that had been given the Indians by the 1868 treaty between the federal government of the United States and the Sioux Indians. It was, said the defense, the United States government that had broken the law "by seizing the land from the Sioux."

United States Federal District Judge Fred J. Nichol ruled that Lane and Kunstler "could not base their defense on an alleged violation of the 1868 treaty." He did, however, rule that witnesses could be questioned about the treaty. Moreover, if shown to be relevant, the Treaty of 1868 could perhaps be entered as evidence. It was never made clear to me what circumstances could trigger the "perhaps"—and allow the Treaty of 1868 to be used in this case.

From the very opening of the trial an almost carnival atmosphere prevailed in the courtroom, highlighted by several outbursts from the defense attorneys.

During the sessions, however, Judge Nichol directed his most scorching criticism toward the government's prosecuting team. The government, he implied, seemed to be attempting to deceive the court and, further, the prosecution seemed interested more in a conviction or a mistrial than in justice. (Judge Nichol wasn't far wrong with his conjecture. As far as the prosecution was concerned, justice *demanded* a conviction; and a mistrial would have resulted, in all likelihood, in the assignment of another judge to the case.)

The judge accused the FBI of "stooping to a new low" in investigative methods. He felt that portions of the prosecution data for the trial were obtained illegally by the Bureau.

This charge led to one of the most challenging moments of my tenure as director of the FBI.

Judge Nichol, while critical of the conduct of both sides, was apparently most disturbed by what he called "raw data" evidence supplied by confidential informants to the FBI—but not available to the court. This is common practice in any investigation. (Promises of confidentiality are given—and these promises must be kept; protection of informants is the key to this basic, traditional method of gathering information.) The judge wished to examine our confidential files and then make a judgment on possible FBI improprieties . . . and whether any of the data should be accessible to the defense lawyers.

What the judge was proposing here was simply a general fishing expedition into the results of an FBI investigation. It was unthinkable. No legal need-to-know had been demonstrated by the defense; only generalized, unsupported allegations of government misconduct. I didn't like the tone of this.

I moved swiftly, ordering Special Agent Trimbach to Washington for emergency consultation. He was at Bureau headquarters the next morning. Together, we agreed we must protect our informers. Their very lives could have been endangered if their identities became common knowledge.

My feelings were very strong then and now about this issue and my defense is a very simple one. America is not a police state. Therefore, the FBI does not, and cannot, coerce any citizen to provide it with investigative information or evidence. The FBI frequently must rely on a network of informants, many of whom are paid. Informant confidentiality is essential to the best use of FBI methods of investigation in a free society; we were now on the verge of losing a crucial point of order. If the principle of informant confidentiality was violated, then the Bureau's primary method (and that of all other investigative agencies, for that matter) of gathering information would be destroyed. The names of informers and confidential sources cannot be revealed without their expressed permission.

None of this should be confused with the defense's right to cross-examine a witness. A witness is one thing. An informant is something else. I felt that Judge Nichol, in lumping them together, was actually attempting to rewrite the law.

The meeting on the confidentiality of our Wounded Knee files and sources on March 28, 1974, was tense. Attending were Attorney General William Saxbe, various government attorneys, other Justice Department officials, myself, and members of my Wounded Knee task force. Justice Department officials suggested that the Wounded Knee trial was so unusual that I should perhaps make an exception and release our so-called "raw files" to the judge for his review.

I was adamant. My answer—the FBI answer—was no.

"Mr. Director, you might be jeopardizing our entire case here. The judge hasn't gone beyond *requesting* the raw data . . . until now. He might *demand* it next," a young Justice Department attorney suggested.

"And if he demands it, we'll really have a showdown, won't we?" I replied. "What assurance do we have that he won't hand our entire block of files over to the defense? Do you know what that could mean? Not only would our informants' lives be endangered, but he would overturn a basic right of every law enforcement organization in this country. We simply can't allow this, and in my opinion, the best way to prevent it is to stand firm right now."

My associates correctly got the idea that I was unyielding. For myself, I couldn't understand how Saxbe could waffle around on this issue. He had seen this judge in action. He knew how critical it was to conceal the identity of informants, many of whom were law-abiding citizens who had their own point of view about how much the lawlessness of AIM was doing to help the American Indian cause.

"Mr. Director, you might give the judge sufficient ammunition to declare a mistrial here—and let every one of the defendants go free. I don't know how firm he might stand against you on this one." The young attorney, I felt, was voicing William Saxbe's argument. I believed the young man was convinced I was right, and hoping that I'd not back off.

"The loss of a guilty verdict in this particular trial would be the most unjust outcome to all of this that I could imagine," I said. "But I will not let the FBI be badgered into a compromise with what I know to be the right of privacy for these informants. We will not yield on this point, and if we look like we stand together on it we might win yet."

I didn't say so at the time, but I was prepared to resign my position rather than give those names to the court. Fortunately, I was not forced into that extreme position.

My view prevailed. The group, including the attorney general, agreed. No fishing expedition. Our informants were to be protected.

And the judge did not choose to pursue the matter.

As the trial moved on, the legal proceedings grew even more unorthodox.

On one occasion the judge accused the FBI of "gross negligence," a charge he did not clarify except to say that we should have been more careful about people's feelings. Another time he had defense lawyers Lane and Kunstler jailed overnight. On still another, he allowed defendants Means and Banks to cross-examine witnesses themselves, thus leading me to conclude that neither the defendants nor the court thought very highly of the job being done by the two famous lawyers. In mid-May, following one particularly uproarious melee, Judge Nichol ordered the courtroom cleared. Finally, not to be outdone by their lawyers in boorishness, defendants Banks and Means refused on one occasion to rise when the judge entered his courtroom. Another clearing of the court.

White House tapes that might have related to Wounded Knee were subpoenaed from President Nixon, but unsuccessfully so. The president, in a letter to the court, said the release of the tapes would not be in the national interest. I remember thinking at the time: and neither is the hooliganism going on in this courtroom!

Finally, in July, the government prosecutors, shell-shocked by the ordeal, rested their case.

On September 16, 1974, Judge Nichol dismissed all charges against Dennis Banks and Russell Means.

The reason given: When one of the twelve jurors fell ill during the trial, the Justice Department refused to allow deliberations to continue with only eleven jurors. The judge declared this to be a default on the part of the prosecution, terminating the trial—and freeing the defendants.

So the trial ended. In my opinion, a disgrace from start to finish. A travesty of justice. A blemish on our entire judicial system. It accomplished naught but a massive waste of money. Worse, the U.S. Government had allowed a demonstration of armed rebellion to go unpunished. It was revolution with impunity. People had been murdered, lives uprooted, and the FBI driven almost to the breaking point. In the end, absolution for AIM. Disappointed, I was fearful of what might be ahead. I knew instinctively that nothing good could come from this mockery. But there was more to come.

In February 1975 Judge Nichol dismissed charges against all remaining Wounded Knee defendants.

Then the final irony: A month later the announcement reached me in Washington that Judge Nichol had disqualified himself from future judicial matters related to Wounded Knee or the American Indian Movement. The jurist felt that his personal identification with—and sympathy for—the plight of the American Indian caused him to lose his professional objectivity. Thus, he was removing himself from any future such cases.

Throughout the spring of 1975, after charges against the defendants had been dropped, the violence at the Pine Ridge Indian Reservation intensified. More terrorism, assaults, robbery, and finally, three murders in a community beset by chaos and lawlessness. Nothing we could do eased the internal friction among the Indians themselves.

Although our agents were an ongoing presence at Wounded Knee, they had no direct confrontations with the Indians during the winter and early spring of 1975.

In Washington we watched and waited. And hoped. And it was in vain.

Late in the afternoon on June 26 my secretary buzzed me and said I had an urgent call from our Minneapolis office. I picked up the phone.

The voice was calm, firm, and deadly serious.

"Mr. Director, we've just received word that two of our agents, Jack Coler and Ron Williams, have been trapped and shot near Oglala, South Dakota—on the Pine Ridge Indian Reservation. We don't know the extent of their wounds. We fear the worst, however."

I jotted notes on my yellow legal pad, recording what fragments of information he could give me. I advised him that I would get back to him within the hour, and hung up.

Immediately calling Deputy Associate Director James B. Adams and Assistant Director Robert E. Gebhardt to my office, I relayed the news from Pine Ridge to them. They received the news in silence. No matter how many years you spend in law enforcement, you're never braced for the trauma of seeing men, especially young men, making the ultimate sacrifice in the line of duty.

Even at that very moment, however, dispatches, telexes and phone calls were beginning to pour in, all adding up to the same thing: we had a full-scale tragedy on our hands. After reviewing what information we had, I knew—we all knew—that we had to take the strongest possible action at once.

I called Minneapolis with my instructions: "You must find out if our men are still alive. If they are, be very careful not to endanger them. If they are not, find the people who did this—and get them behind bars."

Joseph Trimbach had swiftly assembled a SWAT team in Minneapolis. He and the team then flew to Rapid City. From there a chartered plane carried them directly to the small airstrip at Pine Ridge. Trimbach called me from the scene that night, at about eleven, and confirmed our fears: "Mr. Director, our two men are dead. Murdered by persons unknown."

"Are they really unknown, Joe?" I asked him.

"Not really, sir. But you know what it's going to be like proving anything. I don't think we're going to find many witnesses here."

"I understand, Joe. Please keep us posted, and let us know what we can do for you."

About two hundred FBI agents, wearing battle fatigues and armed with automatic weapons, arrived at Oglala overnight. Accompanying them were SWAT teams, an armored personnel carrier, Bureau of Indian Affairs' police officers, helicopters, tracking dogs, and a spotter plane.

At FBI headquarters in Washington my badly shaken staff reviewed all information on the killings to determine exactly what had happened. In a short time, we uncovered a tale of unspeakable barbarism.

In early June 1975 Ronald A. Williams and Jack R. Coler, both natives of the Los Angeles area, were transferred to FBI offices in the Pine Ridge Indian Reservation area. The purpose of the transfers, made as a special assignment, was primarily to stem the escalating rate of crime there. On June 26 Agents Williams and Coler were attempting to serve warrants on four Indians, each of whom was believed to be a member of the American Indian Movement—Teddy Paul Pourier, Herman Thunder

Hawk, Robert House, and James Eagle. The four were charged with felonious assault and larceny.

The two agents carried detailed maps of the reservation, which, it was believed, would show them where certain AIM fugitives from justice could probably be found. They traveled in two separate FBI sedans. By late morning they had arrived at their destination, the Jumping Bull compound—an isolated cluster of small houses located some twelve miles northwest of the village of Pine Ridge and about three miles from the little town of Oglala.

Within this enclave, which also included a tent encampment, was a house that was often occupied by AIM leader Dennis Banks. Two of the houses in this small group were set somewhat apart off a dusty road not far from the main highway between Pine Ridge and Oglala. The tiny village is surrounded by about a half-mile of prairie grasslands, which fall off sharply to a dry, wooded creek bed called White Clay Creek.

The agents believed that James Eagle and perhaps other fugitives could be found in one of the houses in the village. The FBI men had also learned that Jimmy Eagle might be traveling in a red and white van.

The agents spotted the red and white van almost immediately and followed it into the compound area. In the van were Leonard Peltier and two passengers. The van stopped near one of the houses briefly; Peltier and one of the passengers got out of the van, noticed that the two FBI sedans were following them, and quickly got back into the vehicle and drove away.

Leonard Peltier later testified that he "knew" the FBI agents were after him. He believed that the agents were trying to arrest him on a charge of attempted murder in another state. In point of fact, Coler and Williams had no idea that Peltier was even in the area; their quarry was Jimmy Eagle.

Agents Coler and Williams drove their cars down the dirt road and stopped at the edge of the grassland meadow, somewhat past the little cluster of houses. Unwittingly, they had pocketed themselves in a cul-de-sac. To leave the area, they would have to double back past the houses to a point where the road forked. The problem: the arsenal of firepower within those houses. They parked their two government sedans, a green 1972 Rambler and a bronze 1972 Chevrolet, together. Each was equipped, of course, with a two-way radio, which was capable of car-to-car as well as car-to-local-FBI communications.

Coincidentally another of our men, Special Agent J. Gary Adams, was in his automobile some fifteen miles away in the reservation and heard the entire episode on his car radio.

As the red and white van was pulling away, Adams heard on his car radio one of the agents say, "There are some people by these houses and it looks like they are leaving."

This was followed by a momentary silence and then the next radio transmission followed, "I hope you have a lot of gas. It looks like they are going to be traveling." Then prolonged silence. The van suddenly stopped abruptly at a fork in the road and parked, blocking the agents' way out.

The FBI men were trapped. The agents stopped their cars and turned off their ignitions. There was no escaping it: They were surrounded and an arsenal of weapons was pointed at them.

Then came the next radio message: "It looks like they are going to shoot at us." Peltier and his companions opened fire on the two agents from the fork in the road where their van had stopped. After that, shooting erupted from all directions.

"We have been hit" was heard on the two-way radio.

It seems certain that the agents then crawled out of their cars and attempted to take cover behind them. Special Agent Adams, still traveling in his FBI sedan several miles away and hearing the radio transmissions, asked urgently: "Where are you? Where are you right now?"

The government's briefs and evidence tell a vivid story: Williams, apparently crouched low to avoid fusillade, hurriedly gave their location and directions to the Jumping Bull compound, scene of the shooting. Rifle fire could be heard on the car radio and Adams, not familiar with the area, had to get directions from two Bureau of Indian Affairs police officers, Frank

Two Bulls and James Pacer, who also accompanied him to the area.

By this time, several other agents and police were racing to the scene. But the distance was simply too great. Rifle fire continued to be heard on the car radio.

Then a desperate Ron Williams called, "Hurry and get on the high hill and give us some cover or we'll be killed." This was the last transmission.

The Indians, firing from several different directions, were using standard-issue M-1 military rifles, AR-15 semiautomatic assault rifles, and other high-velocity small-calibre weapons. The volume of the incoming fire was extremely heavy. The besieged agents could not have lasted long. Williams's only weapon was his standard service revolver; Coler had a shotgun and a carbine in the trunk of his car. The agents were able to get off only five rounds.

While this murderous fire was raining on them from all directions, the agents must have frantically decided to get the rifles from the trunk of Coler's car to return the fire. In fact, Coler's trunk lid was found open.

Both agents were then hit almost simultaneously by long-range rifle fire. The first bullet to strike home traveled through the open trunk lid and struck Coler's right arm, nearly tearing it off at the shoulder. Though his immediate blood loss was massive, he somehow managed to crawl through the dirt and gravel to another side of his car out of the line of gunfire. He then surely lost consciousness.

Agent Williams had been hit almost the second after he had dispatched the last radio communication for help. The bullet tore through his left shoulder, traveled under his arm and into his side. However, despite his excruciating pain, Williams tore off his own blood-drenched shirt and attempted to apply a tourniquet to Coler's arm. At this point, Williams was, for all practical purposes, alone.

Rescuers racing in furiously from several directions could still hear the sharp, cracking sounds of rifle fire on their car radios.

Then Williams was hit again, this time in the foot. The force of this injury undoubtedly knocked him to the ground. Now his right leg was useless and his left arm hung limply at his side. Agent Williams then, it seems, attempted to surrender.

The Indians, realizing there would be no further resistance from the injured agents, moved in for the kill.

Coler was lying on the ground, unconscious but alive. Williams was bleeding from four different wounds and could only rise to his knees. He saw Leonard Peltier, Dino Butler, and Robert Robideau striding toward him. The AR-15 of Peltier was then pointed at Williams's face. As a last gesture of defense Williams extended his right hand to protect himself and turned his head slightly to the right.

With Ron Williams's hand touching the barrel, the killer fired. The bullet or bullets tore through the agent's hand, into his face, and then ripped away the back side of his head. Mercifully, death was instantaneous.

The murderers then moved to Coler, who was prostrate. Peltier pointed a weapon at his head at point-blank range and fired. The bullet demolished most of the agent's forehead and splattered blood in all directions. Despite the massive damage, the shot was not fatal. The killers realized this. Again the gun, only a few inches from the agent's face, was fired. This time the bullet entered through his jaw and exploded inside his head. The two FBI men were now dead.

Special Agent J. Gary Adams, racing at top speed most of the way, arrived just after Coler and Williams had been slain. As he and the Bureau of Indian Affairs officers with him approached the first house in the Jumping Bull compound, their cars were sprayed with rifle fire. Adams was pinned down most of the afternoon by a torrent of gunfire. Because the law enforcement officers did not know the fate of Special Agents Coler and Williams until late in the afternoon, they kept in mind my orders to avoid open warfare. Little firing was done by them. A great deal of firing, however, was done by the Indians in the compound. Finally, at approximately 5:00 P.M., it was determined that Coler and Williams had been dead since early afternoon.

At that point authorities opened up with every weapon they had. The volume of firepower and tear gas was too much for the Indians. They fled into the darkness to a complex of hills and ravines beyond the grasslands. One Indian was killed in the fire-fight.

Horror-struck, we at the FBI had to contain our anger. Despite our feelings, it was our duty to conduct ourselves as responsible officers of the American law-enforcement community. I called the families of the slain agents and expressed my condolences and the sympathy of the Bureau. I then made plans to attend the two funerals in California.

For the next day or so, however, I stayed at my desk in Washington, closely following one of the most intensive manhunts in FBI history.

I flew to Los Angeles on June 30 to attend the funerals of Jack Coler and Ronald Williams. This was one duty of my position that was always most difficult for me to deal with.

My heart went out to the families of these young agents, both only twenty-six years old. During a brief graveside service in Los Angeles, I presented Jack's widow, Peggy, with the American flag that had draped her husband's casket.

As I handed it to her, I said that it is the custom in this country to present the flag to the family of a man who has given his life for his country. Her husband was a brave man, I said, and we were thankful for his service and would cherish his memory.

I also presented the flag to Lloyd and Ellen Williams, the parents of Ronald Williams, whose funeral was held the same day. As I did so, I recalled a comment Rose Kennedy had once made: that it seemed somehow fundamentally improper for an older person to bury a younger person. I told Ron Williams's parents that their son lived as a good man and died as a valiant man.

The next day, July 1, I held a press conference at the Century Plaza Hotel in Los Angeles. With me were James B. Adams, deputy associate director of the FBI, Joseph Trimbach, Minneapolis special agent-in-charge, and Special Agent J. Gary Adams. We discussed Pine Ridge and Jumping Bull. Explaining what we knew about the sequence of events leading up to the shooting, I told reporters that the Bureau and other law-enforcement agencies were now working round the clock in this investigation. No matter what happened, I stressed, those responsible for the killings would be brought to trial.

As might be imagined, my journey to California had been a very sorrowful one. As I recall, it was pouring rain when I boarded the plane that night to return to Washington. I was exhausted—both physically and emotionally.

Back in Washington I kept my ear to the investigation. Our men conducted a sweep of the entire Pine Ridge area and ultimately inspected virtually every village and remote settlement in the 4,300-square-mile reservation. The search resembled, in many ways, an infantry operation. Our agents toted automatic weapons and were accompanied by helicopters, jeeps, and spotter planes. All roads leading to Pine Ridge were sealed off.

The investigation was also national in scope. Local FBI field offices and Bureau headquarters researched the background of every imaginable suspect. Finally, on November 25, 1975, after a painstaking investigation over a period of many months, a federal grand jury in Rapid City indicted four members of the American Indian Movement for the premeditated murder of two FBI agents during the performance of their official duties. Those charged were Leonard Peltier, 31; Robert Eugene Robideau, 29; Darrelle Dean Butler, 33; and James Theodore Eagle, 20.

When the indictments were handed down, all four were either serving time or being sought for a variety of law violations.

Eagle was serving a six-year sentence following his conviction for another crime. (Ultimately, murder charges were dismissed against Jimmy Eagle because the government felt that the evidence against him was not sufficient to assure a conviction.)

The very day the Jumping Bull murder indictments were returned, Darrelle Butler was convicted in U.S. District Court in Pierre, South Dakota, and sentenced to a two-year imprisonment for the unlawful possession of a firearm.

Robideau was incarcerated in Wichita, Kansas, awaiting trial stemming from the explosion of a station wagon containing ammunition and homemade bombs.

The fourth, Leonard Peltier, was a federal fugitive who had been wanted by the FBI since August 1974 for unlawful flight to avoid prosecution for an attempted murder in Milwaukee. On December 19, 1975, we added Peltier to the FBI's ten-most-wanted list.

Less than two months later, on February 6, 1976, Leonard Peltier was apprehended by the Royal Canadian Mounted Police near Hinton, Alberta. The United States requested that Peltier be returned to this country to face a variety of charges, including his participation in the murder of the two FBI agents at Jumping Bull. On December 18, 1976, following the usual delays attendant to extradition proceedings, the Canadian government returned Peltier to the United States to face trial for his crimes.

Though I wouldn't have said so at the time, it's fortunate that his return to the U.S. came too late for him to be tried with his codefendants, Robideau and Butler.

During this same period, government prosecutors had begun the immense task of sorting through a mountain of evidence and background information to prepare their case against AIM defendants Robideau and Butler. The trial was slated for summer 1976. Before it began, however, still another tragic event associated with Wounded Knee came to my personal attention.

Anna Mae Aquash, a thirty-one-year-old Canadian Indian known to be active in AIM, mysteriously died. Her death remains, to my knowledge, a mystery. Let me recount what we do know.

The body of an unknown woman was found by a South Dakota rancher on his property located on the Pine Ridge Indian Reservation about seventy miles from Wounded Knee.

Roger Amiott said he was repairing a fence on his property about 3:00 P.M. on February 24, 1976, when he spotted a fully clothed woman's body at the bottom of a thirty-foot embankment. Amiott did not recognize the woman and contacted the Bureau of Indian Affairs police. BIA officials and an FBI agent were dispatched to the ranch. The decomposed body was taken to Pine Ridge Public Hospital for an autopsy and, we hoped, for identification.

At the request of the Bureau of Indian Affairs, Dr. W.O. Brown, a pathologist who had performed several postmortem examinations for the BIA, conducted an autopsy. Brown determined that she had been dead for seven to ten days and that "she died of exposure." An FBI agent was present during the customary photographing of the body. Photographs of the dead woman were circulated on the Pine Ridge Reservation. No one recognized her.

Because of the difficulty of obtaining fingerprints, the FBI agent who had assisted with the photography suggested that her hands be removed and sent to our Identification Division in Washington for examination. This macabre-sounding procedure is used frequently in cases where identification is difficult. After the autopsy and removal of hands, the body was buried at Holy Rosary Cemetery at Pine Ridge on March 3.

The Identification Division swiftly completed its work, determining that the dead person was one Anna Mae Aquash, a Canadian Indian from Nova Scotia and a federal fugitive wanted for violations of the National Firearms Act and a bond default. A dispatch with this information was sent immediately to our liaison representative in Ottawa, with the request that Canadian authorities notify the next of kin.

On March 5 the relatives of Anna Mae Aquash were apprised of her death and we released the story of her demise to the news media. That day we, the FBI, also contacted the U.S. attorney's office in Rapid City to request a court order for exhuming the body. Four days later, March 9, the court permitted exhumation for "purposes of obtaining X-rays and further medical information." The Aquash family lawyer, Bruce Ellison of the Wounded Knee Legal Defense Offense Committee, requested that an "independent" autopsy of Anna Mae's body be conducted by Dr. Garry Peterson of Minneapolis. On March 11 her body was exhumed and the second autopsy was performed.

Dr. Peterson made a discovery that caused all of us significant embarrassment. A bullet wound was found below and to the rear of the right ear. Dr. Peterson said that Anna Mae Aquash had been shot at close range and that this kind of wound was common in "execution-type" slayings.

A storm of protest followed. It was predictable and justified.

"What goes on here?" was a reasonable question to ask in a case like this, and it seemed every newspaper in North America was asking it.

The Canadian government demanded an immediate investigation by the U.S. Justice Department, as did the U.S. Civil Rights Commission.

Senator James G. Abourezk of South Dakota called upon Attorney General Edward Levi to investigate thoroughly "the activities of the FBI in the entire affair."

The simple truth was the bullet wound in the woman's head somehow went unobserved by an experienced pathologist, Dr. Brown. Nonetheless, many believed we at Bureau headquarters were attempting to cover up the real cause of her death. Some were actually convinced that since Anna Mae Aquash was associated with AIM and knew Dennis Banks, an Oglala murder defendant, the FBI had murdered her in retaliation for the slaying of Agents Coler and Williams. Others thought she had been an FBI informant and was executed by vengeful members of AIM. Suggestions also had it that, since she had been so active in Indian affairs, she would almost certainly have been identified immediately by BIA and FBI officials.

Thus, upon orders from Attorney General Levi, the Aquash matter came under review by the General Crimes Section of the Justice Department Criminal Division.

On May 18 Thomas O. Enders, the American ambassador to Canada, called me at my office in Washington. Enders said he was concerned that the AIM group might use violence in forthcoming demonstrations as a result of the Aquash case. He asked me if our people were actively investigating the matter. I told him that her case was high on our list of priorities but that we had been unsuccessful so far.

Nine days later, May 27, I issued a lengthy statement to the media about the mysterious circumstances of Anna Mae Aquash's death. I provided a fairly extensive chronology of the case and, insofar as I could determine, the involvement of the FBI in the entire matter. The case was under intensive investigation, and the FBI officials involved in the discovery, and photography, of the body could not possibly have recognized her because of her advanced state of decomposition.

Furthermore, I pointed out, after the positive identification and autopsy, the follow-up investigation—including the exhumation request—was actually initiated by the FBI. The FBI investigates violations of thirteen major types of crimes on Indian Reservations, I explained, but such investigations commence only after the fact. The FBI is an investigative organization, I stressed, not a police force or a protective organization.

Though the investigation into the eerie demise of Anna Mae Aquash continued for a long time, as far as I know neither the FBI nor the General Crimes Division of the Justice Department ever solved the case.

The trial of Robert Eugene Robideau and Darrelle Dean Butler for the shooting deaths of FBI Agents Coler and Williams began June 7, 1976, before Judge Edward McManus, United States District Court, Northern District of Iowa, Cedar Rapids. I was subpoenaed by AIM defense attorneys (including William Kunstler) as a defense witness. Also called for the defense were Senator Frank Church of Idaho and Representative Otis Pike of New York. Judge McManus ruled that testimony from myself, as FBI director, and the senator and congressman, would be necessary for Robideau's and Butler's adequate defense.

Defense lawyers hoped to demonstrate that FBI agents and other government officials had been involved in a campaign of harassing AIM members and that the FBI itself had created an atmosphere of provocation and confrontation that finally led to the two slayings. The defense would prove that "the Indians lived in a constant state of fear of FBI intervention in their private affairs, and even FBI persecution." This forced the Indians to not only arm themselves but to use those arms whenever their emotions got the best of them.

The government, of course, disagreed with this line of reasoning. Furthermore, there was unmistakable physical evidence that connected defendants Robideau and Butler to the crime. Finally, both defendants, said the prosecution, had admitted to jail cellmates their direct participation in the crime. The prosecutor stressed it was nearly impossible to conceive that mere FBI investigations had actually caused the murders.

I testified at the trial on July 7 for more than four hours. In response to questioning by Kunstler I denied that, during my term as director, the Bureau intentionally harassed or disrupted Indian activities. I informed the court that the counterintelligence programs known as Cointelpro—FBI undercover activities directed against certain groups in our society—had been discontinued in 1971 and that no other programs had replaced it.

At another point, Kunstler asked why helicopters, aircraft, and battle gear had been supplied to FBI agents at the Pine Ridge Indian Reservation.

The question was manifestly absurd and he knew it. I told the court that the special equipment was issued, obviously, to protect the lives of our agents.

Kunstler's next question was even more inflammatory: Was life on the reservation more dangerous than in other parts of the country?

I replied sharply that life on this particular reservation was evidently dangerous to FBI personnel. Two of our agents had been murdered there. I strongly defended the Bureau's conduct in dealing with the Native American population in general, and with the people of Pine Ridge in particular.

Under direct question, I informed the court that the Bureau had issued a nationwide alert about potential violence by American Indians during the preceding July 4 weekend.

"Did you have proof of such a threat?" William Kunstler asked.

"Proof, no. But our informants had notified us that AIM was talking about using Independence Day to make their own statement. In my opinion, this was enough to issue an alert."

I defended this action by explaining that the Bureau was in the profession of preventing violence, and the issuance of such an alert was standard law-enforcement precautionary procedure.

"And how might law-enforcement officials respond to such an alert from FBI headquarters in Washington?" Kunstler asked.

"By being alert," I replied. "An alert is not a call to arms. Law enforcement officials are not easily stampeded into a defensive action. No guns would be drawn. This kind of memo was for purposes of internal safety only, to alert officials of the possibilities of violence."

Attorney Kunstler then asked me about the use of FBI informants.

I told him that we regularly used informants to provide us with information on individuals, but not necessarily on organizations.

At one juncture Kunstler asked me if citizens have a right to protect themselves.

"Certainly," I replied. "If individuals are threatened or feel threatened."

"Exactly, exactly. No more questions, Your Honor," he said, satisfied.

The point he was making was obvious: The Indians inside the cluster of houses near Jumping Bull compound felt threatened by the arrival of Agents Coler and Williams on June 26, 1975; and because of this they shot the two agents in self-defense. That reasoning was so preposterous that I could not even imagine it being advanced in a court of law. Carried to its logical extreme, it puts every law enforcement officer in the country in the position of being a "threat" to the public—and therefore a fit and justifiable target for any kook carrying a gun.

I was glad when the questioning concluded. It was my feeling then, as it is now, that little, if anything, was proved or disproved by my testimony.

In the end, after five days of deliberation, a jury of four women and eight men found the defendants not guilty.

Thus, for whatever the role they might have played in the murder of our two agents, defendants Robideau and Butler would not be punished.

While it is, of course, difficult to second-guess jury verdicts, there are several factors that I am sure contributed to the government's loss in this trial.

The judge had allowed the defense to, in effect, put the government on trial for all of the wrongs, both real and imagined, that had been done to the Indian people in the last 285 years.

Also, a lengthy recess was declared after the government's case had been completed but before the presentation of the defense case. Thus, once both sides had been presented, the facts concerning the defendant's guilt were no longer fresh in jurors' minds, whereas the facts concerning the defense contentions were.

Most importantly, two of the government's best witnesses, Michael Anderson and Angie Long Visitor, could never be found by the government to be served their trial subpoenaes. It was the opinion of the government's chief trial counsel that both had been hidden away by friends of the defense. Without the testimony of these two witnesses, the evidence implicating Robideau and Butler was largely circumstantial. In fact, the eyewitness testimony established little more than that they were present.

Only Leonard Peltier remained as a defendant in the case. Following extradition from Canada, Peltier stood trial in the United States. On April 18, 1977, in the United States District Court for the District of North Dakota—in Fargo, North Dakota—he was convicted, following a one-month trial, of murdering Agents Coler and Williams. On June 1 Judge Paul Benson sentenced Leonard Peltier to two consecutive life terms in prison.

The reason for the different outcome of the Peltier trial becomes apparent when one examines the record. Both Angie Long Visitor and Michael Anderson testified at the second trial. This didn't come easily. To ensure her appearance, Angie Long Visitor had to be arrested as a material witness.

With their testimony and the fact that Judge Benson did not allow the trial to be sidetracked onto irrelevant issues, the proof of Leonard Peltier's guilt was overwhelming. He was the leader of the group living in the Jumping Bull compound. He was in the vehicle that the agents followed into the area. He started the fire-fight that ensued. He was observed repeatedly firing his rifle from the area where the red and white van was parked. While no witness would admit seeing the final coups de grace of the two agents, he was observed down by the agents' bodies. A ballistics expert testified that a shell casing, ejected into the open trunk of Agent Coler's Bureau vehicle was from Peltier's rifle. Finally, following the murders, he took Jack Coler's revolver and kept it in his possession for several months.

And so, at long last, the tragic events of Wounded Knee ended. I still recall the passion and fury of those times. I know, according to Census Bureau statistics and to what I've personally seen, that American Indians are the poorest and most troubled minority group in the United States. I recall well the temper of those times. Nonetheless, I simply cannot forget the truly savage attack on our men at Wounded Knee. The memory of this incident haunts and saddens me to this day.

10

The Death of John Fitzgerald Kennedy

My Appraisal after Leaving the Director's Chair

IN 1963 I was the chief of police in Kansas City.

On my agenda for November 22 were the routines of a normal working day—attending committees, reviewing reports, and a regular Friday morning meeting with city officials.

I recall the day as being clear and crisp, with a hint of Indian summer in the air. I had just returned from a quick lunch following the city fathers' meeting, and was shuffling through some mail when my normally reserved secretary, Margaret Richardson, burst into my office.

"Chief, President Kennedy has been shot in a Dallas parade. They think that Lyndon Johnson was also hit . . . !"

For a reason I do not understand to this day, I assumed that President Kennedy had been shot in the right arm near the elbow, and that Vice-President Johnson had been hit in the shoulder. All would be well, I thought.

Nevertheless, I turned on the radio. It was chaos. No one knew exactly what had happened. Each news flash was more urgent than the one before—all conflicting with one another. Margaret and I listened to this for perhaps ten minutes before deciding it would be a while before the facts were known. We agreed to check on the story in ten or fifteen minutes. I turned off the radio and we both went back to our desks.

I next sorted through some departmental correspondence. At

about half-past the hour I walked out to her desk. She was gazing out the window, her back to me as I entered her office. I put my correspondence on her desk and asked, "Any news?"

She turned and looked directly at me. Her eyes were flooded with tears.

"He died."

"Who died?" I couldn't believe we were having this conversation.

"President Kennedy," she replied. "He was shot in the head. Isn't it terrible?"

In my career I had, like most law-enforcement personnel, witnessed a considerable amount of heart-wrenching tragedy. Sadness goes with the territory. One becomes not necessarily immune to it, but, in some way, insulated against it. Not this time. President Kennedy's death staggered me.

I said nothing, nor did Margaret. I returned to my office, opened the blinds, and looked out over downtown Kansas City. I stood there in silence for about fifteen minutes. As Eric Sevareid expressed it later, "One simply cannot accept the fact that such grace and intellect can be shattered in just an instant of time."

By this time the whole story had begun to unfold. In addition to the president, Governor John Connally of Texas, not Lyndon Johnson, had also been hit. The governor would live, however.

The next four days in American history represented, from a mass-communication standpoint, the greatest single tragedy witnessed by the greatest number of people in history. In its culmination, every section of the globe watched, prayed, and wept as the Roman Catholic sacraments for the soul of John Fitzgerald Kennedy were administered that terrible November day so long ago.

I, like millions of other Americans, read many of the books on JFK after his death. The very bulk of the literature about him made him seem, in many ways, larger than life itself. In connection with this, another phenomenon also developed in time: The questions and theories and doubts about the assassination itself—with all the events leading up to it, and the circumstances surrounding it.

To unearth the ultimate truth of the assassination, insofar as the truth could be known, the Warren Commission conducted an extraordinarily intensive ten-month investigation into the entire episode.

At last the Commission completed what turned out to be the largest investigation of its type in American history. Having assembled more than three thousand documents, photographs, and objects related to the assassination, together with twenty-six volumes of testimony and interviews, its final report comprised more than ten million words.

Ironically, even this gargantuan quest for the truth did not answer all questions about the assassination. Many doubts linger even today. But that shouldn't surprise us; there's precedent for this, too. Facts surrounding the Lincoln assassination still defy understanding.

In early 1975, while serving as FBI director, I looked into the bizarre new charge that the Central Intelligence Agency was somehow involved in the killing. A photograph of a man identified as E. Howard Hunt placed the former CIA employee at the scene of the shooting in Dallas. We examined this matter completely, and concluded that Hunt was not the man in the picture—and the CIA was in no way involved in the president's death.

In the summer of that year talk of the assassination surfaced again. This time it concerned a startling piece of information about Lee Harvey Oswald and the Dallas field office of the Federal Bureau of Investigation . . . data withheld from the Warren Commission by the FBI.

Let's begin at the beginning.

I was contacted on July 7, 1975, by Tom Johnson, the highly respected newspaperman who was then the editor of the *Dallas Times Herald.* Johnson said that he had obtained—from a confidential source—some previously unknown facts about one of Lee Harvey Oswald's activities immediately before the assassination.

"This information has been buried for twelve years . . . and it directly involves the Bureau," he said. "I thought you should see it first."

"I agree," I said. "But what do you mean by *buried*?"

"We have conclusive proof, developed from previously untapped sources, that the FBI withheld information from the Warren Commission, and every other assassination investigation since."

"Can you be specific?" I asked.

"It seems that Lee Harvey Oswald had actually visited the FBI office in Dallas just two weeks before he shot the President," Johnson said. "Before he left the office he dropped off a threatening note to the FBI agent who was investigating the case at that time," he added. "Have you heard this story?"

I told Johnson I'd heard a lot of Lee Harvey Oswald tales over the years, but never one that started like this.

Bit by bit he told me the whole story, as he knew it to be.

Following a brief but stormy call at the Dallas FBI office, Oswald left an anonymous note for James P. Hosty, Jr., the agent responsible for maintaining surveillance and files on Oswald, in which he threatened Hosty if the FBI agent insisted upon continuing to investigate both Lee Harvey, and more especially, Marina Oswald.

Though the exact wording of the note has been lost to us—thereby causing much debate as to precisely what the note did say—it apparently made very clear Oswald's objections to the continuing FBI investigation of his family. The fact that the agent had contacted Marina was of paramount concern to Lee Harvey Oswald. He didn't want his wife questioned. If contact was absolutely necessary, contact him.

"As I understand the situation, this is exactly what he went to the FBI office to say. And that's about what the note said. But we'll never know. The FBI never reported the visit by Oswald—and then they buried the note after the assassination!" Tom Johnson concluded.

Shocked by this revelation, I asked him to send me the full story in writing, and give me some time to check on it. Johnson agreed, requesting only that I get back to him first, when I felt comfortable about releasing it to the media.

I understood that, and agreed.

I immediately called Attorney General Edward Levi about the matter. He agreed that I should check it out right away. I soon learned that the worst of it was painfully true.

On the day of Oswald's death, Gordon Shanklin, special agent-in-charge of the Dallas field office, reportedly told Hosty that he never wanted to see that Oswald note again. At that point only a few people in the Dallas field office knew of Oswald's visit and note. And the field office people hoped to keep it that way. They certainly did not want Washington headquarters to hear about it.

Buried for twelve years was this FBI coverup. Why did the FBI people do this? The reason, at least in the beginning, was easy enough to understand: hide the news from Hoover.

Nobody, especially the head of the Dallas office, wanted to make it appear that the FBI had been delinquent in the performance of its surveillance duty, particularly when the death of a president of the United States may have resulted.

To the world at large, they must have reasoned, it might look as if the FBI had the assassin within its grasp, and then let him get away. To J. Edgar Hoover in Washington it most certainly would have looked that way. Such a story would have ignited an inferno of retribution in Hoover. Immediate dismissals and demotions would have followed. No questions asked, no explanations allowed.

Coincidentally, just before this information reached my desk in 1975, Gordon Shanklin decided to retire from the FBI, ending his career one week prior to my call from Tom Johnson.

In a brief conversation with Shanklin, I ascertained that he didn't know the answer to the key question: Did Bureau headquarters in Washington ever find out about Oswald's visit? Frankly, he said, he doubted it. If they had, he wouldn't have left the Bureau at his convenience.

"How about the Oswald note?" I asked.

"Note? What note?" Shanklin replied.

Finding more corroborative evidence seemed an impossible task. In November of 1963, Hoover and Clyde Tolson ran the FBI. By the fall of 1975 both men were dead.

However, in an effort to get any information that might be available on the story, I contacted Al Belmont, who as special assistant to Hoover at the time of Kennedy's death, was the highest ranking FBI line officer now living.

Sadly, Al Belmont was terminally ill. Nevertheless, I flew to California to talk to him. He was unable to add anything to the information I already had. He told me he had never heard the story about the Oswald visit to our field office. Nor was he aware of the threatening note left by Oswald.

Officially, and for the record, the matter had been squelched in Dallas. And although I still had my lingering doubts, I decided I could not give any more of my time to the episode. Whatever coverup there was, it clearly got no further than the Dallas group, who just plain didn't want Hoover coming down on them during all the heat of that post-assassination period.

I put through a call to Tom Johnson in Dallas.

"Mr. Johnson, feel free to release the story, and please accept my thanks for the way you handled it."

The story broke on the front page of the *Dallas Times Herald* on August 31 and then in the *New York Times* on September 1. It was a sensation from coast to coast.

Following the disclosure of the Oswald visit and note—and the subsequent destruction of the note by the FBI—the Civil and Constitutional Rights Subcommittee of the House Judiciary Committee looked into the matter in some detail, as did the Senate Intelligence Committee. Both groups ended up exactly where I did. Having questioned those involved, and finding little that could be added or deleted, both decided that this was a matter that "cannot be resolved."

Since 1975 I have been asked countless times about my views on the Kennedy assassination.

Many theories have been advanced and many questions raised. My own thoughts have remained constant. Lee Harvey Oswald, a classic loser, motivated by a twisted desire to "punish" a society that would not find a place for him, acting alone, assassinated John F. Kennedy. But Oswald, over the years, has not been my primary concern. Not Oswald, not his bent mind. Nor have I become involved with the ballistics elements of the case, or the precise nature of the president's injuries, or the various post-assassination theories about the Mafia, the Orient connection, the true Jack Ruby role, etc. To this day I am troubled not so much by how it happened as how it *could* happen, particularly in light of all the significant information on Lee Harvey Oswald before the assassination.

Lee Harvey Oswald's record was known for several years by the FBI, by the CIA, by the State Department, by the Office of Naval Intelligence, and by the U.S. Consulate in Moscow. He had a dishonorable discharge from the Marines, had been a self-proclaimed Communist for years, had renounced his U.S. citizenship in 1959, had lived in the Soviet Union, had married the niece of a Soviet secret police officer, had a pro-Castro profile as long as a billy club—and was outspokenly anti-American. Any way you look at it, those are noteworthy credentials on anyone's record. Notwithstanding, the various government intelligence agencies did not pool—or, worse, disseminate—their knowledge of the man. Thus, nobody ever came to the conclusion that Oswald could be a threat to the life of JFK.

During 1975 and 1976, two congressional panels—the Subcommittee on Civil and Constitutional Rights of the House Judiciary Subcommittee and the U.S. Senate's "Church Committee"—examined the assassination once again. More hearings were held and more research undertaken. New ideas emerged, old ones were revived (including that of the more-than-one-assassin theory). I was not convinced, however, of the likelihood that any of these rehashes would ever surface anything important. Though my schedule didn't permit me to personally follow up on any of this material, nothing substantive came out of them.

In 1978 I released 100,000 pages of the FBI's Kennedy assassination files in response to the first such request under the Freedom of Information Act. When I retired as Bureau director that year, I regarded the Kennedy assassination as a piece of personal unfinished business. Though the subject was never an obsession with me, over the years the matter would lie dormant in my mind for months at a time, only to resurface again nagging for my attention.

Might there not be, I've often mused, an entirely new approach to the subject that would yield new information on, and as a result, a new conclusion about, the assassination? Somewhere there must be a missing link. A career in investigative work taught me to be wary of loosely assembled solutions. I felt that these pieces didn't quite fit together. The solution to what vexed me, however, was not necessarily in finding any missing pieces, but in better understanding the nature of the puzzle itself.

As mentioned, the material available is probably unreadable in one lifetime. In addition to the Warren Commission's ten-million-word report, the FBI file on the assassination is the largest ever created by the Bureau on any single subject. As director, I had access to all of it and, as time permitted, I reviewed portions of it. I also read any number of the so-called "assassination books." At some point I became aware that one man had never fully told his story from his own vantage point: FBI Agent James P. Hosty, Jr., the Dallas-based agent assigned to the Oswald case in July 1962, who had tracked the Oswalds for nearly a year-and-a-half—and later was an agent under me when I was FBI director.

Hosty's name is a permanent part of the Oswald-Kennedy drama. His phone number was listed among Lee Harvey Oswald's personal effects when the assassin was captured by the Dallas Police Department. The agent's story reveals elements of the tragedy in Dallas that have never been explored before.

His experience helps, in some measure, to answer for me the critical question: How could the assassination have happened?

And, with an eye to the future, its companion question: How could it have been prevented?

To answer these questions we must go back to the fall of 1959 when Lee Harvey Oswald renounced his citizenship and left for the U.S.S.R. He was, he boasted, "defecting to the Soviet Union."

"I hate the United States and all that it stands for," Oswald said at the time.

Because Oswald was a Fort Worth native, news of his defection made the Fort Worth papers. The FBI, the CIA, the State Department, and the Office of Naval Intelligence all opened files on him when his defection became known. Observing all of this from within the Dallas FBI office was Agent Jim Hosty.

For Oswald, getting into Russia permanently was a complicated and discouraging business. The Russians did not welcome him with open arms, at least not in the manner that Oswald felt they should have. Once in the U.S.S.R., Oswald disappeared briefly, from November 1959 until January 1960. Then he surfaced in Minsk where he had been sent by the Soviet government to work in a radio factory. There, in 1961, Oswald met Marina Prusakova. They were married on April 30, 1961. And there he stayed until he began preparing for his return to the United States in May of 1962.

Marina had been raised by her aunt and uncle in the Soviet Union. Her uncle, Ilya Prusakov, was, as we later discovered, a Soviet MVD colonel—the MVD being the Soviet Union's Ministry of Internal Affairs. The MVD is "Big Brother," the police state apparatus by which the Soviet government maintains control of Soviet society.

The FBI kept tabs on Oswald by regularly reviewing the State Department and Naval Intelligence files. The Oswald intelligence file contained all the information on his attempt to renounce his U.S. citizenship, his application for Soviet citizenship, and his declared willingness to give the Soviets any technical information he may have learned as a radar technician in the Marine Corps. Soviet gratitude was apparently less than overwhelming—and the Soviet Union, for that matter, was somewhat less than the utopia that Oswald had expected. As early as the spring of 1961 he told our embassy in Moscow that he wished to return to the United States.

All things considered, our State Department treated Oswald with avuncular kindness. Rejecting his "defection" of barely two-and-a-half years earlier, it first cleared the way for his return. Then it provided him with the money to get home. (To his credit, Oswald paid it all back.)

He arrived at Love Field in Dallas on June 14, 1962, just thirty months after his melodramatic departure.

The State Department advised the FBI of this return. The Bureau was also in regular contact with U.S. Immigration and Naturalization Service concerning the return of this native son.

FBI Special Agent John W. Fain, of Fort Worth, saw Oswald's picture in the Fort Worth newspaper, contacted Oswald's mother and brother to determine when and where he could locate Lee Harvey Oswald, and began to prepare his list of questions. The FBI's primary concern then was to ascertain if Oswald had, in some way, been recruited by Soviet intelligence, what precisely he had been doing in Russia, and exactly what he had in mind to do now that he was back in the United States.

Oswald's FBI file had been assigned to Agent Fain because he had handled some matters about Oswald's defection in 1959. It was FBI policy to interview and prepare reports on returning defectors from Iron Curtain countries and report any unusual discoveries to the CIA. Thus, FBI policy dictated an immediate fact-finding interview with Oswald upon his return.

The first FBI–Oswald interview took place on June 26, 1962, twelve days after his return to the U.S. The interview was a disaster. In fact, it almost turned into a fistfight.

For an interview of this type to be useful, Bureau policy specifies that agents must develop the proper setting and mood. Usually an agent prepares himself carefully for such an interview, particularly so when intelligence matters of an Iron Curtain country are the focus. Thorough preparation is aimed at making the interview as productive as possible. Fain had been trying to set up a preliminary fact-finding meeting with Oswald when, suddenly, Lee Harvey Oswald walked into the Fort Worth FBI office unannounced.

"Here I am," he said. "What do you want to talk to me about?"

Agents Fain and Tom Carter were in the office when Oswald arrived. Oswald's surprise visit caught Fain completely off guard.

From the outset Oswald was so hostile and aggressive that Fain was unable to control the interview. Oswald denied that he had attempted to renounce his citizenship, denied that he attempted to obtain Soviet citizenship, and denied that he offered the benefits of his Marine radar training to the Soviets.

Asked why he defected in the first place, Oswald replied, "Because I wanted to see the country." He refused a lie detector test, saying that he resented the intrusion of the FBI into his private life. Oswald also declared that he had no connection with any Soviet intelligence activity.

"I don't want to relive the past," he shouted at the agent.

Fain and Oswald nearly squared off right there in Fain's office. From the beginning, dealing with Lee Harvey Oswald was no picnic for the FBI.

Agent Fain reported to the special agent-in-charge of the Dallas office that the interview had been most unsatisfactory, that he was less than trusting of Oswald's answers, and that he would attempt another interview with Oswald.

It was at this point that the Dallas-based FBI Agent Jim Hosty first became involved with Oswald's security file. Fain asked Hosty to check on Marina Oswald with the Immigration and Naturalization office in Dallas. This was in July 1962.

Agent Hosty went to the Immigration and Naturalization office in Dallas where Mrs. Oswald's records were kept. At that time she had been in this country almost a month. Hosty noted that she fit the criteria of an FBI regulation that required monitoring immigrants from Iron Curtain countries to ensure that they were not working in an industry vital to U.S. security. The Bureau also was always concerned when young, well-educated individuals came to this country from the Soviet Union or from Soviet bloc countries. Marina, still in her twenties, was a college graduate with a degree in pharmacology. Thus, from an age and educational standpoint, she fit the criteria correctly.

The FBI was, as always, looking for "sleepers," (or secret espionage agents) from the Soviet bloc. Agent Hosty thought it somewhat unusual that Marina was allowed to leave the Soviet Union with Oswald and come to the United States. The Soviets, not terribly generous about such matters, allow very few of their people to so casually leave the country. At that time Marina was only the third known case of a Soviet spouse to leave the U.S.S.R. with a non-Soviet spouse. Noting this, Hosty wrote a memorandum for her file. In it he recommended that she be interviewed in her own right, separate from her husband, according to regulations. He wanted her file to be kept open.

In the same month, July of 1962, our New York field office learned that Lee Harvey Oswald had sought information from the Soviet Embassy in Washington, D.C., about Russian newspapers and periodicals. The records show that in October he renewed his subscription to the *Daily Worker*, the U.S. Communist Party newspaper.

The second FBI–Oswald interview took place on August 16. This time Fain was accompanied by Agent Arnold J. Brown. The interview was held in Fain's car in front of Oswald's residence on Mercedes Street in Fort Worth. The session lasted nearly two hours. Again the FBI was concerned with Oswald's having been within the Soviet Union for nearly thirty months. The Bureau wanted to be certain that Oswald was not a KGB recruit, particularly in light of the fact that Oswald's wife still had close family ties in the Soviet Union. The Bureau's primary purpose was, of course, counterintelligence. Oswald, though much more placid this time, still evaded as many questions as he could.

Agent Fain and officials at FBI headquarters, however, were apparently satisfied that Oswald was not a security risk, that he was not violent, and that, as a sheet metal worker in Fort Worth, he was not working in a sensitive industry in this country. They, therefore, recommended that his file be placed in an inactive status, a decision routinely made by officials within the FBI's Soviet espionage section.

Two interesting sidelights, however, developed from this interview. First, Agent Fain had acquired Oswald's Fort Worth address from Oswald's brother, Robert. As a result, from that day forward, Lee Harvey refused to give his home address to his brother—and he began using a post office box as his address. Second, as Marina Oswald later testified before the Warren Commission, her husband had found the second FBI interview to be extremely upsetting. Though he clearly did not know what to do about it, he made it known to his wife that he didn't like being the object of FBI surveillance—and she was never to give them any information. By that time, August of 1962, Lee Harvey Oswald had already developed a strong antipathy toward the FBI and its agents—if he didn't have it before.

In October, when John Fain retired from the FBI, the Lee Harvey Oswald file was not reassigned. In fact, it was officially closed. At the time the Oswald case was regarded as merely routine, unworthy of any further attention.

Notwithstanding, it seemed curious to Agent Hosty in the Dallas office that the file was allowed to be closed. There were, in fact, two Oswald files, and both had been misclassified according to Jim Hosty. Marina's file was categorized as Pending/Inactive. Hosty thought her file should be held open, too. Her Russian birthright as well as her youth and her college education qualified her as a person to be monitored. Hosty later said he saw no reason to close the file on Lee Harvey Oswald. "The retirement of John Fain was certainly no reason to close it," he said.

"At that time," he has said, "we simply knew too little about either of them. Both cases called for more in-depth investigation. Both should have been kept open, actively pursued with in-depth interviews—and then a determination could have been made on the merits of knowledge gained."

We know that Oswald soon quit his sheet-metal job, and went

to the Texas Employment Commission in Dallas. Then, on October 12, he started work for a commercial advertising photography firm, a job he held nearly six months—a remarkable feat in light of his spotty employment record and obstreperous personality.

That same month Agent Hosty was given the assignment of reopening Marina Oswald's file. His instructions were to interview her in six months, which meant the FBI agent was to contact her in March of 1963.

As scheduled, on March 4, Jim Hosty turned his attention back to Marina Oswald. Her file, he noted, contained only a single memorandum, giving background data on Marina, plus her immigration card.

The memo revealed that she was Russian-born and college-educated. What the document failed to reveal was Marina's relationship to a colonel in the Soviet secret police. We weren't to learn that until after the assassination. Though Marina had nothing to do with the assassination (according to the Warren Report), this is one of the facts about her that supports Jim Hosty's "we-didn't-know-enough-about-either-one-of-them" charge.

Her immigration card proved that she had registered with U.S. immigration authorities in January 1963, as she was required to do by law. It also stated that she was living in Dallas, with an address on Elsbeth Street. Her file automatically cross-referenced to Lee Harvey Oswald, whose file contained the two reports written by John Fain concerning his two unsuccessful Oswald interviews, information about his defection from and return to this country, and the memo from the New York field office stating that Oswald was a recently renewed subscriber to the *Daily Worker.*

The Oswalds were not well-known in the Russian-speaking community of Dallas or Fort Worth. In early February 1963 they had, however, been invited to a party in Dallas which was attended by several Russian-speaking people.

There, the Oswalds met Ruth Paine, a Quaker who lived in Dallas. Mrs. Paine was studying the Russian language and eventually hoped to be fluent enough to teach it. She and Marina became close friends.

At about the same time, Oswald began pressuring his wife to return, without him but with their infant daughter, to the Soviet Union. We've never known what he had in mind. On February 17 Marina sent a request to the Soviet Embassy asking if she and her child might be allowed to return to the Soviet Union. The Soviet government said that the procedure would take about six months.

On March 11, 1963, Agent Hosty went to the Oswald's Elsbeth Street address, the one listed on Marina's immigration card. He discovered that Lee, Marina, and their child, June, had moved on March 3. Oswald's ex-landlady, Mrs. Mahlon Tobias, told Hosty that she had, in effect, kicked them out.

In her opinion, Mrs. Tobias said, the Oswalds had a bad domestic situation. They constantly fought. Oswald, she was certain, beat his wife. Too many loud arguments had forced Mrs. Tobias to expel them from her building. Hosty, speaking with Mrs. Tobias on her front porch, asked her the quickest way to the new Oswald residence.

"Right up there—214 West Neely," she replied, pointing.

Agent Hosty, deciding that the apparently tense Oswald domestic situation would not be conducive to a proper interview, jotted a note in his file to come back and interview the Oswalds in forty-five to sixty days. He notified his superiors at the Bureau of his follow-up activity on Marina. Also, in view of Oswald's newly opened subscription to the Communist newspaper, *Daily Worker,* Hosty recommended that Lee Harvey Oswald's FBI file be reopened. And it was, on March 26, just eight months before the Kennedy assassination.

About this time Oswald apparently began to think seriously of assassinating retired Major General Edwin A. Walker of the U.S. Army, a Dallas resident. General Walker was a staunch right-wing anti-communist and doubtless anathema to Oswald.

Klein's Sporting Goods Company in Chicago received an

order on March 13 for a 6.5-millimeter Mannlicher-Carcano Italian bolt-action rifle with a Japanese telescope. The rifle, bearing serial number C-2766, had been ordered by coupon, clipped from the February 1963 issue of *American Rifleman.* The order was shipped to A. Hidell, P.O. Box 2915, Dallas, the post office box rented by Lee Harvey Oswald. (Oswald used the alias Hidell for many of his questionable activities.)

All of this took place, it is important to remember, during the domestic cooling-off period that Agent Hosty had allowed the Oswalds after his March 11 discussion with Mrs. Tobias. So neither Hosty nor anyone else from the Bureau was in a position to observe Oswald's activities during this time.

On March 31 Marina took the now-famous picture of her husband holding his new mail-order rifle. The picture was snapped in the backyard of their rented Neely Street house in Dallas. This is the rifle that Oswald bought to kill General Walker—and used to kill John F. Kennedy.

Oswald lost his job at the photography firm on April 6. His self-esteem having suffered another blow, we can only assume that he brooded on what he might do to prove to himself that he could succeed at something. Four days later he attempted to kill General Walker.

Hiding in a wooded area across the street from the general's home, he fired a shot from about one hundred feet away. He missed, the bullet whizzing over the general's head and imbedding itself in a living room wall.

Oswald returned home extremely shaken by the experience. He told Marina what he had done, swearing her to secrecy—which she honored. Not until she was questioned under oath after the assassination did Marina Oswald discuss the matter.

On April 21 the New York FBI field office learned that Oswald had been in touch with the Fair Play for Cuba Committee in New York City. He had written and apprised the group of his distribution of Fair Play for Cuba pamphlets in Dallas.

Later that month Marina and daughter June went to live with friend Ruth Paine in Irving, and Oswald moved to New Orleans to look for work. There, on May 10, he took a laborer's job with a coffee-processing firm in that city.

Agent Hosty knew nothing of any of these activities. However, when he returned to the Neely Street house in Dallas on May 15, he found the Oswalds gone, this time with no forwarding address.

We now know that on May 9 Oswald rented a place to live in New Orleans. He called Marina at Ruth Paine's home and asked his wife to join him. Two days later Ruth drove Marina and June to New Orleans.

Early in June, Oswald opened another post office box, and on June 10 he wrote to the *Daily Worker* announcing that he had formed a branch office of the Fair Play for Cuba Committee in New Orleans.

An FBI informant picked up this information and notified Agent Hosty of where Oswald was living in New Orleans. Oswald's presence there also was verified by the New Orleans field office. Hosty then notified FBI headquarters in Washington that the Oswald file was being transferred to New Orleans. The New Orleans field office assumed control of the file in early September, now less than ninety days before the assassination.

Oswald lost his job in New Orleans on July 19, barely two months after he was hired. From then until August 9 no record of him exists. On that day, however, he again surfaced. Distributing Fair Play for Cuba literature in New Orleans, he was arrested for disturbing the peace. One week later, he was again arrested for disturbing the peace; this time he had been heatedly arguing politics with anti-Castro Cubans.

The New Orleans field office, now in charge of the Oswald case, had been investigating Oswald after his second arrest for disturbing the peace.

He was interviewed by New Orleans FBI Agent John Quigley. The interview was of little value. Oswald confirmed that he now lived in New Orleans and described many of his Fair Play for Cuba activities. During most of the interview Oswald was sullen, uncooperative, and evasive.

On August 17 and 21 Oswald appeared on a New Orleans radio program as a spokesman for the Fair Play for Cuba Committee. John Garabedian, a former editor with *Newsweek,* listened to those tapes some years later and wrote:

> Oswald's tone of voice was nasal, nervous, occasionally sing-song with a slight Southern "cajun" accent. The flow of words was rapid, rambling, evasive. The sentences were at times surprisingly articulate, but in their midst there was a strange emphasis on violence. Oswald saw forces working against liberty everywhere—in China, in the U.S. His views seemed those of a frustrated, besieged man who wanted desperately to be free. Oswald said he admired Fidel Castro because, he said with emotion, Castro was an "independent person" and not anyone's "puppet." He said "Russian imperialism was a very bad thing," and so was the "extreme . . dogmatic Communist system of Red China," but so was the "dog-eat-dog economy" of the U.S. Oswald became very emotional when speaking of people with whom he clearly identified—the exploited, the cheated, the losers. The phrases he chose take on startling significance in light of the assassination. The U.S., Oswald said, slashed the Cuban sugar quota, and cut the throats of Cubans. The U.S. was trying to destroy Cuba. Oswald's bitterness at his life exploded again when he talked about a "dog-eat-dog economy," though he wasn't, he insisted, condemning capitalism. "In the U.S., people do not depend on each other," said Oswald. "They have no feeling of nationality, no feeling of culture, no feeling of any ties whatsoever on a high level. It is every man for himself. That's what I mean by dog-eat-dog."

Following this, it appears, Lee Harvey Oswald began the final cycle of his lifelong erratic behavior.

Oswald said goodbye to Marina in New Orleans on September 23, 1963, and soon departed for Mexico. We know that he earlier told Marina that he was planning a trip to Mexico City as soon as possible. On September 17 he obtained a tourist card for the visit. Oswald insisted that Marina tell nobody about the trip. He wanted to go to the Soviet and Cuban embassies there to apply for visas, for Marina and June to return to Russia and for himself to travel to Cuba.

If we can follow his thinking at all, he must have felt that Marina and June could join him later in Cuba, or that he could join them in the Soviet Union. In any event, he was without a job in New Orleans, without money to pay the rent, and almost literally, a man without a country.

Ruth Paine, Marina's faithful Russian-speaking friend, picked up Marina and June and drove them back to Irving. And Oswald left for Mexico City two days later, arriving there September 27.

We've learned through several sources that Oswald lugged quite a bit of Communist propaganda with him to Mexico City, including newspaper clippings of his Fair Play for Cuba activities, background notes on his life in Russia, and Communist correspondence. All of it was no doubt designed to document his loyalty and importance to both the Cubans and the Russians.

The Bureau again lost touch with Oswald when he left New Orleans. Agent Hosty was not advised that Oswald was missing until October 3.

Oswald's stay in Mexico City apparently shaped the man's thinking irrevocably. He was there, we know, for one week, from September 27 through October 2. How he spent all of his time we don't know, but that he made numerous visits to the Cuban and Soviet embassies we are certain. The information was gathered through informants, wiretaps, surveillance cameras, and other types of foreign intelligence techniques.

We know that Oswald's first visit in Mexico City was to the Soviet Embassy. He informed the Russians, in effect, that he would like to have Soviet visas for himself and his family so that they could go to the Soviet Union as soon as possible. To an acquaintance he confided that the main reason he wanted the Soviets to expedite his visas to their country and also to Cuba was because "the FBI is making my life miserable" in the U.S.

According to Marina Oswald's later testimony before the Warren Commission, Oswald loathed the FBI and said so many times during the period the Bureau maintained a file on him. He came eventually to detest Agent Hosty, a man he had never met until the afternoon of November 22, 1963.

It was known at the time by members of the United States intelligence community, including the Central Intelligence Agency headquarters, and the FBI's Soviet espionage section— but not by the Dallas or New Orleans field offices (thus not by Agent Hosty)—that Oswald spoke with Valery Vladimrovich Kostikov at the Russian Embassy in Mexico City.

The importance of Kostikov cannot be overstated. As Jim Hosty wrote later: "Kostikov was the officer-in-charge for Western Hemisphere terrorist activities—including and especially assassination. In military ranking he would have been a one-star general. As the Russians would say, he was their Line V man— the most dangerous KGB terrorist assigned to this hemisphere!"

"When I first heard about the Oswald–Kostikov meeting, Kostikov was identified to me as a vice-consul," Hosty adds. "He was a lot more than that."

The information that Oswald talked to Kostikov at the Russian Embassy was obtained variously. One method was through CIA wiretaps of the embassy's phone in Mexico City. Oswald's call from the Cuban to the Russian Embassy, for instance, was tapped by our government. The Soviet Embassy was also being watched by ultrasensitive CIA surveillance cameras. What's more, the agency had some very highly placed informants within the embassy itself. Thus, the fact that Oswald met with this particularly dangerous KGB official is certain. Later testimony verified it. And various commissions, investigatory committees, and researchers have detailed Kostikov's functions.

It appeared that Oswald confided to the Soviets and the Cubans that he had information on a CIA plot to assassinate Fidel Castro. He would, he promised, provide all of this highly classified information in exchange for Soviet and Cuban visas for his family and himself respectively. It is possible to assume that at the Soviet Embassy he offered to kill President Kennedy.

The Soviets could have responded to Oswald in one of three

ways. First, they could have said, "No, you are crazy." Second, they could have said nothing. Or, third, they could have said, "Yes, we will help you."

Despite the Kostikov meeting I personally think the Soviets informed Oswald that they wanted no part of his scheme. In hindsight, it's apparent that the Soviets were less than impressed with Oswald. They advised him that it would take several months to process the visas for his family. The Soviet Embassy in Mexico City contacted the KGB authorities in Moscow for instructions. There was a substantial delay on the Oswald visa request, though we don't know exactly why.

However, the Cuban Embassy was told by its government in Havana that Oswald could receive his visa if he had actual proof showing that he had in fact received a Soviet entry visa. By the time this Cuban decision was made, Oswald had already returned to Dallas.

Oswald, as indicated, told the Cuban Embassy officials much the same. But here he definitely offered to kill President Kennedy. He may have made the offer because of the efforts by the Kennedy Administration to destabilize the Castro regime. Oswald may also have been influenced by Castro's public threat on September 9 against American leaders. In any event, our informant "Solo," a double-agent, met with Castro after the assassination.

Castro himself verified that Oswald had offered to kill the American president and that the offer was made directly by Oswald to Cuban officials at their embassy in Mexico City. The dictator thought at the time that the offer might be a deliberate provocation by the U.S. government or that Oswald was simply a madman. It seems certain that Castro just didn't know what to do with him. And not knowing, they dismissed him.

Very likely Oswald was in a dangerous frame of mind at the conclusion of his Mexico City adventure. Consider what thoughts must have been going through his head.

He probably had spent his last dime to go to Mexico City— only to learn that the Communist world had no interest in him. Doubtless, anger welled within him when the Soviets informed him that it would be months before his family could obtain visas. Nor did he know when he would receive his Cuban visa. He had no reason to believe it would be soon.

He had demonstrated his incapability of holding a job for any length of time. Now he must face the prospect of not only finding a job, but also keeping it. His life at this time, we must realize, was barely above the poverty line.

On top of all that, Oswald, evidently disillusioned by his years in the Soviet Union, had returned to the United States with a wife about whom he now apparently cared very little—a wife and a baby.

And now, dissatisfied again with the United States, he tried to leave a second time, only to discover that he wasn't wanted in the Soviet bloc.

Where, he must have been asking himself, do I turn now?

The ride back from Mexico City was long and grim for Lee Harvey Oswald. His life had no purpose. He was at wit's end. I'm inclined to believe that by the time he set foot back in this country he had made a decision to do something dramatic. One thing is certain. He was a walking powder keg in early October 1963.

Oswald returned to the U.S. on October 3, 1963. A few days later he learned that Marina was still with Ruth Paine in Irving, Texas. He journeyed there to see his wife, and then went into Dallas to seek work. Oswald moved into a rooming house and started work for the Texas School Book Depository as an order processor in the textbook warehouse. He was paid one dollar an hour.

Central Intelligence Agency headquarters in Washington knew of the Oswald-Kostikov meeting in Mexico City right after it happened. On October 10, a week after Oswald's return to this country, the CIA informed Bureau headquarters, the State Department, Naval Intelligence, and other members of the intelligence community that Oswald had visited the Russian Embassy while in Mexico City. The Dallas field office, however, was not notified of anything. The New Orleans FBI office was still in control of the Oswald file. Thus, all developments on Oswald were sent there in the normal course of business.

Eight days later the CIA released to the FBI the news that Oswald had met with V.V. Kostikov at the Soviet Embassy. In this communique—addressed solely to the FBI—Kostikov was identified as "vice-consul," with no reference made to his high-level KGB connection. Forwarded to the New Orleans office with explicit instructions "to advise no other agency of this Oswald–Kostikov meeting," this memo underscores the reluctance-to-share attitude prevalent throughout all government agencies at that time. Not only did the CIA withhold the true identity of Kostikov, but they also made it clear that the information they were willing to mete out was of "the highest confidentiality," and should go no further.

Jim Hosty, who probably had spent more time with the file of Lee Harvey Oswald than anyone else, learned of Oswald's historically critical trip to Mexico City by accident. Here's how that came about.

Agent Hosty heard from an informant that Marina Oswald had left New Orleans in a car bearing Texas license plates on September 23. She was traveling with her daughter, June, in a car going west being driven by another woman. It was not hard for Hosty to guess who the driver was, or where the trio was bound.

Lee Harvey Oswald was not with them, however. No concern. Without the information about Oswald's visit to the Russian Embassy and his meeting with a high-ranking Soviet KGB official, Hosty continued to look upon the Oswald case as routine. In point of fact, of course, the various pieces of information on Oswald that then existed at the highest levels of our government—at the CIA, at Bureau headquarters, at Naval Intelligence, and elsewhere—were anything but routine.

Nevertheless, as part of his regular work schedule, Agent Hosty went to the Dallas immigration office and began reviewing another file.

While thus engaged, he was approached by an Immigration

and Naturalization Service official who exclaimed, "That's really something about Oswald contacting the Russians in Mexico City!"

Stunned, Hosty replied, "Oh, I didn't know about that. Is that where he is now?"

"I thought that you knew."

"No, I didn't know. But I would like to know where he is now—if you know that," said Hosty.

"Jim, I thought you knew all about this, or I wouldn't have brought it up. I'm sorry. You know I can't say anything," stated the INS man.

Agent Hosty didn't press the issue. He knew the "Third Agency Rule." He knew his friend from Immigration and Naturalization didn't have the authority to tell him what he'd learned from another agency. In this case, the CIA.

(What a tangle of red tape. New Orleans had become the FBI office of record on the Oswald case, so when Bureau headquarters in Washington learned of Oswald's trip to Mexico City from the CIA, it transferred the information to New Orleans. But the INS file on Oswald was still in Dallas. The INS received the Oswald–Mexico City information in Dallas at about the same time the FBI office in New Orleans heard it. No word reached the FBI office in Dallas. So Jim Hosty had no record yet that Oswald had been in touch with the Russians in Mexico City.)

The date of this chance meeting between Hosty and the INS man: October 22. Exactly one month to go.

Agent Hosty returned to the Dallas office and sent an immediate wire to FBI–New Orleans. What can you tell me about Lee Harvey Oswald in Mexico City? In a response via registered mail, New Orleans shared with Hosty all that they knew: the Central Intelligence Agency had advised that Lee Harvey Oswald had in fact been in contact with the Russian Embassy in Mexico City where he met with "Vice-Consul" Kostikov. Period. No mention was made of Oswald's visit to the Cuban Embassy. Worse yet, no identification of Kostikov as a high-ranking assassination specialist was given to New Orleans. Or to Agent Hosty.

On October 29, the New Orleans field office told the Dallas field office that it had the forwarding address that Lee Harvey Oswald had left with the New Orleans post office. The forwarding address was 2515 West Fifth Street, Irving, Texas, identified as the home of a Ruth Paine. This confirmed Agent Hosty's guess that the car with the Texas plates leaving New Orleans heading west was that of Ruth Paine.

Hosty, now aware of Oswald's Mexico City visit, wanted to determine where Oswald was living, update his file, and determine if Oswald was working in a "sensitive" industry. At this time, November 1, he took the necessary steps to reestablish the Dallas field office as the office of origin for the Lee Harvey Oswald file.

Consider what had taken place by this date, three weeks before the assassination.

Lee Harvey Oswald had met in Mexico with a dangerous Soviet official. The highest levels of our intelligence community knew this. And yet the full import of this information—the exact nature of the Oswald contact in Mexico City—had not been conveyed to FBI field people in either Dallas or New Orleans. Why not? The reasons given add up to "top secret." Translated that means either information was deliberately withheld for "prerogative" reasons, or it was merely a bureaucratic oversight.

Thus, word never reached the one man responsible for reactivating the Oswald file. And because the Washington intelligence community was probably not yet aware of the president's planned trip to Dallas, it saw no urgency or special need to relay this information to the FBI there.

Oswald met with the Soviets. This we now know for sure. He may well have offered to kill President Kennedy for the Soviets. This we will probably never know for sure. Oswald did offer to kill President Kennedy for the Cubans. This we also know. At the time, the Cubans did not take Oswald seriously. Or if they did, they did not tell us. Because none of this information reached Dallas, Agent Hosty still viewed Lee Harvey Oswald as a curious—but not dangerous—surveillance subject.

Hosty had plenty of other cases to work on. Even though he

had never met Oswald and even though Oswald seemed like a somewhat bizarre person with Communist leanings, no intelligence available at the Dallas field office warranted his thinking that Oswald was given to violent behavior.

Had Jim Hosty and the Dallas office known the nature of the Russian with whom Oswald had met at the Soviet Embassy in Mexico City, the FBI in Dallas would have (after learning that the president was coming to Dallas) undoubtedly taken all necessary steps to neutralize Oswald—perhaps by interviewing him on November 22. And history would have taken a different turn.

Agent Hosty drove out to Ruth Paine's home on November 1, 1963, arriving late in the afternoon at a small single-story house in Irving, a growing community between Fort Worth and Dallas.

He was met at the front door by Ruth Paine, to whom he showed his FBI credentials. She was very cordial, inviting Hosty into her living room.

"What can I do for you, Mr. Hosty?" she asked.

Jim explained that he was preparing a background report on Lee Harvey Oswald and he needed some very basic information on Lee and Marina.

"What kind of information?" Mrs. Paine asked.

"Well, for one, I have to confirm whether Marina Oswald is staying with you here in your house, at least for the time being?"

"Yes," Mrs. Paine replied. "She is living here until she and Lee can get enough money together to get a place of their own."

"And do you know where Mr. Oswald is living?" Jim asked.

"No, we only know that he's in a rooming house somewhere in Dallas."

"Could you get his address for me?"

"I can try, but I'm not sure he'll give it to even Marina," Mrs. Paine said.

"Why not?" Jim asked.

"Because he's afraid she'll tell the FBI—you."

"Lee Harvey Oswald has nothing to fear from us," Jim said.

Ruth Paine didn't respond to that, so Jim tried another question on her.

"Can you tell me where he's working?"

"Oh, I couldn't tell you *that!*" Mrs. Paine said.

"Why?"

"Marina would never forgive me," Ruth said. "He's told Marina and me that you've gotten him fired from other jobs. She's told me several times that we must never tell you where he works."

Jim was taken back by this, but Mrs. Paine was obviously sincere.

"Mrs. Paine, you don't believe those stories, do you?" he asked.

"Well . . . I'm not sure."

"Mrs. Paine, it's not in the FBI's best interest to have Lee Harvey Oswald moving from job to job and from city to city this way. We wish he would settle down. It would make life a lot more pleasant for all of us, wouldn't it?"

Jim let the question sink in for a moment, then asked again if Mrs. Paine would please tell him where Lee Harvey worked.

"Well, I guess so. He works for the Texas School Book Depository as an order processor."

If Ruth Paine's story was true—and Hosty believed it was, even though he'd have to check it out—it only confirmed that Oswald was not working in a sensitive industry. In view of Oswald's erratic, highly questionable behavior and his years in the Soviet Union, the FBI was continuingly concerned that Oswald might find some specialized job in a sensitive, classified, or even top-secret, industry in this country. Not only was this not the case, but Oswald was unable to hold even the most commonplace of jobs in the most mundane of industries.

Suddenly, while Jim and Ruth Paine were talking, Marina Oswald walked into the room. Ruth introduced him to Marina, explaining in Russian that Agent Hosty was with the FBI.

At this, and observing Hosty's notepad, Marina looked quite alarmed.

As an agent, Hosty had dealt with many refugees and newly arrived immigrants to the U.S. Her apprehensiveness was not at all unusual. Such persons initially think of the Bureau as the KGB, the Gestapo, or the like.

In addition, he was certain that Oswald's own hostility toward the Bureau had been assimilated by his wife. Hosty tried to assure Mrs. Oswald—with Ruth acting as interpreter—that his visit was not an unfriendly one. The Bureau, he explained, was really an organization that would protect her rights. After Ruth translated, Marina seemed to calm down.

At that point, Marina told Hosty that she did not know exactly where her husband was living. She knew only that it was "a rooming house somewhere in Dallas." She said that her husband was no longer distributing pro-Castro literature. However, she said she believed that the Castro government was being treated unfairly in the American press. It did please her that her husband now had a job. Agent Hosty assured her that the Bureau was also pleased her husband was working. He further explained that it was certainly within her husband's constitutional rights here to demonstrate for political causes of his choice as long as his activities did not endanger the security of the United States government.

They continued talking a few more minutes. Ruth then asked him if he was planning to conduct an extensive interview with them at this time. No, he said. He was there only to verify where each of the Oswalds was living. He would return at a time convenient to everyone to get Lee Harvey's address.

Agent Hosty, before a more complete interview could be conducted, needed to review the updated New Orleans field office file on Oswald so as to be abreast of any additional information. He gave Ruth Paine his name and telephone number and asked her to contact him as soon as possible with Oswald's address and phone number. He told both women that he would be back in a few days. He thanked them for their time and left.

Several things about Oswald caused Hosty some concern, but not alarm, at this time. First, Oswald had been a defector to the Soviet Union and now had a Soviet-born wife living in this country who had relatives living in her homeland. Second, Oswald had a dishonorable discharge from the U.S. Marine Corps. Third, Hosty knew about the Mexico City trip, but was unaware of its importance. Fourth, he had received a copy of the FBI report on an interview with Oswald on August 10 in New

Orleans. Oswald clearly had lied throughout that interview. Fifth, Hosty also knew about Oswald's Fair Play for Cuba Committee activities and his subscription to the *Daily Worker.* There was no doubt that Oswald was at least a Communist sympathizer. These concerns were sufficient to keep the file active, but not enough to merit unusual attention. Furthermore, Oswald, to be sure, was strange, even bizarre, but Hosty had no evidence Oswald was prone to violence. And he did not now have a sensitive or secret occupation.

Agent Hosty, as mentioned, was waiting to see the complete New Orleans file on Oswald before conducting an in-depth interview with Marina Oswald. According to FBI regulations, he could not interview Lee Harvey Oswald without permission from headquarters. That permission was certainly obtainable, but at this point his instructions were only to verify where Oswald was living and working.

However, as Hosty has said many times since, even if he had talked to Oswald, it is not likely that the interview would have been productive. Hosty didn't believe he had the necessary background information he needed to trigger a meaningful response from Oswald. In retrospect, the one thing he could have done was make Oswald blow his top: mention the two words "Mexico City." But Jim Hosty wasn't to discover this until a few hours after the death of JFK during a grilling of the assassin at the Dallas Police Department.

Both Marina and Ruth Paine later testified that Oswald was extremely distressed to learn that an FBI agent was checking up on him. Oswald instructed his wife that if the agent should return, she should say absolutely nothing—but somehow get the agent's license number.

Hosty returned to the Paine house four days later, November 5. He was there only about five minutes, checking to see if Ruth or Marina had obtained Oswald's address for him. Neither had. While the agent was conversing with Ruth, Marina slipped out the back door and took down his license number. Interestingly, Ruth told Hosty during their brief discussion that Oswald had described himself as a "Trotskyite Communist," which, in view of Leon Trotsky's fate at the hands of the Stalinists, she found amusing. Hosty asked her if she thought that Oswald had a mental problem of some sort. Marxism, she felt, had become very nearly a religion for Oswald, but he did not appear to be unbalanced in any way.

The day before, Hosty had verified that Lee Oswald was an employee of the Texas School Book Depository. Also that day, the Secret Service was first officially notified of the presidential trip to Dallas, although there had been a lot of publicity about the trip in the Dallas papers as early as mid-September.

On November 8 Lee Harvey Oswald went to the FBI office in Dallas in search of Jim Hosty. This was the same trip to the FBI office by Oswald, two weeks before the presidential assassination, that much later created headlines across the U.S.A. on Labor Day weekend in 1975.

Oswald was irate with the Bureau for many reasons, but the crowning blow seems to have been the FBI's direct contact with Marina. Oswald must have been terrified at what his wife could have told the FBI. Marina knew all about the high-powered rifle he had purchased earlier that year. She knew all about his attempt to kill General Walker on April 10. She knew too much about his Mexico City trip. As Hosty was the person who made the contact, he was the focal point of Oswald's wrath. Unfortunately, the agent was at lunch when Oswald walked into the FBI office on Commerce Street that day.

"Where's Hasty?" is the way Oswald opened the conversation. "I have something for him!"

Receptionist Nanny Lee Fenner explained that Agent Hosty would be back after the noon hour. Oswald then handed her a plain white envelope bearing the name "Hasty."

"Here, give this to Hasty," he said.

With that he strode out of the office, not identifying himself. She then handed the envelope to the Assistant Agent-in-Charge Kyle Clark.

Clark read it and said, "There's probably nothing to it. Just give it to Jim when he comes back from lunch."

It is important to be aware of the fact that Jim Hosty, in the Dallas field office, dealt primarily with right-wing fanatics—Ku

Klux Klansmen, neofascists, and other "group" extremists. Oswald, a notorious loner, was therefore something of an oddball for Jim. Hosty, like almost all FBI agents, was accustomed to getting off-the-wall phone calls and mail. So receiving a strong letter in itself was not that unusual.

When Jim returned from lunch that day, Nanny Fenner handed him the envelope. "Here. One of your nutty friends came by to see you and left this."

This note, the one Tom Johnson called me about in 1975, has been the subject of much conjecture and controversy. Though its exact wording has been lost forever, it is reported to have said, in effect: "If you have anything you want to learn about me, come talk to me directly. If you don't stop contacting my wife, I will take appropriate action." It was not signed. Hosty tossed the note in his in-box. Not knowing who it was from, he gave the note no further thought until midafternoon on the day of November 22.

The same day, November 8, in Washington, D.C., the Protective Research Section of the Secret Service reached a fateful conclusion. The PRS, responsible for compiling an advance list of potentially dangerous persons in the Dallas–Fort Worth area, completed its review of the names submitted by every branch of government, including the Bureau. The list came up blank.

As the Warren Commission later pointed out, the capabilities of the Protective Research Section in 1963 were absurdly inadequate. But so far as President Kennedy was concerned, there was nothing to fear from the crank element in the Dallas–Fort Worth area. There was none. Normal security arrangements would suffice.

Based upon the procedures followed by the FBI in 1963, there was no way that Lee Harvey Oswald's name could have made the Secret Service's list. The Bureau handbook then had a very narrow interpretation of what constituted presidential danger: "Threats against the President of the U.S., members of his immediate family, the President-elect, and the Vice President." The Dallas field office had no knowledge of Oswald or anyone else who had threatened President Kennedy.

All together the intelligence community in Washington, however, had enough combined information on Oswald's trek to Mexico City to put his name in lights on a presidential security list. But for reasons of their own, the headquarters of all intelligence organizations concerned failed to convey that information. Thus, the one FBI agent responsible for maintaining surveillance on Oswald was kept in the dark. That fact prevented Oswald's name from being on the Secret Service's Protective Research Section list. And that omission cost JFK his life.

Two other significant things marked November 8. First, that evening Oswald learned of Jim Hosty's second visit to the Ruth Paine home. This apparently sent Oswald into a frenzy. Second, the lead story in the Dallas and Fort Worth papers was about President Kennedy's planned trip to Texas. Who knows what effect this had on Oswald.

The next day, November 9, Oswald wrote his now famous letter to the Soviet Embassy in Washington, D.C. It was typed on Ruth Paine's typewriter. In it Oswald refers to his visit to the Soviet Embassy in Mexico City and his meeting with "Comrade Kostin" (spelled incorrectly; he meant "Kostikov.") He mentioned "Agent Hasty" (another misspelling) and "the notorious FBI." Oswald also inquired about Soviet entrance visas for himself and his family. Ruth Paine discovered a draft of the letter the next day, November 10. Deeming its contents a figment of Oswald's unusual imagination, she told no one of it. The letter was postmarked November 12, 1963. Ten days before the assassination.

On November 13 a Secret Service agent from Washington came to Dallas to begin his advance presidential security check of the area. The local papers announced that the Dallas Trade Mart had been officially selected as the site of the president's luncheon, which was to be held on November 22. The route of the presidential motorcade was announced in the Dallas papers of November 18, the same day the Secret Service advance agent from Washington completed his work.

Because everything was in perfect order and no mishaps were likely, very little contact took place between the Secret Service and the FBI before November 22.

The Bureau, via Agent Hosty, did pass along to the Secret Service a certain amount of unsolicited security information, a portion of which dealt with right-wing elements in Dallas, and which was hand-delivered on November 21.

The FBI delivered nothing to the Secret Service concerning Lee Harvey Oswald. Based on the information the FBI had in its Dallas field office, Oswald did not, by any criteria, "represent a threat against the safety of the president." In fact, nothing had surfaced that would suggest to the Dallas field office that Oswald was given to—or had any potential for—violence.

On November 19, 20, and 21, the Dallas newspapers mapped and described the route of the presidential motorcade. Jim Hosty learned of the precise motorcade route on November 21. Then handling a forty-case workload, the agent later said he did not realize Oswald's work place (the Texas School Book Depository) was along the parade route. "Even if I had, that fact alone would not have led me to think that Oswald represented a threat to the president," he has said.

During the final days before the assassination, while working at the book depository, Lee Harvey Oswald was living at a rooming house in Dallas under the assumed name of O.H. Lee. Each weekend he would visit, as he had since his return from Mexico City, Ruth Paine's house in Irving to be with his wife. On the weekend of November 15, however, the Paines were planning a party for one of their youngsters. Marina told Oswald that he should not come to Irving that weekend.

On November 17, a Sunday, Ruth and Marina decided to phone Oswald at his rooming house in Dallas. They could not reach him because of his assumed name. Whoever answered the phone did not know anyone by the name of Lee Harvey Oswald.

For Marina this was the last straw. When Oswald telephoned her on Monday night, November 18, they had a loud argument about his alias, only one of several he used.

She asked him why he used all those strange names. Didn't he know that in doing so he was hiding from her?

He insisted that his aliases protected him—and her—from the probing sessions with the FBI.

Marina inquired if he was concerned about how upset this made her. His answer was another plea for her to understand that he had to stop the FBI from snooping into their lives.

Exasperated, she told him that she thought he was crazy.

Oswald did not try to contact Marina on Tuesday or Wednesday. On Thursday, November 21, he changed his usual schedule and got a ride from work in Dallas to Irving to stay with Marina. Allegedly, he went there to patch things up with his wife. (His normal schedule, you'll recall, was to stay at his room in Dallas during the week and go to Irving for the weekend.) But in light of his plans for the next day, Oswald had made up his mind to spend the evening with his family.

The scene conjures up the macabre. Oswald looking forward to a few peaceful hours with his wife and child, like any ordinary working man after a day at the office. With one dramatic difference—Oswald spent the evening with the crime of the century brooding in his heart. With mind set, with no turning back, a quiet evening with Marina and June. Tomorrow he will attempt to end his own lifetime of failure and frustration. Tomorrow he will show them all how big and important he really is.

The President began his Texas trip by flying from Washington to San Antonio, then to Houston, then to Fort Worth, where he spent the night of November 21.

He arrived at Love Field in Dallas at 11:39 A.M. the next day. In his large entourage were Mrs. Kennedy and Vice-President Lyndon Johnson. The day was a balmy seventy-six degrees, bright and sunny. The presidential motorcade, a half-mile long, was hailed by huge, enthusiastic crowds lining the streets.

At almost exactly 12:30 P.M. three shots rang out from the Texas School Book Depository. The president slumped forward, mortally wounded.

The motorcade then raced, at speeds of up to seventy miles per hour, to Parkland Hospital, where frantic efforts to save the president's life failed.

President Kennedy's body left Dallas at 2:47 that afternoon

aboard *Air Force One,* and his one-thousand-day presidency became a chapter in American history.

Lee Harvey Oswald's day began differently. He awoke early in the morning at the Ruth Paine home. In a parting gesture, Oswald left what little money he had, together with his wedding ring, with his wife. He rode to work with a neighbor, B. Wesley Frazier. Oswald was carrying a large wrapped package with him. When Frazier asked him what was in the package, Oswald replied that it contained curtain rods.

The two arrived for work at the Texas School Book Depository at 7:56 A.M. Oswald carried the brown package into work. Excitement permeated the workplace because the president's motorcade would travel by the building around noon. Oswald and the other employees went to work early and filled book orders until about 11:50. All the employees then left for lunch early so they could catch a glimpse of JFK as the motorcade passed.

All, that is, but Oswald.

Lee Harvey Oswald did not leave the premises with the other employees but remained on the sixth floor near a window at the easternmost corner of the building, facing Elm Street. He carefully surrounded himself with book cartons, then unwrapped his Italian bolt-action, clip-fed, 6.5-millimeter Mannlicher-Carcano rifle. He loaded the gun, and waited.

At almost exactly 12:30 Oswald fired three shots, killing the thirty-fifth president of the United States.

Oswald then fled the building, leaving his rifle behind. He walked seven blocks to the corner of Elm and Murphy streets. Here, at 12:40, Oswald boarded a city bus. He rode to a point between Poydras and Lamar streets and then got off at 12:44.

Oswald walked to the corner of Commerce and Lamar streets, where he hailed a taxicab. The taxi took him to the corner of Beckley Avenue and Neely Street. He got out and paid his fare at 12:54. From there Oswald walked to his rooming house at 1026 North Beckley Avenue. He left a few minutes later, having picked up a handgun.

Then Oswald walked to the corner of Tenth Street and Patton Avenue, where he was confronted by Officer J.D. Tippit. Tippit was responding to an "all points" bulletin alerting police to look for a suspect described as "a white male, medium height, slender build, about age thirty." No mention was made of the suspect being armed.

Oswald shot and killed Officer Tippit at 1:16.

From the site of the murder, Oswald walked to the Texas Theatre on West Jefferson Boulevard, where he was apprehended by the Dallas police at 1:50 P.M.

At the Dallas Police Department Oswald was questioned intermittently for a total of more than twelve hours, between 2:30 P.M. on Friday and 11:00 A.M. Sunday. Captain Will Fritz of the Homicide Bureau of the department did most of the questioning. Fritz was joined by other teams of interrogators from the Dallas Police Department, FBI, and Secret Service.

Charges were filed against Oswald at 6:00 P.M. on November 22 by Captain Fritz for Officer Tippit's murder. At 11:26 that night he was formally charged with the murder of President Kennedy.

Until the end of Oswald's life which came at 1:07 P.M. on November 24, barely forty-eight hours after the Kennedy assassination, he denied all charges except that of carrying a revolver into the movie theater.

For Agent Jim Hosty, that Friday began with an 8:30 meeting with his boss, Gordon Shanklin, and about forty other agents assigned to the Dallas field office. Shanklin had talked to the agents several times about security arrangements for the president's visit to Dallas. Now he reminded them that if they had any indication, any indication at all, of potential violence against the president, this would be the last opportunity to alert the Secret Service. The meeting surfaced nothing that suggested any direct threat to the president.

The record shows that Agent Hosty did not feel, based on the information he had, that Lee Harvey Oswald was a threat to the security and well-being of President Kennedy, and thus he said nothing. In fact, the possibility of an assassination attempt never occurred to him.

The Dallas Police Department had worked hand-in-glove with the Secret Service and, insofar as it could be determined, tracked down every lead of concern. The police were alerted to possible demonstrations by right-wing elements. That accounted for the hefty security at the Dallas Trade Mart, the one location where the president would stay for an extended time. The demonstrations, police believed, would erupt there, if anywhere in Dallas. All things considered, however, the Secret Service believed Dallas was reasonably safe for the presidential motorcade.

The meeting at the Dallas field office, Hosty recalls, lasted about half an hour, ending around nine o'clock that morning. He then departed for a meeting on another matter with an army intelligence agent and a treasury department official in downtown Dallas. That meeting over, Hosty and the intelligence officer, a personal friend, strolled down to the 1100 block of Main. They knew that the presidential motorcade would be passing there soon. The crowds were abuzz with excitement.

When the president did pass, Hosty noticed that many Secret Service men surrounded other cars in the motorcade but that the president's limousine was entirely unprotected. He was concerned about this. But the night before, the president had given the Secret Service strict orders to stay away from his car. He wanted to be as visible as possible to the people of Dallas.

"There he is!" shouted Hosty's friend.

The crowd by now was tumultuous, cheering, waving, applauding, throwing confetti and streamers. JFK was overjoyed. Hosty, standing some four blocks from Dealey Plaza, calculated that he saw the president pass by three or four minutes before he was slain.

After the parade was past, Hosty crossed the street to the Oriental Cafe for a bite of lunch. He scanned the menu and ordered a cheese sandwich and a cup of coffee. He had just started to eat when he heard sirens screaming down Main Street. The FBI agent says he thought to himself—Oh, boy, those right-wing fruitcakes are really raising a ruckus down at the Trade Mart.

Moments later, a waitress dashed from the kitchen crying, "They've shot the president! My God, they've shot the president!"

"How do you know?" Hosty asked, "Where did you get this information?"

"The radio in the kitchen," she said. "A news bulletin just interrupted all the programs."

The cafe was now in turmoil. Hosty hoped the news was false or the injuries minor. He quickly paid his bill and hurried out of the restaurant. On the street he encountered Dallas FBI office supervisor, Joe Loeffler, also running back to the office. They stopped momentarily.

"Get into a car real quick, turn on the radio, and stand by," Loeffler instructed him.

Hosty double-timed it to the office garage, pulled out a Bureau sedan, and turned on the two-way radio for instructions.

In seconds a supervisor ordered, "We want four cars at Parkland Hospital, immediately!"

Hosty turned on the siren and flashing lights and streaked for Parkland Hospital. He made it in fifteen minutes. It was then about one o'clock.

Parkland Hospital was chaotic. Police and Secret Service cars were everywhere. The hospital was completely sealed off. Patrolmen surrounded the emergency entrance. Nobody then knew how serious the president's injuries were. There was talk of head injuries. The mood was grim.

Agent Hosty got on his two-way radio to ask for instructions.

"Jim, get back to the office immediately!" Supervisor Ken Howe ordered.

Hosty wheeled out of the hospital parking lot and raced back to headquarters.

Events were breaking fast. Jim heard a constant chatter on his radio. He passed the Texas School Book Depository on the way back to downtown.

"It has been established that the shots came from the Texas School Book Depository," said the voice on the radio.

The Texas School Book Depository, Jim Hosty reflected. That's where Ruth Paine said that Lee Harvey Oswald was working.

At approximately 1:16, crackled Jim's radio, a police officer had been shot and killed. Several FBI agents came on the air and said they were heading over to West Jefferson Boulevard to check it out.

Hosty mused: a policeman shot in broad daylight in a quiet residential neighborhood, following so soon after the shooting of the president, also in broad daylight. It had to be the same person or persons.

Under direct orders to return to headquarters, Hosty did not assist the investigation of the police officer's death. He arrived at the Bureau office at 1:20 P.M. Thirteen minutes later it was announced to the world that John Fitzgerald Kennedy, President of the United States, had died. Unthinkable. But true.

The atmosphere at the Dallas FBI field office was tense, angry. Agents scurried in all directions. Phones jangled incessantly. One line remained open to Bureau headquarters in Washington. Special Agent-in-Charge Gordon Shanklin had just used this line to call J. Edgar Hoover with the assassination news. Little did the agents in the Dallas office, including Jim, know that at that moment Agent Hosty was the principal Dallas repository of information on the assassin. He was the one and only field person with an active file on Oswald.

Dallas FBI Supervisor Ken Howe, acting on Teletyped orders from Alan H. Belmont, special assistant to Hoover, instructed Hosty to identify right-wing individuals in the Dallas area to be used in conjunction with a similar list being developed at that very moment by the Dallas police. They believed the assassin's name might be on one of these lists. This was a logical assumption since it was well-known that the right-wing elements in Dallas had always made clear their very hostile feelings about the president. The name Lee Harvey Oswald was never mentioned.

Jim was working on the list when an agent called from the Dallas Police Department. Ken Howe took the call. Upon hanging up, he turned to the others in the office.

"A Lee Harvey Oswald has been picked up," Howe said. "Do we know anything about him?"

A chilling, ghastly feeling nearly overwhelmed Jim Hosty. He had trouble getting his thoughts together. He could hardly speak. "I might have something. Let me check the files," he managed to reply.

Hosty straightaway made for Gordon Shanklin's office where he repeated the call they had just received. Then he announced that the active file on Lee Harvey Oswald was in his possession.

Shanklin was stunned. He couldn't believe that his office had an active file on Oswald.

"Jim, get that file for me right away. What *do* we have on Oswald?"

Hosty got him all of the background information he had. Shanklin flipped through it, then called Al Belmont in Washington for instructions.

Belmont, too, was shocked by this information.

He ordered Shanklin to dispatch Hosty, the man most knowledgeable about Oswald, to the Dallas Police Department to be of any possible assistance.

As Shanklin hung up, he turned to Hosty for the file.

Jim was reading it himself, shaken by what he'd just found in it. That very day a brand new piece of information had been added, information Jim Hosty had never seen before. It was a confidential letter from the Washington field office saying that on November 9 Lee Harvey Oswald had written to the Soviet Embassy in Washington, mentioning Kostikov by name, but not his KGB connection.

This was the second time Jim Hosty had come across the name Kostikov. Exactly one month earlier, on October 22, Kostikov was identified as a "Vice-Consul" in the Soviet Embassy in Mexico City. This time no identification was given.

At last the Washington field office had transmitted the letter to the attention of Agent Hosty in Dallas. It arrived via registered mail, in the ordinary course of business. So there it was, 2:30 in the afternoon of November 22, and finally in Jim Hosty's hands. Only then did the Dallas field office learn of the November 9 letter. Hosty still recalls his thoughts at that moment: What difference does it make now? The president is dead.

The obvious question is: Why the delay? My feeling, having been so close to the FBI for so long, and having seen the whole picture, is that after Oswald's letter was intercepted, it was passed on to the Soviet espionage section at FBI headquarters. The transmittal process probably took a few days. This was the routine method of transmitting information of this type. At the time, there was no special urgency attached to this information.

The espionage section would have taken a few days to read and react—and get back to the Washington field office, suggesting that the letter be sent to Dallas. Two or three more days.

Apparently, within the machinery of the Bureau, those responsible just did not put two-and-two together fast enough. That delay, together with the decision to withhold from the Dallas office information on the true identity of the Soviet agent Kostikov, was a human judgment, and human miscalculation. With acute hindsight, one can say that without the delay and the withholding of the critical Kostikov–Mexico City data from key Bureau personnel in Dallas, President Kennedy's life might well have been saved. The Bureau, I'm sure, didn't know when it intercepted this letter that the president was even going to Dallas. I'm not making excuses for it. I just know how a large bureaucracy works—slow. At times too slow.

Agent Hosty showed Special Agent-in-Charge Shanklin the Oswald file and discussed it with him in detail. Shanklin, as instructed by Al Belmont, called Captain Fritz at the Dallas Police Department.

"Captain, this is Gordon Shanklin, Dallas FBI. We have an agent here who has background information on Lee Harvey Oswald. He might be of some help to you. Would you be interested?"

"The department would welcome any assistance from the FBI. Could the agent come over right away?" Fritz replied.

Hosty now knew of two top-secret pieces of information: the Oswald–Mexico City data, and the November 9 letter Oswald had written to the Soviet Embassy in Washington, D.C. He still did not have, however, nor did anyone else in Dallas have, the extraordinary information about the true identity of KGB agent Kostikov. But he had his instructions from Al Belmont, assistant to J. Edgar Hoover, and from Special Agent-in-Charge Shanklin to cooperate fully with the Dallas Police Department. He was prepared to help in any way he could.

Despite the cordial reception accorded President Kennedy, many in Dallas strongly disliked the president, including numerous Dallas police officers. One of them, Lt. Jack Revill of the Dallas Subversive Unit, had only the day before argued with Hosty about the merits of JFK. The lieutenant had expressed a certain chagrin over having to guard the president during his visit.

Hosty arrived at the Dallas Police Department at 3:05. He parked his car in the large underground garage, then walked over and got on the elevator. Revill and a couple of other Dallas officers were there.

Jack Revill cornered Hosty and said, "We've got a hot lead on the Kennedy killing, Jim. There's only one guy missing from the Texas School Book Depository. His name is Lee!"

"His name is Lee Harvey Oswald and he's in custody here right now," Jim Hosty replied, "and he's a Communist."

Revill screwed up his face, as if in pain. Without cracking a smile he implied that he didn't want to believe the FBI agent. Did Hosty know what he was saying?

"Damn it, Jack," retorted Hosty, "of course I know what I'm saying. Oswald's here in this building, and I think he's the one who did it."

Jim based his statement on information he had learned from 12:30 to 3:00, not on what he knew from Oswald's file.

Revill, guessing that Hosty was basing his remarks on data he had before the assassination, grew irate. He wanted to hear more.

"Jack, you know federal law prevents me from supplying classified information to local authorities. Where can I find Captain Fritz?" Hosty asked.

Revill calmed down and led Hosty to the office of Captain Fritz.

When Jim got off the elevator at the third floor, pandemonium greeted him. How could so many newspeople and police officers be crammed into one space? The police department had imposed virtually no restrictions on media coverage. Now it seemed as if the National Press Club was inhabiting the hallways, all jabbering and shouting at the same time. The police looked frantic, a condition that was not helped by the constant ringing of dozens of telephones. Never had he seen anything like this.

Captain Will Fritz actually had two offices—an outer and an inner office. The interrogation of Oswald was being conducted in the small inner office, nine-by-fourteen feet. Captain Fritz, Oswald, two detectives, and FBI Agents Jim Hosty and Jim Bookhout were present at this part of the interrogation. Hosty's participation began at 3:15.

The prisoner appeared much smaller than the agent thought he would. Hosty had been viewing Oswald's picture for many months without actually seeing him. In fact, Oswald's slight stature was Hosty's first impression of the man.

The prisoner was wearing a T-shirt at the time and was handcuffed. A sizable bruise marked his forehead; he had received it when apprehended by the Dallas police in the movie theater. Captain Fritz, a skilled interrogator, questioned Oswald in a low-key manner. Oswald continued to deny everything, allowing only that he did carry a loaded pistol into the movie theater.

Hosty showed Oswald his identification. Oswald glared at him with cold hatred and screamed, "So you're Hosty! I know about you. You're the one who questioned my wife twice!" He was now on his feet, shouting. "Oh, I know all about you, Hosty."

Jim Hosty was stunned and puzzled by the man's instant display of rage.

Captain Fritz grasped Oswald's arm and ordered him to sit down. The captain then asked, "What are you talking about?"

"Hosty threatened my wife," thundered Oswald. "He told her she could defect. He wouldn't leave her alone—with all those questions of his. I'm going to fix you, FBI!"

Only then did Hosty realize that it was Oswald who had left that anonymous note for him at his office. He was using the same threatening language about his desire to be left alone—and that his wife be left alone—by the FBI.

Oswald calmed down. Fritz asked him more routine questions for ten to fifteen minutes. During this time, the prisoner emphatically denied that he had purchased a mail-order Italian rifle. Fritz asked Oswald about his time in Russia. Oswald quite placidly replied that he had lived there for three years.

Then Hosty apparently struck a nerve. "Have you ever been to Mexico City?"

Oswald abruptly arose and demanded, "How did you know about that?" He went into a tantrum and pounded his manacled fists on the desk. Again, Captain Fritz ordered Oswald to sit down, quiet down, and answer Agent Hosty's question. Oswald then vehemently denied ever having been in Mexico City.

Fritz then queried Oswald about his role in the Fair Play for Cuba Committee.

At this, Lee Harvey pointed his finger at Hosty and spat, "Ask Hosty. He seems to know everything!"

Hosty informed Fritz that he would fill him in on everything he knew about these activities. A lengthy give-and-take between Oswald and Fritz followed. Oswald was now cool. (Hosty seemed to be the only person in the room who rankled Oswald.) All in all, Captain Fritz was handling the interrogation well.

The session ended at 4:05, when one of the detectives stuck his head into the office and announced, "Captain, we're ready for the lineup now."

"Okay, let's get him downstairs," replied Fritz.

Two eyewitnesses quickly identified Oswald as the killer of Officer Tippit.

At this point, things began to change direction for Agent

Hosty. As he emerged from Fritz's office, he was immediately approached by a senior squad member from the Dallas FBI field office. The man, Agent W. Harlan Brown, informed Hosty that he was not permitted to attend the next interrogation session with Lee Harvey Oswald. Nor was he to divulge anything to the Dallas police or cooperate in any way with them. In fact he was ordered to return to Dallas FBI headquarters. So, when the second interrogation of Oswald began, Hosty was absent.

From our vantage point now we can probably determine why Jim Hosty was so instructed by the Bureau.

The specialists in the Soviet espionage section of FBI Headquarters in Washington were doubtless reviewing the Oswald file. Agent Hosty had received his instructions from Gordon Shanklin to cooperate fully with the Dallas police. Shanklin's instructions had come from Alan Belmont, special assistant to J. Edgar Hoover. But Belmont undoubtedly issued those instructions without knowing everything in the Oswald file. Or what it all meant.

But Bill Sullivan knew.

William C. Sullivan, assistant director in charge of security in Washington, was probably the highest FBI official, at that point, to review the Oswald file. What he discovered there must have astounded him. He read the data on the meeting between Oswald and Kostikov (Sullivan would have known at once exactly who Kostikov was), surmised the Cuba connection, reviewed CIA surveillance data on the Soviet Embassy in Mexico City, studied FBI wiretaps involving Oswald and Kostikov, then read the November 9 follow-up letter from Oswald to the Soviet Embassy in Washington. This information, it would surely have struck him, had such dire international implications that the White House must be informed immediately.

Sullivan probably went straight to Hoover and then hastened to the National Security Council at the White House. No doubt, President Johnson was then apprised.

In fact, a number of researchers, including Anthony Summers and Edward Jay Epstein, have reported that LBJ warned that "these rumors (of the Oswald–Soviet–Cuban connection) could lead us into a war that could cost forty million lives."

The president went on to say that "given the mood of the nation right now, if the public became aroused against Castro or Khrushchev, there might be war." So, it seems, the silence imposed on Jim Hosty originated at the highest level—the White House.

But Agent Hosty, not privy to the behind-the-scenes meetings in the nation's capital, was understandably a bit bewildered. Not only was he suddenly ordered out of the Oswald interrogation, but he was also enjoined from supplying FBI intelligence on Oswald to either the Dallas police or the Secret Service. This after he had been so pointedly instructed to cooperate with the Dallas police.

On the night of November 23 the Dallas field office received a tip from an unknown source that Oswald would be killed. The information was immediately relayed to Dallas police, who chalked it up as another crank call. Who could get to Oswald —in Dallas Police Headquarters?

The next day, Sunday, Oswald was gunned down in the halls of police headquarters—on national TV. His killer was Jack Ruby, a stripjoint owner who was distraught over the murder of the president. Because Ruby was known by most members of the Dallas police force, he was able to enter headquarters and walk about at will.

Within several hours of the Oswald murder, Jim Hosty was called into his superior's office. "Jim, I don't ever want to see that Oswald note again. Oswald's dead and there can't be a trial now."

Hosty, following what he thought was an explicit order, went into the men's room and flushed the note down the toilet. Thus was a critical piece of the assassination puzzle lost forever.

President Johnson had placed the FBI in total command of the assassination investigation. Thus, on Saturday, Jim Hosty was back at the Ruth Paine household in Irving interviewing members of the family. It was during this interview that Ruth Paine turned over to Agent Hosty the original draft of the Oswald letter to the Russian Embassy in Washington.

On Monday, Hosty returned to the Dallas Police Headquarters to comb through the effects of Lee Harvey Oswald, looking for anything that might cast more light on the killing of Kennedy—and/or Oswald himself. (Already rumors of a Ruby-Oswald connection prior to November 22 were being circulated throughout Dallas.)

Hosty found, among other things, his own name and telephone number, and the stub of Oswald's bus ticket to Mexico City.

As the scope of the FBI's investigation widened, teams of additional agents were sent from various Bureau field offices to assist in the search for more information relevant to the JFK assassination. When the preparation of data for the Warren Commission is included, the case eventually became the largest in the Bureau's history.

Numerous FBI officials were called to testify before the Warren Commission in 1964. When his call came, Agent Hosty discovered, to his horror, that the two Soviet-related documents he needed were missing. The cable from the Central Intelligence Agency dated October 18 concerning Oswald's Mexico City visit, and the November 19 Washington field letter about Oswald's correspondence with the Soviet Embassy, had vanished. Without these documents, he could not testify about their contents.

In the meantime the Secret Service had mistakenly informed the Commission that there were "two secret agents." In truth, there were not "two secret agents" but two pieces of secret information that Agent Hosty could not substantiate because the documents had been lifted from his Oswald file. When he returned from the Warren Commission hearings, the documents were back in his file with a note attached to them: "Removed from Hosty's in-box on November 22."

It has since been learned that the two documents apparently had been removed by Supervisor Ken Howe of the Dallas field office upon the instructions of Assistant Special Agent-in-

Charge Kyle Clark. Clark received his directive from Assistant Director William C. Sullivan in Washington. The latter almost certainly received his orders from the White House. The withholding of that information from the public was thus complete— all because the White House seemingly considered the risk of a confrontation with the Soviet Union over the Kennedy assassination too great.

The Warren Commission concluded that before the assassination, Agent Hosty should have known who KGB agent Kostikov really was. After all, reasoned the Commission, the CIA and FBI Headquarters knew. Therefore, Hosty knew.

Today, Jim Hosty says, "I never knew what the Warren Report was trying to suggest. There's no question but that I *should* have known about Kostikov, who he was, and the threat he represented. I first heard of the Oswald meeting with Kostikov a full month before the assassination—but somebody forgot to let Dallas know exactly how dangerous Kostikov was." The Third Agency Rule again! All records and correspondence support Agent Hosty in this. If only Jim Hosty *had* known. . . .

In any case, the Warren Commission learned of the true nature of the Oswald–Mexico City connection, but did not immediately reveal the information to the public. The head of the Secret Service Protective Research Section testified before the Commission that, before the assassination, the U.S. government had at least eighteen pieces of derogatory information on Lee Harvey Oswald. Further, the record suggests that both FBI offices—in Dallas and in New Orleans—did, under the circumstances, everything that could have been expected of them.

How, then, could the assassination have taken place?

The system itself, as it then existed, permitted it. The various intelligence agencies of government, with four years of surveillance data behind them, simply did not put two-and-two together and say, "This man could be dangerous. He should be neutralized." As a result, one lone madman filtered through our intelligence net, and then through our presidential protection system.

Had our intelligence communities pooled their information on Oswald, had the Oswald–Kostikov–Mexico City information been distributed among the various agencies (assuming the facts about Kostikov were as explosive as they indeed appeared to be), had the Secret Service Protective Research Section been aware of all the Oswald data, and had the information been distributed to the New Orleans and Dallas FBI field offices in time for them to act then, without doubt, JFK would not have died in Dallas on November 22, 1963.

11

In Reflection

"I served with the best"

I TELL THE FOLLOWING STORY because in my mind it so clearly marked the end of one era and the beginning of another.

Everything I had always believed about law enforcement was put to the test by a man named Wilburn K. DeBruler one day in 1974. Will forced his way into my conscience that day and made me decide whether the FBI was going to press an investigation of a governor of one of our states—or allow political expediency to prevail. At the time I was not certain I was being very sophisticated. I was certain I was right in the decision I made. I was also certain that I—and the FBI—stood at a crossroad.

The Oklahoma City field office needed an answer.

They had a tip that the governor, David Hall, was taking kickbacks on construction jobs. Preliminary investigations all supported the story. There was no solid proof of anything yet, but something was up. Did headquarters want to hear more about it?

FBI–Washington wasn't so sure. Probably not. For years the FBI's unwritten policy had been unswerving: no involvement in local politics or politicians. A long time ago, J. Edgar Hoover had discovered that congressional support for his programs was tough enough to come by without making people mad. And the surest way to make politicians mad at you was to put their friends in jail. Worse yet was this looking too closely at their own affairs. Bad business, investigating politicians. Don't do it.

In fact, if there were two kinds of criminal investigations that the FBI traditionally shied away from, they were (1) the sins of politicians, and (2) white-collar crime. Kickbacks in the Oklahoma governor's mansion thus qualified for looking the other way on both scores.

Wilburn DeBruler, special agent-in-charge of the Oklahoma City field office, was upset. He thought things had changed. With Hoover gone, Will DeBruler thought field office people were expected to pursue investigations of this sort. Was this new director going to correct things—like he said he was—or was that just some more talk out of Washington? The evidence gathered so far suggested the worst; why shouldn't headquarters want to know where it all led?

DeBruler's men—Special Agent Paul A. Baresel and Supervisor Travis W. Muirhead—had heard kickback rumors. The story was a familiar one. A construction firm, the low bidder on a particular project, was approached, after being awarded the project, by a staff member from Governor Hall's office. The staffer asked for a $125,000 payment for the governor from the contractor. Clearly, an illegal kickback.

After consultation with other members of the construction firm, the contractor decided to pay the kickback. He then went to his bank, borrowed the $125,000, and, as instructed, met an official from the governor's office at a local motel. The cash was laid out on a bed and counted. The man from Governor Hall's office then took the money to a bank, purchased money orders in varying amounts, and paid off several of the governor's personal expenses.

The governor's apparently bleak financial condition and his difficulties with the Internal Revenue Service already had Hall in hot water. The IRS, Baresel ascertained, was attempting to launch tax-fraud charges against the governor. However, local IRS people in Oklahoma City were having their own problems with Washington: the Justice Department was dragging its feet in granting approval to proceed on the matter.

Following standard FBI operating procedure, the agents in the Oklahoma City field office prepared a summary of their completed investigation to date, together with allegations requiring further inquiry, and sent it to FBI headquarters in Washington. In the meantime they had contacted the U.S. attorney's office in Oklahoma City, where they received full support, and a commitment to follow up—as soon as Washington got behind the effort.

Normal FBI Headquarters procedure in a matter like this would call for a Bureau supervisor initially to study the communication from the field office. If the supervisor had questions about the investigation, he would either send it back to the field for clarification, or contact his unit chief. The latter might approve the planned investigation or, if he had reservations, route the case all the way up to an assistant director. From this point, in rare instances, the matter could reach the director's desk. Somewhere in this process the facts were usually sent over to Justice for legal review. The whole procedure, depending on the urgency, took from two days to two weeks.

In the case at hand, a telephone call was made to Oklahoma City from headquarters in just a couple of days. Running true to form, headquarters ordered the field office to shut down the investigation—and submit a closing report in ten days. These were the instructions relayed to Special Agent-in-Charge DeBruler. And DeBruler exploded. He had no intention of shutting anything down, not on orders from a headquarters supervisor who didn't know things were different now.

DeBruler called Washington.

"All the evidence here suggests that this could be an extremely important case. It warrants full FBI attention. And if I understand what the new director is telling us, the FBI should pursue this matter to its conclusion. Until somebody else tells me to leave this one alone, we are going to continue the investigation of Governor Hall." DeBruler was adamant.

And because the special agent-in-charge outranked the supervisor, there was no argument at this point.

Early the next morning, however, DeBruler received a call from the office of the assistant director. The caller said, in no uncertain terms, that the FBI would not get involved in a case regarding the governor of Oklahoma. DeBruler was to get out of it, get his people out of it, and submit the closing report at once.

Now the special agent-in-charge was just plain mad. Outranked and overruled, he could see that the case was following an all-too-familiar pattern. An FBI field man found a hot one; FBI–Washington felt the matter was too controversial. Wanting no part of it, Washington ordered the case closed. Everybody knew the source of the dictate—even though Hoover himself rarely saw any of these cases. And now DeBruler was being stonewalled by an upper-echelon manager who, even though Hoover was gone, was doing exactly what the former director would have wanted.

DeBruler, though, was not to be denied. He knew what my directions were. He had read the "Green Book." (This publication, issued from FBI Headquarters at my direction, contained the 200-page transcript of my confirmation hearings. My commitment to investigate crime wherever the FBI found it, it had been sent to all agents.) In addition to the "Green Book," I had mailed to all special agents-in-charge a series of letters making it as clear as I could that I personally wanted to be involved in their problems, whatever they might be.

DeBruler decided to take me at my word.

He called me directly.

In the past, such a move by any agent had been deemed a career risk. In fact, in all my years with the Bureau, I heard of but one field agent who had the temerity to call the director. On November 22, 1963, Gordon Shanklin, special agent-in-charge of the Dallas office, called Hoover to inform him that John F. Kennedy had been shot. I myself had never even considered calling Hoover from the field . . . for any reason.

Even though my management philosophy was vastly different from Hoover's, and even though I'd done everything but run television commercials to make clear the policy differences between the old Bureau and the new, DeBruler was told that a call to me from the field would be ill-advised. No matter, thought DeBruler. Whatever the risks, he wanted to pursue this case.

Had things changed or not? Since I was the only person left who could approve such an aggressive investigation, he was determined to get through to me.

DeBruler's first call was diverted to an assistant director and did not reach me. He called again—and was again turned aside, this time reaching a staff member in my office who asked the nature of the call. DeBruler explained that he wanted to talk to me and why. He was put on hold for a minute, and finally put through on my line.

"Mr. Director, they tell me I shouldn't be doing this, but I think it's what you would want me to do." He paused for a moment. "I'm Will DeBruler, special agent-in-charge in Oklahoma City. I'm onto a very hot lead here that might involve the governor of this state in a kickback scheme. I've got to know from you whether to pursue this or back off. If we're right, it's headlines across the country. And if we're wrong, well, I guess that's another kind of headline. I need your advice."

"You have to do your job, Mr. DeBruler. And it's not your job to protect the interest of any political party or personality. What can you tell me about this case over the phone?" I asked.

He outlined the facts as he knew them, explained that he was getting enormous resistance within the Bureau, and hoped that I'd understand.

"Mr. DeBruler, I understand two things. One, making a telephone call like this is almost unprecedented around here. For that, I appreciate your courage. Two, I understand that you are following up on evidence that does seem to lead to the governor's mansion there in Oklahoma City. For that, I appreciate your determination to do your job—as you and I both see it."

"Thank you, sir. I think this is one of your high-priority cases. If I am right, it's real quality, Mr. Director."

I had to smile to myself. He was playing back the new party line, all right. And he had both my admiration and appreciation. My campaign to emphasize quality-over-quantity in FBI work was paying a dividend in Oklahoma City.

"Mr. DeBruler, I have no doubt that you're on to something

here. I think it's time to jump into it with both feet. And don't worry about the splash."

I could hear a sigh of relief through the wires from Oklahoma City.

"Thank you, Mr. Director," he said. "I'll be sure to send you a telex outlining what we have discussed."

For many months thereafter, the Oklahoma City field office and a tough-minded U.S. attorney pursued the case against every obstacle. As so often happens in cases like this, it grew. While investigating the original allegations against Hall, the FBI uncovered other illegal activities which, combined with the kickbacks, ultimately resulted in an indictment that sent the governor to prison for more than three years.

The case was a monumental success in the fight against political corruption. For the FBI, it was a giant success of another kind: a new philosophy—quality-over-quantity—had taken a giant step forward.

The Hall case was probably the first in which the Bureau had deliberately entered into a high-priority investigation of that nature with full force. FBI agents across the nation watched the case and its every turn, waiting for Washington to back off.

When it finally became apparent that there was to be no back-off, and in fact an unknown agent-in-charge had gone directly to the director to see if the battle would be engaged and heard that the new man at headquarters was behind him, word spread like wildfire throughout every field office. When the line was held and the case was won, I knew that headquarters had just become something different—and more—to the men and women in the field who wanted and needed that kind of support.

In the "Green Book" I had made my declaration of independence. It was, after all, the sum of everything that I had said to the Senate Judiciary Committee that approved Nixon's recommendation of Clarence M. Kelley as director of the FBI back in the summer of 1973. I felt I had to do something to live up to that 96-0 vote of confidence given to me by the U.S. Senate.

Even more than that, however, was the need I felt to make sure the men and women of the FBI knew that I was going to stand behind them in the performance of their duties. As Archibald Cox could not compromise with the White House in his responsibility as special prosecutor, I believed that I could not compromise with what I believed in during those five years in Washington from 1973 to 1978.

If the episode in Oklahoma City turned out well for me, so did all my days in Washington. In spite of the rugged months in the beginning—Watergate, the tragedy of Wounded Knee, the ordeal of Patricia Hearst—I was fulfilled by the feeling of accomplishment that the directorship gave me.

As I pushed past my mid-sixties, I knew the time had come to make room for the next director. I felt, after almost five years, that things were on course.

My last day as director was also my last day in law enforcement, February 15, 1978. It had been nearly thirty-eight years since that very first day with the FBI in 1940.

Although I had a degree in law, I had never practiced. Nor had I experience in the world of business. Frankly, I felt somewhat alone and apprehensive about the prospects of entering the arena of free enterprise. After a few false starts, however, I did find a niche for myself—a combination of security work and private investigation for law firms, businesses, and private citizens. In all, it has been a fitting sequel to all of my previous experiences.

All things considered, I have been very fortunate. I have enjoyed all the good things our country has to offer. I am deeply grateful.

Much has happened—to me, to the country—during those years since my assignment in Huntington. But so quickly did the years pass, I seldom had time to reflect on history in the making. Now, however, there is time to reread, ponder, and reflect.

The FBI was a solid, responsive, world-famous organization when I arrived in Washington in summer 1973. Nearly fifty years under one man's leadership, however, can cause some problems in any organization. The outside pressures for change in the Federal Bureau of Investigation had become great— especially during the previous ten years.

In retrospect, it is difficult to imagine how one person could have done a better job than Mr. Hoover. Notwithstanding, a one-man band does have certain limitations. Systems were outdated. Management structure, dictated by tradition and precedent, was not in tune with the realities of the 1970s. Richard Nixon's earliest conversations with me made it very clear what my mission had to be: implement the changes I thought necessary; discount the measured traditions of the past. Do what was so long overdue.

Freedom to change is one thing. Producing change is another. The Bureau itself was comfortable with the leadership style of Hoover. I discovered early that reforms would not come easy. Too many people liked things the way they were. Indeed, it took my entire term as director to make many of the internal reforms, a number of these coming to pass only because of retirements. We had to proceed slowly, heedful both of Hoover's reputation and the structure of the organization he had built. I proceeded with care and caution—and the greatest circumspection.

My initial reform was aimed at making our operations more responsive and more relevant to the day-to-day conduct of business. Thus, the creation of the division of Planning and Inspections.

Next, and almost simultaneously, I set out to update the Bureau's computer and data management systems. Woefully antiquated, they couldn't compare with the computer systems I had left behind in Kansas City.

Once again, however, seeing the need for change—and accomplishing that change—were two different things. The machinations I employed to update data systems in Washington provided insight into Bureau thinking at that time.

First, I felt the need to stamp these changes as Bureau decisions, not Clarence Kelley's. So an internal review committee studied the overall requirements of all FBI data processing. Privately, I was convinced that a comprehensive D.P. system, utilizing the most sophisticated equipment and programming, would enhance the Bureau's efficiency dramatically—and immediately. So, when the committee recommended that an outside person should coordinate this effort, I at once approved the move. Not so fast, I heard very clearly. Outside assistance wasn't the answer; the coordinator needed FBI experience. Years of experience were needed because the FBI's needs were *different*.

I took another tack. I decided that, one way or another, our own personnel must be used, or we'd never get this project off the ground. A man from our Laboratory Division was selected to coordinate the project. In the final analysis, he did a good job. However, had we used outside company consultants, we undoubtedly would have had the benefit of the latest planning and technology—at far less time and cost.

Another area demanding attention, from the very beginning, was the relationship between the FBI and the news media.

The tradition of openness with the media in this country traces to the earliest days of colonial government. The media almost seems like a fourth branch of government because it has always played an irreplaceable role in protecting our constitutional freedoms.

Over the years, the Federal Bureau of Investigation had become an entity unto itself, apart from—and above—media attack, it thought. The time had come, I thought, to review that point of view.

"We must revise our relationship with the press," I said to members of my executive staff on more than one occasion in 1973 and 1974. "The FBI they write and talk about is not what you see it to be. I think the way to resolve that difference in our favor is to open our doors to them."

As a result, our public information staff was soon doubled. In the fall of 1973 the External Affairs Division was established. We invited the media people into our organization. Officials at FBI headquarters and agents in the fifty-nine Bureau field offices were questioned almost daily about FBI activities. Legitimate requests for information came from all segments of society, from private to media representatives.

Under my direction the Bureau became as open and as accessible to public and press as was proper and reasonable. The number of our news conferences and radio and television appearances increased tenfold. My notes and files show almost sixty major national news releases during my term. We also began training our field-office personnel and agents in media relations.

When I became director, I discovered that personnel operations and management procedures had always been the responsibility of J. Edgar Hoover himself. Alone—just as we always thought. Thus, the autocratic approach to people's careers. I knew firsthand that the human needs of Bureau people often took backseat to inviolate Bureau rules. Substantial changes were in order.

It might have been more prudent for me to come aboard, creep along, and continue the Hooverian style of personnel management. But I knew I couldn't do it that way. What's more, neither could Hoover have done so. Not anymore. Though this approach worked for him for almost a half-century, had he lived, his days of arbitrary management were numbered. The times made the change inevitable, no matter who sat in the director's chair.

In that first summer, 1973, we revised and substantially improved the requirements for the all-important selection and evaluation of special agents.

On the heels of that, we initiated changes in the position classification and advancement procedures for our army of clerical and secretarial personnel.

Next we established, for the first time, a comprehensive Career Development Program, which would affect the working lives of virtually all of our people. Under this program, career review boards were created both at headquarters and in field offices to assist in selecting supervisory and management personnel.

The following year we created the well-formulated and highly beneficial Management Aptitude Program to be utilized at the FBI Academy.

With all of these new programs it was my intent to provide clear performance guidelines so that all employees knew precisely what was expected of them by FBI management. I intended to encourage initiative and the highest level of performance by every employee. Self-starters with outstanding performance records would be rewarded.

Disturbed by the incidence of some good people leaving the FBI in their middle years, we stressed that excellent life-long career opportunities were available within the Bureau. And in the new FBI, you could succeed in one of two ways. Our system would channel into administrative areas those men and women with qualified managerial skills. At the same time the system encouraged those who wished to stay in investigative work to do so—without feeling that their growth or earning potential were limited. I wanted to get more emphasis on "investigation"—and less on "bureau"—in the Federal Bureau of Investigation.

At the very top of the organization, the FBI needed the very best people. I was determined to surround myself with people whose skills, whose integrity, whose knowledgability were all unquestioned.

By the time I retired, the entire top management organization of the Bureau had been changed. In addition to a new associate director and deputy associate director, I appointed new assistant directors to head up eleven different divisions of the Bureau: Laboratory, External Affairs, Training, Computer Systems, Administrative (later changed to Finance and Personnel), Inspection, Intelligence, Legal, General Investigative, and Special Investigative Divisions, as well as the Office of Planning and Evaluation.

By changing the FBI management team we also changed (for the better, I believe) the management style. What had been an essentially autocratic, almost militaristic, rule became within a few years one of participatory management.

Not everyone applauded. I was often roundly criticized by

those still loyal to the Hoover philosophy. In view of the fact that some of my key moves either replaced or bypassed Hoover's people, this was not surprising to me.

In my confirmation hearings I expressed my strong support for congressional oversight of the FBI. During my fifty-five months as director, I spent more time before congressional committees than Hoover did in forty-eight years. In fact, during 1975 we cooperated in an unprecedented way with members and staff of the Senate Committee on Intelligence Activities. In the most exhaustive study of the FBI's intelligence and security operations ever undertaken by anyone outside the Department of Justice, the members and staff of the committee had unrestricted access to our files. They talked not only to FBI executives but also to Bureau personnel who conduct security-type investigations and were themselves personally involved in day-to-day intelligence operations. Congressional committees had greater access, during my term of office, to Bureau personnel, data, and operations than ever before. In balance, I found the Congress to be composed of conscientious, well-informed, hard-working American citizens.

I was criticized by some for being too cooperative with Congress. I assume there are those who still feel that way.

But the Bureau under Hoover had become too independent, I believed. So much so, it seemed to me, that constitutional and congressional checks and balances no longer applied to the FBI. Such a state of affairs was not good for the public, the Bureau, or our constitutional form of government. In any case, we cooperated fully with Congress. In 1975 we established the Office of Congressional Affairs within the Bureau's Legal Division, whose primary purpose was to facilitate closer liaison with congressional committee staffs and to analyze proposed or enacted legislation from an FBI point of view.

I felt for many years that because it was the nation's leading investigative agency, the FBI should be at the forefront in cooperating with police and other investigative agencies throughout the United States. My feelings trace in part to the many sides of law enforcement I have known. Within reason, the Bureau should set the standards in law enforcement.

With that in mind, on taking office I directed that FBI services become more widely available to other policing and investigative agencies, especially in the areas of fingerprint identification technology, criminal information dissemination, and scientific and laboratory services.

Additionally, we broadened the Bureau's participation in the Police Foundation, and began to hold regular symposiums and seminars in technical areas such as crime laboratory development, specialized scientific training, and communications. Also, advanced courses and training are now offered on a regular basis for chiefs of police at the FBI Academy at Quantico, Virginia. In line with this thinking, I also felt that the FBI not only should be the nation's leading investigative agency but also should regain its rightful position as a division within the Department of Justice, reporting to the attorney general.

Certainly the most far-reaching reform I instituted in Bureau operations was overhauling the basic strategy of investigation. That reform fundamentally altered the FBI's day-to-day method of operations, and did so permanently. If it can be said that I left a legacy with the Bureau, the quality-over-quantity investigative approach would be it. What was that concept and how did it affect the FBI?

In summer 1973 one of the most serious problems the Bureau had to face was the traditional month-by-month, year-by-year FBI method of developing and reporting statistics on its own performance. The system that had evolved over the years was almost comical.

From my experience as field agent I knew firsthand that a distorted Bureau-wide method of reporting statistics had existed for many years.

By long-standing custom, the FBI regularly maintained five specific categories of investigative accomplishments: stolen property recovered, money saved, fines levied, fugitives located, and convictions completed. This sounds fine in theory. But the main fault of this method of keeping score was that it gave equal weight to every case. Thus, a major investigation involving hundreds of agents (as in the Hearst kidnapping) would be reported as one case in the FBI stats. As well, the recovery of somebody's 1961 Dodge would be one case.

This type of reporting developed from the Bureau's near obsession with not only maintaining the previous year's stats, but actually improving on them every year. Thirty years of this and what do you have? Numbers that for all practical purposes are meaningless, except for self-promotion . . . and budget-boosting. The impetus for all of this came, naturally, from the director himself. In the field, all of our numbers had to be kept up—"just like the Ford Motor Company," as noted earlier.

Every special agent-in-charge in the field had to keep his statistics moving higher in at least three (of the five) categories each month. Thus, some special agents-in-charge, concerned with maintaining high caseload levels, built successful careers out of the pursuit of inconsequential cases. By and large, field office statistics had to be hiked at the field level to reflect the proper level of accomplishment. (Sometimes numbers had to be adjusted *down*. If your numbers soared too high, there was always next year to worry about.)

This game-playing system, as might be imagined, was a waste of manpower. And worse. It meant that the toughest cases, often the most important, were either pursued indifferently—or not pursued at all.

Bureau statistics were used as background material for news releases to the press. This publicity advised the public, through the broadest kind of media coverage, that the Federal Bureau of Investigation was recording higher numbers of successes with each passing year. This meant to the American people that the Bureau was doing a better job every year.

J. Edgar Hoover then presented these statistical accomplishments annually at congressional budget hearings as proof of ever-increasing FBI excellence. "Be aware, however," Hoover repeated every year, "in order for us to improve still further on this marvelous record the Bureau will need an even larger budget this coming year."

It was a classic Hoover routine. And it worked every year.

It was in connection with this numbers-first thinking, and the budget approval implications behind it, that we experienced the great aversion to anything controversial. No activity was to be encouraged, no investigation was to be pursued, that might "embarrass the Bureau."

And because all of this thinking came from headquarters, it permeated the morale of the entire field organization. If an ambitious (and uninformed) agent initiated aggressive action in a controversial area, his career could be stymied; if he did it twice, his career could be ended.

"For the sake of your job," I heard repeatedly in one form or another, "you better follow the safe, don't rock-the-boat investigative strategy." It may be that when you hear "don't rock the boat" enough times, pretty soon you want to get out of the boat. I think that's what happened to me by 1961.

From my earliest days as director I insisted that the Bureau must reassign its investigative resources.

"Gentlemen, our priorities are bent. We count three stolen cars as being 300 percent more important than one kidnapping. And we won't even touch a white-collar crime or a political fraud case. We must turn our efforts to the areas of maximum *need*— not maximum *numbers*!" It was a speech I made in Washington and in the field dozens of times during 1973 and 1974.

As things stood then, the FBI was actually losing the battle against many types of crime: we were wasting our most valuable commodity, manpower, on frivolous cases.

New resource systems were needed to help select priority crime targets. Only when proper targets were chosen on a continuing basis could we concentrate our efforts where they would do the most good.

The new philosophy soon became known as "quality-over-quantity."

Shortly after becoming director I initiated the quality-case program. This required a comprehensive reassessment of all FBI caseload priorities.

I directed that the FBI was to concentrate on only extreme

high-priority crime targets such as kidnapping, espionage, organized crime, political corruption, and the like.

"Leave the stolen cars to local police," I instructed.

In time, caseload quantities decreased by the thousands as
field offices began to turn away from the easy, numbers-only
investigative assignments. All of a sudden, field offices directed
their firepower against priority targets.

Beginning in late 1974 my reforms were being tested in four
field offices. Three of the four reported extraordinary results.

To be sure, there were those agents, particularly some of the
veterans, who fought the new directives to the end. On the
whole, however, the new strategies were well supported, and
came to be extremely productive. Areas of emphasis under the
quality-over-quantity approach were: white collar crime, organized crime and racketeering, subversion, and foreign-terrorist
activities. Special training in computer-type crimes was given to
agents investigating white-collar crimes. Emphasis was placed
on the use of imaginative approaches for penetration of professional hoodlum and racket operations, including the use of
undercover special agents . . . and outlays by the FBI of "front
money" for information.

The results? Increases in convictions for white-collar crime, as
well as vice and racketeering figures, in those cases investigated
by the FBI. Our aggressiveness took hold. Today FBI caseloads
are but a fraction of what they were in the early 1970s.

The FBI's internal information systems were also restructured
so that convictions and investigations were classified by individual case quality . . . as well as by quantity. As Harvard professor of government, James Q. Wilson, has observed: "Each
FBI field office was authorized to close out all pending investigative matters that had little prosecutive potential and to develop
priorities that would direct its resources toward important
cases."

After the trial period in four field offices, in September 1975
we expanded the concept to all field offices. Instructions were
issued to the field offices to (1) conclude as expeditiously as possible cases of "marginal importance," (2) establish investigative

priorities in conjunction with the local U.S. attorneys, and (3) concentrate on quality cases and on major criminal and security problems within their respective territories.

In fall 1976 the General Accounting Office completed a major study of the FBI's methods of developing and reporting criminal investigative statistics. "The quality-over-quantity concept of conducting investigations and managing resources represented a major step forward," GAO noted.

Late the same year I announced, in a speech in New Orleans, that investigations handled by the Bureau had declined by more than 135,000 from the previous totals. The aggressive approach had enabled us to direct our maximum efforts where it most benefitted the United States.

The new approach increasingly involved us in ambitious undercover operations, stings, cases the magnitude of Abscam, and, after I had retired, Abscam itself. The last resulted in the convictions of six congressmen and one U.S. senator for conspiracy, taking cash bribes, or conflicts of interest.

Because of the development of the quality-over-quantity concept, the FBI no longer wasted its resources and manpower on cases of local jurisdiction. Even the most serious of these—such as arson, robbery, and murder—are usually best handled by local authorities. The Bureau can, should, and will assist local authorities with training, specialized education, consultation, and information. The Bureau, however, must concentrate on multistate and national concerns, especially foreign counterintelligence, organized crime and labor racketeering, and political corruption.

Law enforcement now has passed to a new generation, however, and I have a few concluding observations. We, of course, need more law enforcement capabilities to meet America's needs. We now have the best personnel ever. But law enforcement authorities by themselves cannot stop crime. The broad range of personal freedom in this country has its price: responsibility. Every citizen has a responsibility regarding crime, if only vigilance in attempting to prevent it, and diligence in seeking to eradicate conditions that encourage crime.

The critical problem in law enforcement is easily enough stated: How do we fight crime with every possible weapon while protecting the liberties of all Americans, as guaranteed by the Constitution? Such an undertaking requires the very best law enforcement professionals our society can produce. To that end, law enforcement must offer to our talented young people career opportunities to compare with law, medicine, business, and similar occupations.

In reflecting on my thirty-eight years as a law enforcement professional, I believe that there are four primary requirements that must be met by American law enforcement for it to be effective. First, there must be complete integrity. Second, there must be proper and judicious use of limited manpower and physical resources. Third, the best professional standards must be established, then complied with. Fourth, our constitutional liberties must be protected.

I count myself most fortunate to have worked with high-quality professional men and women with both physical courage and outstanding ability. Their efforts, more than mine, have contributed to the improvement and advancement of law enforcement in this marvelous country. I am personally satisfied that I was always able to be at my best—because I served with the best.

Acknowledgments

WHEN WE BEGAN TO RESEARCH the materials and data for this book our first task was to sort, file, and catalog the vast amounts of correspondence, memoranda, newspaper clippings, books, and other papers acquired during a very active thirty-eight year career in law enforcement. This initial research took about six to eight months, and when completed, we had approximately 150 different subject files. From these original files eleven chapters have been written. Considerable effort has been made to ensure the historical and factual accuracy of the text.

We are indebted to numerous individuals who kindly provided us with valuable assistance. In preparation of the chapter "KC COP," Marjorie Kinney, department manager, and the staff at the Missouri Valley Room of the Kansas City, Missouri, Public Library supplied us with Kansas City source and background materials. Kansas City Police Department Lieutenant Colonel Lester N. Harris and Lieutenant Colonel James R. Newman (retired) provided commentary based upon their years of experience with the department. Captain Frederic Smith of the Kansas City Police Department's South Patrol Division assisted with proofreading certain episodes. Retired Kansas City newspaperman Fred Kiewit, who wrote the definitive accounts of the Kansas City riots in 1968 for the *Kansas City Star,* also proofread and made suggestions. Captain Tom Moore of the Roeland Park, Kansas, Police Department made several excellent suggestions for the book.

Edward S. Miller, deputy associate FBI director (retired), because of his historically unique position at Bureau headquarters on Saturday, October 20, 1973, was extremely helpful in supplying his special insight and information for the chapter "The Saturday Night Massacre."

William D. Ruckelshaus, former deputy attorney general, director of the Environmental Protection Agency, and acting FBI director added significantly to the Watergate chapters.

Assistant Director of the FBI W. Raymond Wannall (retired), an expert on American domestic counterintelligence matters, read the "Cointelpro" chapter and gave us the benefit of his many years of study.

Special Agent-in-Charge Charles W. Bates (retired), who headed up the Patty Hearst kidnapping case, supplied a great deal of information, including his firsthand knowledge of the case.

Special Agent-in-Charge Joseph H. Trimbach (retired), in charge of the FBI contingent during the first dramatic confrontation at Wounded Knee, gave us the benefit of his firsthand knowledge of the entire episode. To Assistant United States Attorney Lynn E. Crooks, District of North Dakota, we are indebted for critical proofreading, suggestions, court transcripts, and appellate briefs regarding the Wounded Knee murder litigation. Mr. Crooks suggested a significant expansion of the chapter "Wounded Knee" and we followed his recommendation. Susan R. Duenow, deputy clerk, United States District Court, Northern District of Iowa, researched and gathered trial transcripts for us from the first Wounded Knee trial. A number of officials from the Department of the Interior, Bureau of Indian Affairs, provided us with Pine Ridge Indian Reservation maps and topographical data.

Special Agent James P. Hosty, Jr. (retired) devoted considerable time and energy to assisting us with data on the Kennedy assassination.

Assistant Director of the FBI Wilburn K. DeBruler (retired) gave us the benefit of his unique thinking regarding the Quality-over-Quantity investigative concepts.

Mary J. Patton, head of information services, Metropolitan Library System, Oklahoma City, researched their archives and gathered the background data for the text on the scandal involving the prosecution and conviction of former Oklahoma Governor David Hall.

Rhonda Johnston, Dolores Otto, and Valerie Schroer—from the Kansas City staff of United States Senator John Danforth—kindly and expediently fulfilled many of our requests for government materials and information. Transcription of tapes, cassettes, and the typing of manuscripts was very capably handled by Mylene Larson, Mary Ann Luther, Linda Gerber, Jean M. Walker, and Marti L. Campbell. We also received help from the research librarians at the Antioch Branch of the Johnson County, Kansas, Library, and at the General Library located on the University of Missouri–Kansas City campus. Shirley Dyckes Kelley read the text and made excellent suggestions, as did Nancy A. Davis. Hazel M. Garrison assisted in planning and appointments. And a special thanks to James E. Cox for arranging the initial meeting between us that led to our collaboration here.

Finally, our thanks to Ellen Parker for her editorial help during the year-end holidays, 1986.

—CLARENCE M. KELLEY

—JAMES KIRKPATRICK DAVIS

Bibliography

Alexander, Shana. *Anyone's Daughter: The Time and Trials of Patty Hearst.* New York: The Viking Press, 1979.

Baker, Marilyn with Sally Brompton. *Exclusive! The Inside Story of Patty Hearst and the SLA.* New York: Macmillan Publishing Company, 1974.

Baron, John. *KGB: The Secret Works of Soviet Secret Agents.* New York: Bantam Books, 1974.

Bishop, Jim. *The Day Kennedy Was Shot.* New York: Greenwich House, 1983.

Brown, Dee. *Bury My Heart at Wounded Knee.* New York: Washington Square Press, 1970.

Connell, Evans. *Son of the Morning Star.* San Francisco: North Point Press, 1984.

Davidson, Jean. *Oswald's Game.* New York: W.W. Norton & Company, 1983.

Demaris, Ovid. *The Director: An Oral Biography of J. Edgar Hoover.* New York: Harpers Magazine Press, 1975.

Drury, Allen and Fred Maroon. *Courage and Hesitation.* Garden City: Doubleday & Company, 1971.

Ehrlichman, John. *Witness to Power.* New York: Simon and Schuster, 1982.

Epstein, Edward J. *Legend: The Secret World of Lee Harvey Oswald.* New York: McGraw-Hill Book Company, 1978.

Felt, Mark. *The FBI Pyramid.* New York: G P Putnam's Sons, 1979.

Hearst, Patricia C. *Every Secret Thing.* New York: Crown Publishers, 1976.

Perkus, Cathy and Noam Chomsky. *Cointelpro. The FBI's Secret War on Political Freedom.* New York: Monad Press, 1975.

Schlesinger, Arthur M., Jr. *The Imperial Presidency.* Boston: Houghton Mifflin Company, 1973.

Sidey, Hugh. *A Very Personal Presidency: Lyndon Johnson in the White House.* New York: Atheneum, 1968.

Sirica, John J. *To Set the Record Straight.* New York: W.W. Norton and Company, 1979.

Sullivan, William C. *The Bureau: My Thirty Years in Hoover's FBI.* New York: W.W. Norton and Company, 1979.

Summers, Anthony. *Conspiracy.* New York: McGraw-Hill Book Company, 1980.

Ungar, Sanford J. *FBI: An Uncensored Look Behind the Walls.* (An Atlantic Monthly Press book.) Boston: Little, Brown & Company, 1975.

Weed, Steven. *My Search for Patty Hearst.* New York: Doubleday and Company, 1976.

Weyler, Rex. *Blood of the Land: The Government and Corporate War Against the American Indian Movement.* New York: Vintage Books, 1982.

White, Theodore H. *Breach of Faith: The Fall of Richard Nixon.* New York: Atheneum Publishers, 1975.

White, Theodore H. *The Making of the President 1964.* New York: New American Library, 1966.

White, Theodore H. *The Making of the President 1968.* New York: Atheneum Publishers, 1969.

White, Theodore H. *The Making of the President 1972.* New York: Atheneum Publishers, 1973.

Woodward, Bob and Carl Bernstein. *All the President's Men.* New York: Simon and Schuster, 1974.

Woodward, Bob and Carl Bernstein. *The Final Days.* New York: Simon and Schuster, 1976.

Index

321

324 · Index